Thérèse
of
Lisieux

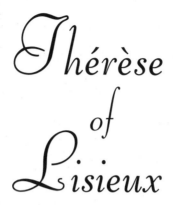

Thérèse of Lisieux

A Life of Love

Jean Chalon

Translated by Anne Collier Rehill

Liguori

LIGUORI, MISSOURI

Published by Liguori Publications
Liguori, Missouri

Library of Congress Cataloging-in-Publication Data

Chalon, Jean.
  [Thérèse de Lisieux, une vie d'amour. English]
  Thérèse of Lisieux : a life of love / Jean Chalon : translated by Anne Collier Rehill.
    p. cm.
  Includes bibliographical references and index.
  ISBN 0-7648-0111-2 (pbk. : alk. paper)
  1. Thérèse, de Lisieux, Saint, 1873–1897. 2. Christian saints—France—Lisieux—Biography. I. Title.
BX4700.T5C4813 1997
282'.092—dc21
[B]   97-9983

Photographs courtesy of Office Central Lisieux, 51, rue du Carmel, 14100 Lisieux, France. Used with permission.

Printed in the United States of America
First U.S. Edition
01 00 99 98 97   5 4 3 2 1

Acknowledgments

My thanks go first to Françoise Verny, who was able to overcome my reservations about writing a biography in which the heroine is so different from those to whom I had previously devoted myself.

Thanks as well to Charles-Henri Flammarion and to Father Nicolas Sed, who believed me capable of carrying out this enterprise, of which I thought I would never see the end.

Finally, thanks to all those who, for other motives, helped me in my labor. In alphabetical order: Carlos de Angulo, Sister Anne Marie du Christ, Aimée Bederian, Sophie Berlin, Marie-Thérèse Bouley, Madeleine Cornuault-Falque, Claude Daillencourt, Claude Delay, Jacqueline Demornex, Ghislain de Diesbach, José Escoda, Marie Guérin, His Excellency Guy Gaucher, Anne Jaffrezou, Danièle Jay, Karl Lagerfeld, Jacques Lonchampt, Sister Marie-Lucile, Anne Muratori-Philip, Marie-Claire Pauwels, Monique Pivot, Isabelle d'Ornano, Liliane de Rothschild, Silvio Saragossi, Irène Stecyck, and François de Teyssier.

Contents

List of Illustrations   xi

 1: A Celestial Marriage (13 July 1858)   1

 2: The Miracle of Saint Joseph and of Rose Taillé
    (11 March 1873)   6

 3: Child of the Sémallé Countryside
    (16 March 1873–2 April 1874)   10

 4: An Inexplicable Crying Fit (Easter Monday 1875)   14

 5: A Holy Family (Summer 1876)   18

 6: The Child Spoiled by God and by Zélie Martin
    (Spring 1877)   24

 7: The Death of a Mother (28 August 1877)   28

 8: Post-Zélie (15 November 1877)   32

 9: The Happy Island of Les Buissonnets
    (Winter 1877–Spring 1880)   36

10: Prayer at Age Nine (Autumn 1881–Winter 1882)   45

11: The Miracle of Pentecost (13 May 1883)   50

12: The Strength to Suffer (14 June 1884)   58

13: Interlude at Saint-Ouen-les-Pins and Trouville
(August 1884–May 1885)   63

14: "The Most Unhappy Creature in the World"
(May 1885–September 1886)   66

15: The Miracle of Christmas (25 December 1886)   72

16: A Memorable Month of May (May 1887)   75

17: Thérèse's First "Child" (August 1887)   80

18: An Obstacle Course (October 1887)   84

19: The Trip to Italy (November 1887)   90

20: Jesus' Plaything (20 November 1887)   97

21: An Incomprehensible Delay (1 January 1888)   103

22: The Death of the Little Lamb (15 February 1888)   107

23: The Thorns of Carmel (Spring 1888)   112

24: "You Have Never Committed a Single Mortal Sin"
(28 May 1888)   118

25: A Father's Misfortunes (23 June 1888)   121

26: A Fighting Reed (December 1888)   125

27: A Mirror of Snow (10 January 1889)   127

28: A Roughly Handled Treasure (Spring 1889)   131

29: The Discovery of the Holy Face (July–December 1889)   136

30: An Interminable Engagement (Summer 1890)   139

31: The Wedding of the Child Jesus and the Child Thérèse
(8 September 1890)   143

32: Thérèse's Three Obsessions
(Autumn 1890–Summer 1891)　146

33: A Flower of Suffering (Autumn 1891)　151

34: The Beneficial Effects of an Epidemic
(January–February 1892)　156

35: A Time of Grace (Summer–Fall 1892)　158

36: A Euphoric Election (20 February 1893)　163

37: Thérèse's Four Jobs (Spring–Summer 1893)　166

38: The Two Shepherdesses (21 January 1894)　170

39: The Death of a King (29 July 1894)　174

40: The Intrepid in Carmel (14 September 1894)　177

41: Thérèse at the Stake (21 January 1895)　181

42: To Live a Life of Love (22 January–14 June 1895)　188

43: Thérèse the Poet (1895)　192

44: Thérèse's Double Failure (20–21 January 1896)　198

45: The Entry into Night (Easter 1896)　203

46: The Dream of a Soul (10 May 1896)　206

47: Lucifer's Fiancée (21 June 1896)　211

48: Pure Love (6 August 1896)　216

49: Mad Love (8–17 September 1896)　221

50: Jesus' Prisoner (1 November 1896)　224

51: Thérèse's Windows (November 1896)　228

52: The Christmas Spinning Top (24-25 December 1896)　233

53: Saints and Angels (8 February 1897)   236

54: A Good Little Zero (March–May 1897)   239

55: The Little Way and the Elevator (4 June–8 July 1897)   244

56: "Yes, I Want to Spend My Heaven Doing Good on Earth"
    (17 July 1897)   249

57: The Five Sisters (18 July 1897)   253

58: The Pity of God (31 August 1897)   256

59: Joining the Stars (30 September 1897)   262

Afterword   268

Bibliography   271

Index   272

List of Illustrations

Thérèse at age three and a half   20

Thérèse at age eight with her sister Céline   47

Closeup portrait of Thérèse at age eight   51

Closeup portrait of Thérèse at age thirteen   69

Thérèse at age fifteen   109

Thérèse as a novice in a white mantle   133

Thérèse as a novice without the mantle   149

Sister Geneviève near the infirmary porch   152

Thérèse, her sisters, and Mother Marie de Gonzague in the
    courtyard of the Lourdes Grotto   179

Closeup portrait of Thérèse at the Lourdes Grotto   183

Thérèse as Joan of Arc in prison   187

The community gathered for the Feast of the
    Good Shepherd   189

The community at the laundry   193

Closeup of Thérèse and Marie at recreation in the
    Chestnut Walk   196

Thérèse and Céline beneath the cross in the
    cloister courtyard   201

Thérèse standing in the cloister courtyard   204

Family group in the Chestnut Walk   207

Thérèse holding a rosary   218

Thérèse as sacristan, with her sisters and cousin   229

Closeup of Thérèse as sacristan   231

Thérèse with holy pictures   250

Thérèse lying ill at the cloister   257

Thérèse in death—in the infirmary   267

To the memory of
Father Alex Ceslas Rzewuski,
who led me from Liane de Pougy
to Thérèse de Lisieux

"To live in love is to banish all fear."

Thérèse of Lisieux

1

A Celestial Marriage

(13 July 1858)

The saints are God's luxury, His outward signs of wealth, the human beacons upon whom He shines a bit of His infinite light to show the way through the darkness of time, or of the heart, when the need is felt. And France truly needed enlightening at end of the nineteenth century, when Marie Françoise Thérèse Martin was born in Alençon on 2 January 1873. She was to become, in Lisieux, one of these human beacons: Saint Thérèse of the Child Jesus and of the Holy Face.

In Paris as in the provinces, the storms that had been provoked by the fall of the Second Empire were beginning to calm. The National Assembly awarded to Louis-Adolphe Thiers the title "liberator of the territory" for having anticipated the retreat of the German Occupation troops. Shortly afterward, Marshal Marie-Edme-Patrice-Maurice de Mac-Mahon acceded to the presidency of the Republic. France was able to breathe again, as the bourgeoisie triumphed and everything seemed, for the moment, to be restored to order. A moral order, which, of course, Thérèse's parents, Louis Martin and Zélie Guérin, incarnated to perfection.

Louis Joseph Aloys Stanislas Martin was born in Bordeaux on 22 August 1823. His father, a captain in the military, had retired in 1830 and settled in Alençon. Extremely devout, Captain Martin raised his son with one precept: "Always glorify and love God above all else."

Equally pious, Louis's mother constantly preached humility to him, as well as other Christian virtues. At a very early age, Louis Martin aspired to the cloister. In 1843 he wanted to enter the Grand Saint Bernard Monastery but was unable to because he did not know Latin. Thus he became not a monk, but a watchmaker and jeweler. Louis lived like a hermit, but a hermit who loved nature, music, traveling, Fénelon, Lamartine, and Chateaubriand. Above all, Louis loved solitude. To satisfy his taste for isolation, in 1857 he bought an old tower on the banks of the Sarthe, not far from the house in which he lived with his parents on rue du Pont-Neuf.

Christened the Pavilion, this tower sheltered a few chairs, a table, and fishing gear, for the chaste Louis permitted himself just one pleasure—fishing. An expert fisherman, he gave the fish that he caught to the St. Claire Convent of Alençon.

In the enclosure adjoining the tower, Louis placed a statue of the Virgin Mary. A copy of a Bouchardon madonna, she stood three feet tall. Even though she was not smiling, she would later become universally known as the Smiling Virgin. This statue was the only feminine presence in the Pavilion. There were no romantic attachments in the life of Louis Martin, of whom all Alençon proclaimed a virtuousness that could be matched only by that of Zélie Guérin.

Azélie Marie Guérin, called Zélie, was born on 23 December 1831 in Mayenne, in the village of Gandelain. Like Louis's parents, the Guérins were extremely devout. M. Guérin was a policeman, and, like M. Martin, he chose to retire in Alençon, where he settled in 1843. In his *Normandie* (1844), Jules Janin depicts Alençon as "the main town in the department of Orne, a fortified city in the tenth century of our history…situated in the middle of a fertile plain, it is big and well built, and the land's old trees surround it with their antique shade."

In other words, boredom reigned in Alençon, where Zélie came to live at the age of twelve.

"My childhood was as sad as a shroud," Zélie later related. She suffered from frequent headaches, perhaps provoked by maternal indifference and paternal severity. Zélie focused her affection on her sister, Marie-Louise, who entered the Convent of the Visitation of Le Mans, taking the name Sister Marie-Dosithée, and on her brother, Isidore.

Like Louis Martin, Zélie Guérin was tempted by the cloister. She applied to the sisters of Saint Vincent de Paul, who rejected her not because she had no Latin, but because she would be "a perfect Christian mother."

"So I'll get married and have a lot of children," exclaimed Zélie. She chose the trade of lacemaker and mastered the famous Alençon needlework, which, since the seventeenth century, had been the renown of the city.

In 1853, Zélie Guérin set up her own shop, as a "manufacturer of Alençon needlework." She created the designs, which the workers executed at home. To Zélie fell the most difficult part of the job, that of assembly—joining the various pieces by invisible connections.

In a city like Alençon, which numbered at the time some thirteen thousand inhabitants, everyone knew one another and appraised one another at their true worth. The Martins, who were distressed about their son's prolonged celibacy, and the Guérins, who wanted to find a husband for their daughter, decided to arrange a meeting of their children. This was customary at a time when marriages were not celebrated lightly, but only after a discreet investigation of the future husband and wife, including their antecedents, their financial condition, their health, and so on.

Louis Martin and Zélie Guérin saw each other, liked each other, and their virtues were quickly amalgamated. Three months after their first meeting, on 13 July 1858, they were married in the Church of Notre Dame. Zélie brought to her husband a dowry of five thousand francs and seven thousand francs of personal savings; he had twenty-two thousand francs in savings, his house on Pont-Neuf, and his Pavilion. The couple could envision the future with confidence and the assurance that they would be comfortable.

Louis was thirty-five years old. Chestnut-haired, with a vast forehead made even bigger by premature baldness, and with his blue eyes and fine appearance, he looked like a gentleman mystic.

Zélie was twenty-seven. With her brown hair, black eyes, and perfect oval face, she could have been a model for Ingres. With innate elegance, she draped herself in a cashmere shawl that she would wear until her death, unaware of successive styles. Zélie was not frivolous. Nor was Louis. The two agreed to live together as brother and sister, following the example of Saint Joseph and the Virgin Mary, and of a few other, similar, if less well-known, couples. It was a celestial marriage, a union of two souls and two hearts.

After ten months of angelic harmony, and after a discussion with her confessor, Zélie understood that she could not be both virgin and mother. She resigned herself to carrying out the conjugal duty, which Louis performed with a delicacy she never stopped paying tribute to. "My husband is a saintly man; I wish all women could have one just like him," admitted Zélie, who allowed herself another confession: "I have never experienced any pleasure in my life, no, never what is called pleasure."

In this last confidence, we should not give to the word *pleasure* the precise and exclusive meaning it has taken on today. This meaning was generally not known to the wives who tolerated the unpredictable frenzy of their husbands while waiting for it to pass, as a fever passes, or an epidemic or other calamity. Sex was, for a Christian couple like Louis and Zélie, only an instrument of procreation. And if they disdained those pleasures "that are called, lightly, physical,"* the couple knew the happiness of producing children.

And it was a happiness almost without interruption. On 22 February 1860, Marie, their first daughter, was born. On 7 September 1861, Pauline. On 3 June 1863, Léonie. On 13 October 1864, Hélène. On 20 September 1866, their first son, Joseph Louis. On 19

---

*Colette, *The Pure and the Impure.*

December 1867, Joseph Jean-Baptiste. On 24 April 1869, Céline, and Mélanie Thérèse on 16 August 1870.

At the end of the nineteenth century, infant mortality was extremely high. One child out of three died before the age of five. In an effort to check the hecatomb, the Comtesse de Ségur, who had lost one of her own young sons, wrote a work of popular medicine, *La Santé des enfants* [*The Health of Children*], which appeared in 1855. Mme Martin, a great admirer of the countess, certainly must have read it and put it into practice. Which did not stop the premature death of four of her children: Hélène, Joseph Louis, Joseph Jean-Baptiste, and Mélanie Thérèse. Four others remained alive, four daughters—Marie, Pauline, Léonie, and Céline.

In the spring of 1872, Zélie Martin was again pregnant. In September of that year, she asked her brother, Isidore, Lisieux's pharmacist, for "two kilos of good candy" for the baptism of the child who would be named, if a girl, Thérèse, in memory of the great saint Teresa of Ávila and of the very little, too-soon-departed Mélanie Thérèse.

On 15 December 1872, Zélie Martin wrote to her sister-in-law, Céline Guérin: "I'm crazy about the children; I was born to have them. But it will soon be time for it to stop. I'll be forty-one years old on the twenty-third of this month, the age at which one becomes a grandmother!"

But Zélie Martin would never be a grandmother. She would have to be content with being a mother for the ninth, and last, time.

2

The Miracle of Saint Joseph and of Rose Taillé

(11 March 1873)

It is rare that a child remembers the nine months it spends in its mother's womb. So Zélie remembered for Thérèse, and she wrote to her sister-in-law, Céline: "While I was carrying her, I noticed something that never happened to me with my other children: when I sang, she would sing with me...I'm telling this to you because no one else could believe it."

It was a precious confidence, showing that Zélie Martin was not the sinister person obsessed with death that some have wished to show her as. She was sufficiently cheerful to sing when she was pregnant and to sing as well when she was not, to the great satisfaction of her husband and daughters, who constituted her only audience. There was no question of Zélie's appearing in the salons of Alençon, which had hardly changed since Balzac had portrayed them in his *Cabinet des antiques*. The Martins were rarely invited, and when they were, they declined the invitation that would have interrupted the blessed monotony of an existence punctuated by the accomplishment of their religious duties.

Between the daily morning mass and the evening prayer that they recited together, to mention only two of their obligations, nothing could divert the Martins from their pious universe. On Sundays, M.

Martin refused to open his watchmaking-jewelry shop. And Mme Martin did not travel on the day of Our Lord. The couple lived their faith day by day and made sure that their progeny did the same. Marie, Pauline, Léonie, and Céline, who knew no other way to live, did not complain. On the contrary—they blossomed in what could have seemed like a yoke of constraint but was for them a cocoon of pleasant routines. Only Léonie, who was clearly not as docile as her sisters, rebelled sometimes, but she repented right away.

In July 1871, the Martins left their house on rue du Pont Neuf for another on rue Saint-Blaise, number 36 to be exact, which today is number 42. This house, inherited after the death of Zélie's father, was Thérèse's birthplace. It was a grand house, with a reception room, dining room, and kitchen. This was not luxury, but rather bourgeois affluence. They placed it all under the protection of the Virgin, whose statue left the enclosure of the Pavilion to sit enthroned at rue Saint-Blaise.

In April 1870, Louis Martin sold his watchmaking and jewelry business to better assist his wife, who devoted her days and a portion of her nights to Alençon needlework. Louis took care of the business management, the bills with the heading "Manufacture of Alençon Needlework/Louis Martin." He satisfied his taste for travel with regular trips to Paris in search of clients and orders.

Louis and Zélie were satisfied with this arrangement, and with their new house, embellished by an enclosed garden with rosebushes, espaliered pear trees, and a bower. It would have been bliss for Zélie, had she not been sobered by the memory of the four children she had lost, especially the last one, Mélanie Thérèse. "Never will I be consoled over the death of my little Thérèse; it often keeps me awake at night."

Zélie was comforted by the thought that her four little departed ones were now angels who would watch over the child she carried, who was born on Thursday, 2 January 1873, at 11:30 at night. On 3 January she sent her sister-in-law this victory dispatch regarding the newborn: "She is very strong and healthy, they tell me she weighs eight *pounds,* so even if it is really six, that is already not bad; she seems very sweet....I was in pain for barely half an hour; what I felt before that does not count. She will be baptized tomorrow, Saturday, and all that will be missing to make the celebration complete will be you."

On 4 January, Marie Françoise Thérèse Martin was baptized in the Church of Notre Dame, where her parents had been united in what they thought would be a virginal marriage. Thérèse had as godmother Marie, her oldest sister, and as godfather Paul Albert Boul, the son of a friend of Louis Martin's. Marie and Paul Albert were both thirteen years old and highly conscious of the gravity of the commitment they were making in the name of the newborn.

On Tuesday, 14 January, Thérèse smiled for the first time at her mother, who could not believe her eyes: "I thought I was wrong, but yesterday there could be no doubt—she looked at me very attentively, then she gave me a delicious smile."

To the joy of the first smile succeeded the pain of the first sickness. On 17 January, Thérèse showed symptoms of enteritis. Zélie wondered, "Will I have to lose this one, too?" She lost sleep, and only after Thérèse was better did she again sleep well.

On 1 March came a new alarm, this time more serious. "My little Thérèse...was getting stronger before my very eyes, and I was so proud. But today things have really changed, she is doing very poorly and I have no hope whatsoever of saving her. The poor little thing is suffering horribly, since yesterday, and it is heartbreaking to see her."

Since her mother could not breast-feed her, Thérèse was nourished with a milk soup and became steadily weaker. A nurse had to be found without delay. On 11 March, Louis being away, Zélie raced to Sémallé, a hamlet a few kilometers from Alençon, to get Rose Taillé, to whom she had entrusted her two deceased sons. Rose left her own children to follow Zélie, and upon her arrival in Alençon, she saw that she had come on a useless errand: The baby would no longer take in anything.

Zélie invoked Saint Joseph, and Rose offered her breast to Thérèse. Suddenly, she began sucking until she was out of breath; then, after spitting out a few mouthfuls, fell back as if dead. About fifteen minutes later, she revived and gave her mother a smile that filled her with even more joy than the first one had. Thérèse was saved. Saint Joseph and Rose Taillé had united their efforts to accomplish a miracle on this 11 March 1873.

Zélie immediately began a hymn of thanksgiving, and she sang as she had in the blessed days when she still carried her Thérèse, from whom she now had to separate herself. Rose could not desert her husband, their four little boys, their house, and their cow, nicknamed the Redhead. Along with her, she took Thérèse, who would live as a little country girl of the Norman meadowlands.

3

Child of the Sémallé Countryside

(16 March 1873–2 April 1874)

Thérèse's first impressions were not urban but rustic. She spent more than a year, from 16 March 1873 until 2 April 1874, in the meadowlands of Normandy, where each bit of hedge seemed to hide a mystery, where legends and proverbs abounded, such as "windy year, year of apples," or "priests and shepherds are all sorcerers." The Taillés believed in ghosts and in will-o'-the-wisps that led travelers astray. They did not believe in imps. In Sémallé, it was said of a timid man that he was afraid of the imps.

The Taillés were wary of the number 13 and protected the cricket, the lucky charm of the home that sheltered it. They adhered to one of the most charming customs of the Norman meadowlands: giving flowers under any pretext—a wedding, the first day of May, a gathering. It was doubtless in Sémallé that Thérèse was taken by a passion for flowers that stayed with her for the rest of her life.

The flowers' fragrance tried to overcome, without always succeeding, the odor of the stable that was attached to the Taillés' cottage, and, in the courtyard, the stink of a pile of manure that was spread as fertilizer over the fields.

Diverse smells, birds chirping, hens clucking, the cow lowing, the four Taillé boys complaining (the youngest was a year old), opulent meadows, magnificent trees—these were what Thérèse's first months, her first sensations, were made of. As soon as she arrived in Sémallé, she came back to life and prospered for three weeks. And then there was a relapse, a new intestinal crisis accompanied by a strong fever.

Zélie, urgently summoned, hurried to Sémallé with a doctor who concluded that Thérèse's days were not numbered. It appeared that Rose Taillé and Zélie Martin had become alarmed for nothing. Thereafter, under the care of "little Rose" and the fresh air of the meadowlands, Thérèse became "a big baby, browned by the sun."

The big baby could not stand to be separated from her nurse, who, each Thursday, went to sell her butter and eggs at the Alençon market. Rose left Thérèse at the Martins' house. But she cried so loudly, and made such a fuss, that she was taken posthaste back to Rose. "As soon as she saw her nurse, she looked at her laughing, then not another sound. She stayed there like that, selling butter with all the women until noon!" reported Zélie. Thérèse selling butter and eggs at the age of five months—here was a promising start.

During each Thursday visit, a bedazzled Zélie observed her youngest daughter's progress in health, beauty, and weight. On 1 July 1873, she gave this account of Thérèse's weekly visit: "All she did was laugh; she especially enjoyed little Céline. She burst out laughing with her. It seems as if she already wants to play. That will come soon; she stands on her little legs, stiff as a post, and I think she will walk early and be good-natured. She seems very intelligent and has a fine look of predestination."

Thérèse was only seven months old, and already the understanding, the preestablished harmony, between her and Céline was manifest, and would last. As for the "look of predestination," Zélie had no idea how right she was! Thérèse was born on 2 January 1873, at 11:30 P.M. According to her horoscope, drawn up at my request by astrologer Danièle Jay, the stars came to an agreement—even Venus and Mars, for once not at war—to give the child the will to come out of herself and find her blossoming in God, and to "achieve in herself the alchemy of love and forgiveness."* Not wishing to be outdone, Jupiter placed itself in the sign of the Virgin to endow

---

* *Danièle Joy, horoscope of Thérèse Martin.*

Thérèse with a love of the humble and the poor, and with a "sense of the divine lived in the bosom itself of little things."* The "little way" that Thérèse found, a saintliness in daily life and in what is most day-to-day about daily life, was already represented in her horoscope.

It is not the habit of Christian couples to have their children's horoscopes drawn up: The future belongs only to God. But the future prepares itself in the stars, which obey the will of God—the same God whom Zélie Martin never ceased to thank for preventing Thérèse from joining her two angel brothers and her two angel sisters in heaven.

Rose Taillé maintained that "you could not find a sweeter child." Thérèse almost never yelled, and she happily let herself be carried on top of wheelbarrows of grass. At ten months, she stood up and hung on to chairs, demonstrating the clear intention of walking as early as possible and throwing herself into the conquest of the meadowlands.

At eleven months, Thérèse expressed her preferences. When she went to Alençon on Thursdays, she enjoyed only the company of four-year-old Céline and pushed away their nanny, Louise Marais, who in 1865, at age sixteen, had entered the service of the Martins. Louis and Zélie treated their servant with angelic gentleness, and Louise seemed devoted to her employers. Yet, as shall be seen, Thérèse's precocious refusal to look at Louise or to be taken in her arms would be justified.

Thérèse was comfortable only with the country women with whom Rose Taillé associated, or with the workers who surrounded Zélie Martin. The clients of the latter, high and powerful women of Alençon with hats overloaded with feathers and flowers, scared Thérèse, who seemed to have inherited from her mother a horror of people who were subjected to fashion.

Shortly before her first birthday, in mid-December, the little child of the Sémallé countryside "walks almost by herself." She had two

---

* *Ibid.*

teeth, which she willingly showed, since she smiled often. In mid-January 1874, Thérèse at last walked by herself, like a big girl.

Zélie Martin, who, as a Christmas present, had sent to her nieces in Lisieux *Les Petites Filles modèles* by the Comtesse de Ségur, really felt that she had brought into the world a child who also promised to be a model daughter. "She is as gentle and sweet as a little angel. She has a charming character, you can already see it; she has such a sweet smile. I long to have her at home." Thérèse's unforgettable smile was starting to exert its power. Zélie would have liked to see the smile every day, not just once a week. But her last-born's health was more important than any other consideration.

To stave off her impatience, Mme Martin made city clothing for her country daughter: a sky-blue outfit, little blue shoes, blue belt, and white coat. Thérèse was destined to the colors blue and white, the colors of the Virgin, who reigned, in those days, over Catholic France. As a sign of their devotion, Louis and Zélie gave all their nine children the forename Marie.

The time came for Thérèse to leave Sémallé, and the beautiful blue outfit was not enough to console her over the loss of Rose Taillé. Leaving her four foster brothers for her four sisters, and wheelbarrows full of grass for embroideries of Alençon needlework, must not have been easy for the fourteen-month-old child of the countryside. She returned to her native city on 2 April 1874 to cleanse herself of her rusticity and learn the good manners of polite society, and especially to learn the holy ways of her holy family.

4

An Inexplicable Crying Fit

(Easter Monday 1875)

Thérèse went from the Taillé family, who confused the priest with the sorcerer, to the Martin family, who believed only in God and for whom the priest was the representative of God on earth. This was not without merit: Anticlericalism was on the rise and spared no social class. Parisian ladies of the haute bourgeoisie, such as Mme Mesnard-Dorian, refused to sit at the same table as a priest. Workers were deserting the Church for the bistros. Alcoholism and anticlericalism went hand in hand in the eyes of the Martins, who were sobriety itself and rigorously observed the fasts that the Church prescribed.

Zélie belonged to the Third Order of Penance and to countless religious associations, which is why she said, "I belong to all the associations." Louis could have said the same; moreover, he never missed a pilgrimage. Anticlericals openly made fun of the pilgrims, who, when they responded to provocations, were sometimes taken to the police station. Faced with these vexations, end-of-century Christians thought of themselves as those of the first centuries, exposed to the persecutions of Roman emperors. The Neros and Diocletians were replaced by "red" deputies who dreamed of "swallowing priests whole," driving out the Jesuits, and dissolving congregations.

Cardinal Nicholas Wiseman's novel, *Fabiola,* published in 1854, was on everyone's bookshelf and in everyone's mind. Zélie was prepared to follow in Saint Agnes's footsteps and Louis in Saint Sebastian's; these were two saints whose martyrdom Wiseman took pleasure in describing in pages that could have been written by de Sade. It was all whips, rods, and chains. The Martin couple missed the sadism, of course, as Thérèse would miss it later. All things are pure to the pure.

If the Christians of the first centuries had a tendency to let themselves be tortured without complaining, those of the end of the nineteenth century were on the defensive, ready to fight their future executioners. In 1875, in reaction to the prevailing anticlericalism and to redeem the horrors of the Commune, which George Sand herself said was not "a revolution, but positively a crime that is a product of common law," the archbishop of Paris, Monseigneur Guibert, blessed the first stone of the basilica of Montmartre and dedicated France to the Sacred Heart. Catholic France sang, and would sing for a long time, this refrain: "Save, save France, in the name of the Sacred Heart." It was certainly one of the first hymns that Thérèse would have learned, since Thérèse was exceptionally talented, as her mother maintained: "She sings little songs for us, but you have to be used to them to understand them. She is very intelligent and says her prayers like a little angel, it is ideal!"

This maternal hymn to her last-born is dated 8 November 1874; Thérèse was just twenty-three months old. Shortly before Christmas, she received her presents from Lisieux. Her uncle, Isidore Guérin, especially spoiled her, by sending her a miniature ark of Noah. Just the sight of it made her "mute with pleasure." As for Céline, she was delighted with her game of building blocks, and Léonie "very pleased" with her rosary. The elder girls, Marie and Pauline, boarders at the Convent of the Visitation of Le Mans, were allowed to receive the traveling bags they had wished for. Now they were filled with joy, but not as much as was Mme Martin by Thérèse's awakening piety. She gave this account to her sister-in-law, Céline, in a letter dated 14 March 1875:

> Little Thérèse...already knows how to pray to the good Lord.
> Every Sunday she goes to part of the vespers and if, by misfor-
> tune, we ever neglected to take her, she would cry and not be
> consoled. A few weeks ago, we were walking with her on a
> Sunday afternoon. She had not been "to matt," as she says.
> When we got home she began crying loudly, saying she wanted
> to go to mass; she opened the door and ran away under the rain
> that was coming down in torrents, toward the church. We ran
> after her to bring her home, and her sobs lasted a good hour.

At two years and three months, Thérèse escaped to run to the church
and cried for an hour because she had not been "to matt"—this was
promising! To this sobbing, which lasted for a while but was under-
standable, succeeded, a few days later, an inexplicable crying fit, the
backdrop of which was the Convent of the Visitation of Le Mans.

In March 1875, on Easter Monday, for the first time in her life,
Thérèse got on train to visit her aunt, Sister Marie-Dosithée, in Le
Mans.

Delighted with the trip, Thérèse was less so when she entered,
also for the first time, the Visitation. Barely inside, she began to cry
softly, noiselessly, until she was choking from tears. After that she
settled down, arousing the admiration of the convent's nuns and in
particular of her aunt, who commented that she was "very sweet,
and unusually obedient; she did everything she was told to without
hesitation and was so tranquil that you could have had her stay like
that all day, without moving."

This unforeseeable crying fit left Zélie perplexed. Who knows
what goes on in the head of a two-year-old child? Unfathomable
mystery. Later, in her *Histoire d'une âme* (*Story of a Soul*), Thérèse
would relate that in her second year she had thought: I, too, will be
a nun," without knowing much about what that meant, and because she had heard people saying that her sister Pauline was to
become a nun. Was it the acuteness of this thought that provoked so
many tears? The presentiment that this convent in Le Mans, with its
grilles, its cells, its parlor, foreshadowed the one in Lisieux where

she would be a nun? So many questions without answers. This really inexplicable fit was nothing like a tantrum and contrasted remarkably with Thérèse's good behavior during the visit.

Back in Alençon, Thérèse retuned to her games with Céline. They indulged in their favorite pastime of cutouts or in the joys of building blocks. Sometimes they quarreled, and Céline would give in because she was the oldest and wanted "to have a pearl in her crown"—to make a commendable sacrifice. Thérèse was not yet at that point. Sometimes Zélie saw herself obliged to "correct this poor baby who gets herself worked up into dreadful furies; when things do not go as she would like them to, she rolls around on the floor desperately, believing that all is lost."

All was lost except the love that Thérèse had for her mother, which she showed even in her games. For instance, when she walked down a staircase saying *"Maman"* at each step, her mother had to answer, "Yes, my little girl." If by misfortune Zélie forgot, Thérèse stayed in place, without moving, until she at last got her "Yes, my little girl."

Céline, by now six, read easily, and even read aloud *Les Petites Filles modèles,* giving the appropriate voice to each character. Zélie marveled at this. Seized with the desire to emulate, and also wanting to inspire the wonder of her mother, Thérèse "is already starting to read…she already knows almost all her letters." Indeed, Thérèse was doing everything she could to win the attention of her mother, whose death she wished for in an overabundance of love:

> The baby is an imp second to none; she comes to cuddle with me while wishing me death: "Oh! I would love for you to die, my dear little mother!" We scold her, and she says, "It's so you go to heaven, since you say we have to die to go there." In the same way, she wishes for the death of her father.

These "overabundances of love," which would later change Thérèse into Sister Thérèse, appeared in December 1875, shortly before her third birthday. From her earliest years, Thérèse lived a life of love.

5

A Holy Family

(Summer 1876)

An obsession with saintliness dominated the thoughts of Zélie Martin. She prayed constantly that her daughters "will all be saints." She had the same wish for herself. "Me, too, I would love to be a saint, but I do not know where to begin; there is so much to do that I am limited by the desire." As for her husband, no doubt was possible, he was a holy man!

The harmony between Louis and Zélie was held up as an example by their friends Christophe Desroziers, Sister Marie Gertrude Bigot, and Mme Coulombe, the lady of the manor of Lanchal.

It really was perfect harmony. Whenever M. and Mme Martin were temporarily apart, they wrote letters to each other that left no doubt about this perfection. "It would be impossible for me to live without you," sighed Zélie. Louis invariably finished his letters with, "Your husband and true friend, who loves you for life."

The holy family formed by Louis, Zélie, and their five daughters contributed to the edification of the devout in their parish. The regularity of their existence aroused the admiration of neighbors who, about five o'clock in the morning, upon hearing noises in the house on rue Saint-Blaise, would whisper, "It's the Martins getting ready for the first mass, let's get some more sleep."

In her *Histoire d'une âme*, Thérèse repeatedly paid tribute to the excellent upbringing she received from her parents, without which, she wrote, "I would have become quite wicked and perhaps have been lost." Thérèse was boasting. She had a romanticized vision of perdition. She even went as far as saying she could perhaps have been another Mary Magdalene. Impossible! Never would Thérèse d'Alençon have become an Émilienne d'Alençon, a Liane de Pougy, a Valtesse de la Gigne, or a Caroline Otero, to mention only the four most well-known courtesans of her time. And then there was this dreadful admission at the end of her life: "My body has always bothered me, I have never been comfortable in it; even as a small child I was ashamed of it."

But as a young child, Thérèse seemed to get on very well with her body, which was so pleasant to perch on a swing that her father had put up in the garden. This body, seized at times by fits of turbulence, collected cuts and bumps that were healed with compresses and above all with extra affection. At the age of three, Thérèse was all tenderness. Tenderness that she received and returned a hundredfold, which caused her mother to say, "I think I love her more than the others, probably because she is the youngest."

This young body sometimes sprang surprises on Thérèse, becoming so restless at night that it had to be tied down. It was Céline who came to tie the many ropes intended to stop the "little imp" from "driving herself crazy." In a letter of 26 March 1876, Zélie told of this "craziness":

> Last night she woke us up by calling out to her father, telling him she was "touched." Her father answered, "Sleep, my Thérèse," but she said again, "Papa, I'm touched." Finally he got up to see what this craziness was. Her little head was indeed touching the wood of the bed frame, so that each time she moved she banged it. So tonight, I fixed her bed in a way that she should no longer be able to drive herself crazy!

Later, in *Historie d'une âme,* Thérèse told a slightly different version of this incident, saying it was her mother whom she called to help her, not her father, as Zélie reported.

This "craziness," even if it sometimes disturbed Louis's and Zélie's slumber, was nonetheless a source of amusement for the holy family, which also found entertainment in the talent that Thérèse had for imitation. It was the Martins' gardener who often bore the brunt of this talent.

He maintained that he received visits from his deceased wife, who came to "annoy" him, as he said, because he had forgotten to close the door. As soon as she saw the gardener, Thérèse would start to say over and over again: "You're annoyin' me, woman, you're annoyin' me," with such gusto that she had to be hushed up.

But Thérèse was used to being quiet. When Marie gave Céline two or three hours of lessons, the "little imp," in order not to leave her Céline, from whom she was inseparable, sat on a chair in a corner without saying a word, sewing. When she could not thread her needle, Thérèse, who had already learned the power of tears, cried in silence until Marie interrupted the lesson and came to help her.

In May 1876, Zélie drew an interesting parallel between Céline and Thérèse, by now no longer a little imp but a little ferret. "My little Céline is completely inclined to virtue; it is the innermost feeling of her person. She has a pure soul and loathes evil. As for the little ferret, we don't really know how she will turn out, she is so little, so absent-minded, she is more intelligent than Céline but much less gentle, and especially almost invincibly stubborn; when she says 'no,' nothing can make her give in. You could put her in the basement for a whole day and she would spend the night there rather than saying 'yes.' "

Thérèse would later learn to turn this stubbornness that her mother presented as a fault into a good quality. It was because of her "invincible" stubbornness that she entered Carmel and became a saint, as she had decided to, and nothing could make her change her mind!

In 1876, sixteen-year-old Marie, fifteen-year-old Pauline, and thirteen-year-old Léonie behaved like little mothers toward Céline and Thérèse. Léonie, thinking she had arrived at the age when one no longer plays with dolls, gave her two little sisters a basket filled with ribbons and scraps of fabric. Céline picked out a bundle of piping, and Thérèse, regal, decreed: "I choose everything." A magnificent phrase. Thérèse was completely committed to the absoluteness of this choice, to the absoluteness of this "everything." Such a soul could only be completely fulfilled by the Great Everything that is God.

After Léonie, it was Marie's turn to take center stage, as Zélie reported to her daughter Pauline in a letter of 21 May 1876:

> Marie loves her little sister and thinks she is very sweet, but she would be quite difficult, for the poor little one is greatly afraid of upsetting her. Yesterday I wanted to give her a rose, knowing that makes her happy, but she began to beg me not to cut it. Marie had forbidden it. She was red with emotion, but even so I gave her two, and she dared not appear in the house after that. In vain I told her the roses were mine. "No they're not," she said, "they're Marie's." The child becomes upset very easily.

As for Pauline, a boarder at the Convent of the Visitation of Le Mans, Thérèse asked every day when she would be back. And Pauline would have loved to see her two little sisters, whose botched photographs she received: one of Céline with a half-closed eye and one of Thérèse, who had been afraid of the photographer, pouting.

During the summer vacation of 1876, the family indulged together in the joys of the Alençon summertime. They picked strawberries in the Pavillon garden, went on long Sunday walks across the fields, picked profusions of cornflowers and daisies. Like her contemporary Alexandra David-Néel, the explorer, who as a child was fascinated by the line of the horizon, which she wanted to seize, Thérèse, for her part, was fascinated by the distant greens of the Norman countryside:

> Already I loved distances…the space, and the gigantic fir trees with their branches touching the earth, left in my heart an impression similar to what I still feel today at the sight of nature.

During these walks, if the Martins came across a poor person, it was Thérèse's job to give the alms. She learned to give to those who had nothing. She also learned to give to Him who is everything, to God. "Starting at age three, I began to refuse nothing that the good Lord asked of me." But what could God really ask of a child of three, if not to be happy in the most holy family of Alençon?

This bliss was sometimes interrupted by a complaint from Thérèse, who would moan, "I'm so unhappy." But why was she unhappy to the point of shedding tears that made the household rush to her? It was because Céline had just told her: "Your dolls are ill-mannered and you give them everything they want."

This supposed "calamity" occurred on 7 December 1876. The real calamity would occur the next day, when Zélie finally decided to consult a doctor about the tumor she had in her breast, which for some time had been worrying her.

6

The Child Spoiled by God and by Zélie Martin

(Spring 1877)

In April 1865, Zélie Martin had felt the first shooting pains caused by a lump in her right breast. She did not worry about it very much; breast cancer was not watched for in those days, as it is today.

Zélie was a strong woman who treated her body roughly, like something that was of little consequence. She did not worry about what she considered to be a trifle, and she thought of her family's health before thinking of her own. Moreover, she came from a family, the Guérins, in which courage was coin of the realm.

In the middle of the Reign of Terror, her father, Isidore, had defied [revolutionaries who wore a blue "Liberty cap" and were thus known as] the Blues and helped the resisting priests, one of whom was his uncle, the priest Guillaume Marin Guérin, whom he saved from certain death. When one is the daughter of a man who, before becoming a policeman, started out as a soldier at Wagram and went through the battles of the First Empire, one does not become upset about a lump in the breast!

And then there was the will of God, which Zélie followed blindly. Finally, there was Louis, whom she did not want to worry, their daughters, and the Alençon needlework that took up her days. How was she to find a little time to get medical treatment? By the time she decided to consult a doctor, in December 1876, it was too late.

When she came back from that last-chance visit, Zélie, overwhelmed, could not keep herself from upsetting the harmony of the family circle, and she hid nothing about the verdict that burdened her. There followed a scene of appalling distress. Marie and Léonie sobbed, quickly imitated by Céline and Thérèse, who, too young to understand what was actually happening, guessed vaguely that something serious was threatening their beloved mother. Devastated, Louis immediately went up to the attic to put away his fishing gear, realizing that he was too unhappy to allow himself this final pleasure.

It did not take Zélie long to become calm again and envision, with the tranquillity that comes from absolute confidence in the designs of Providence, the post-Zélie. She was convinced that Marie, who was sixteen, could take her place and that she could be assisted in the job by Pauline, who was fifteen. She punctuated her reasoning with an irrefutable "Anything that happens will always be what the good Lord wants." There was not the shadow of a revolt against the divine will. She even found the strength to reassure her family and to declare to her sister-in-law in Lisieux:

> It's really nothing, and if I could not see the lump, I would think it was nothing at all....If the pain gets worse, I'll go on pilgrimages. If I had listened to Louis, I think we would already be in Lourdes, but there is no rush. For now, what I would like is to come and spend a day with you. You could see how well I look, and that I have a good appetite and am in good spirits; it's true that I am not distressed.

Zélie went to Lisieux and took advantage of the visit to consult the eminent Doctor Notta. He confirmed the Alençon doctor's diagnosis: It was too late. There was no hope other than a miracle in Lourdes, where Zélie decided to go on the next pilgrimage.

Since a disaster never comes alone, Zélie's sister, Sister Marie-Dosithée, was dying. She had reached the last stage of consumption.

On Christmas Day 1876, she received extreme unction and waited serenely for death. So as not to disturb her serenity, Zélie hid the gravity of her own condition from her sister. She charged the Visitation nun with delivering various "messages" upon her arrival in heaven; for heaven, to believers at the end of the nineteenth century, was something like our modern department stores. You could find anything there—you had only to ask. It was very simple. Thérèse, following the example of her mother, learned at a very young age to ask with the same simplicity.

Zélie advised Sister Marie-Dosithée, who died on 24 February 1877, as follows:

> As soon as you're in paradise, go and find the Virgin Mary and tell her: "My good mother, you played a strange trick on my sister by giving her poor Léonie; it was not a child like this that she asked you for, and she needs you to put matters right."

"Poor Léonie," as she was called in the family, did not have Marie's good sense, or Pauline's piety, or Céline's virtue, or Thérèse's intelligence. She learned with difficulty, and despite the intervention of her aunt in the Visitation, she was sent home three times from the Le Mans convent. She was the black sheep of the Martin clan and stayed in the background, upsetting Zélie by refusing to obey her, "never having obeyed her except by force, argumentatively doing the exact opposite of what she wanted, even when she wanted to do something, and in the end obeying only the maid."

Yes, Léonie obeyed only the maid. And for a good reason. One month after Sister Marie-Dosithée's death, a horrified Zélie discovered that Louise had been whipping Léonie until she bled whenever the latter did not carry out her orders. It had been a true case of domestic enslavement. Louise's tyranny had been reserved only for Léonie, sparing the other Martin girls, and it had been limitless!

When Zélie told Léonie: "Go ahead and play in the garden, I don't like to see you here when everyone else is having fun," Léonie refused, for fear of the retribution that Louise had promised her: "If your mother tells you to go and play, go ahead, but you know what punishment awaits you after that."

In short, Louise Marais behaved with Léonie like Mina, the evil maid in *François le bossu* [*Francis the Hunchback*], who beats poor Christine. Even though she was fanatical about the Comtesse de Ségur, Zélie did not think of making the connection. Even worse, she took pity on the unworthy servant, whom she kept in her employ, whereas the Comtesse punishes Mina by sending her to Walachia, where each month she is whipped in the presence of a Walachian prince with no hope of escape.

Louise received mercy only on one condition: that she never again speak to Léonie. Delivered from her torturer, "poor Léonie" was all tenderness and obedience toward her mother, who thanked Sister Marie-Dosithée, as was fitting, for having quickly and conscientiously delivered her "message" in heaven.

We have seen that as a baby, Thérèse had felt only repugnance for Louise. The maid carried out her duties flawlessly, all the while regretting that she was not among the rich. One day when the conversation concerned one of the wealthiest men in Alençon, Louise had said: "If only I had all that!" Thérèse, who had just received a box of candies, had immediately replied, "I like my box of candy better than all that." The little imp's retorts and pranks were Zélie's delight; watching them, she forgot about her illness.

A child spoiled by God and by Zélie Martin, Thérèse knew she had nothing to fear when she was in her mother's arms. Not for one instant did she imagine that she could be deprived of this protection. For the time being, she was concerned only with knowing what day it was, repeating with relish, "Today is Sunday, tomorrow is Monday, then Tuesday..." She never missed her prayers and said some of them while jumping for joy. She would not have told a lie "for all the gold in the world," insisted her mother, who asked God every day that all her daughters, including poor Léonie, should become saints.

7

The Death of a Mother

(28 August 1877)

During the spring of 1877, disheartened by Sister Marie-Dosithée's death and by the progression of the disease that was little by little taking Zélie, Thérèse felt, confusedly but intensely, the pain and anguish. She was as emotional as her contemporary, Anna de Noailles, who said, "I am the most sensitive point of the universe."

This hypersensitivity, expressed in frequent and sudden outbursts of tears, was manifested as well in her increase of "practices." These were acts of virtue, the equivalent of our modern "good works," that were carried out each day and counted on a rosary. The "practices" went along with the "pearls," sacrifices made to adorn the crown that would be given to the Lord when, after death, one was placed in His presence in heaven.

During the spring and summer of 1877, Thérèse and Céline played at increasing their practices and pearls. The winner was the one who could count the most of these at the end of the day. They did this to such an extent that a neighbor asked Mme Martin what on earth her two little girls could be doing—in the garden, they spoke only of "practices" and "pearls."

Zélie rejoiced in Thérèse's obvious piety: "This dear little girl is our happiness, she will be good, you can already see the beginnings of it. She speaks only of the good Lord; she would not miss saying her prayers for everything [sic]."

Sometimes during mass, especially during the sermon, the little imp got a bit bored. But at age four, was this not excusable? Thérèse preferred to do the preaching herself. Thus she explained to Céline how the good Lord could comfortably fit into a host. Which gave rise to the following exchange, overheard and reported by Zélie:

"How can the good Lord be in such a little host?"

"It's not surprising since the good Lord is all-powerful."

"What does that mean, all-powerful?"

"It means He can do whatever he wants."

Zélie thought she was already hearing the sort of discussion that must take place in heaven, and she resigned herself to her imminent death.

"At least the good Lord is doing me the favor of not frightening me; I am very calm, I find myself almost happy, I would not exchange my lot for any other....Meanwhile, I am going to do everything I can to make a miracle occur; I am counting on the Lourdes pilgrimage, but even if I am not cured, I will try to sing on the way back."

Zélie left for Lourdes with Marie, Pauline, and Léonie. It was a tedious trip. Marie got dust in her eye and moaned for four hours. Léonie, whose feet hurt, added her moans to her sister's. It was a disastrous sojourn; Mme Martin disliked the accommodations and lost the rosary that had belonged to Sister Marie-Dosithée.

These annoyances, and many others as well, would have been quickly forgotten if a miracle had cured the invalid. But there was no miracle. Zélie came home with her illness. Valiantly, she sang the same hymns on the way home as she had sung on the way there. Marie, Pauline, and Léonie, despairing over this failure, could not bring themselves to join their voices to their mother's, who proclaimed: "I am not sorry that I came to Lourdes. Even though fatigue has made me sicker, at least I will not reproach myself for anything, if I don't get better. In the meantime, let us hope."

Zélie hoped. Which did not stop her from contemplating the

liquidation of her Alençon needlework business in favor of a well-deserved retirement. It was time. Léonie wanted to die in her mother's place. Marie and Pauline increased their novenas, as Thérèse and Céline increased their "practices" and "pearls." As for Louis, he retreated into his grief.

On 8 July, on her bed of pain, Zélie let herself drift into a dream of family happiness:

> The maid absolutely has to leave soon, and I have no one else in mind. Oh! If only the good Lord would do me the favor of curing me, I would not want any more domestics. Marie is very good at running the house, she's the one who makes up the rooms and takes care of her little sisters. Pauline and Léonie could help too, and we would be happier than I have ever been.

The happiness Zélie foresaw would be that enjoyed by Louis and his daughters at Lisieux, at Les Buissonnets. Also presentient was the last mention that Zélie made of Thérèse in her correspondence: "My Thérèse is a charming little creature, I assure you that one will manage well." She had no idea how right she was. In her letters to her brother and sister-in-law, she continually praised her daughters.

Alas, the illness only got worse. On 27 July she wrote to Isidore Guérin: "I have suffered for the last twenty-four hours more than I have ever suffered in my life, and those hours were spent in moaning and crying out."

Thérèse and Céline had to be moved away from the dying woman and her cries of pain; they were entrusted to one of M. Martin's nieces, Mme Leriche. They spent the days at her house, coming back in the evenings to sleep at rue Saint-Blaise.

On 27 August in the evening, Zélie Martin received extreme unction. Thérèse would never forget it: "The moving ceremony of extreme unction was also imprinted on my soul. I still see the spot where I was, next to Céline, all five of us in order of our ages, and our poor dear father was there as well, sobbing."

In the night of 27–28 August 1877, at about 12:30, Zélie Martin breathed her last sigh. In the morning, Louis came to get Thérèse so she could kiss her mother one last time. "And without saying anything, I brought my lips to the forehead of my darling mother. I do not remember crying very much, I did not speak to anyone of the profound feelings that I had...I watched and listened in silence."

At age four, Thérèse understood that silence is the safest of refuges.

8

Post-Zélie

(15 November 1877)

Even when it is foreseeable, as Zélie's was, death never fails to overwhelm the next of kin, who wonder, at that time, about the other life. None of the dead have returned from the hereafter to tell us about what happens there....

If Louis, Marie, Pauline, Léonie, Céline, and Thérèse were convinced that Zélie was in heaven, the six were not any less distraught about the absence of the woman who had been the center of the family circle. Each one of them, to different degrees, was "very sad," as Thérèse babbled when she kissed her mother for the last time. But at age four, what kind of notion could she have of the "last time"?

The death of a mother is a test that everyone faces in his or her own way. Some never recover and are orphans for the rest of their lives; others look for a substitute mother and succeed, after a fashion, in filling the emptiness. Thérèse belonged to this second category.

When the five Martin girls came home from the burial, the maid, Louise Marais, who was still there—she would not leave until December 1877—said what would have been better to keep to herself, for this sort of statement deepens grief: "Poor little girls, you no longer have a mother." Then Céline threw herself suddenly into Marie's arms, crying out: "You will be my *maman*."

Accustomed to imitating Céline, Thérèse turned toward Pauline and declared: "Well, for me, Pauline will be my *maman*." For while Marie was her godmother and Céline her favorite, Pauline represented for Thérèse, according to her own admission, "a child's ideal." Instinctively, every child chooses a model that he or she tries to copy exactly. Thérèse's model was Pauline. Her successes at the boarding school of the Convent of the Visitation of Le Mans, her cheerfulness, the prestige of her age—Pauline was twelve years older than Thérèse—everything made the little youngest girl opt for the sister her father had nicknamed "the real pearl," for she was incomparable, gifted in everything.

The nicknames that Louis gave his daughters, and that he would repeat to ward off his distress, were revealing. Marie was "the diamond," of which she had the purity, or "the bohemian," because she had the vivaciousness of a Gypsy. Léonie was just "good Léonie," to emphasize the fact that she had stopped being mean since escaping from Louise Marais's sadistic treatment. Céline was "the intrepid": Nothing stopped her. Thérèse, always the most spoiled, had earned several nicknames that had no need of explanation, such as "the little queen" or "the little ray of sunshine."

In this predominately female tribe, Louis was obviously "the king." A king without amusements. A king whom the loss of his companion would have rendered inconsolable if he had not found in his faith, and in the company of his daughters, all the comfort it was possible for him to have. In each one of them, a little bit of Zélie yet lived.

Louis continued to follow the wishes of his wife strictly; in the months preceding her final days, she had several times entrusted her children to her brother and sister-in-law. Isidore and Céline Guérin made no secret of how much they wanted to see the Martins move to Lisieux, so that Zélie's last wish could be fulfilled.

To carry out this desire, Louis resigned himself to leaving Alençon, where he had been happy and where he had enjoyed the most agreeable thing in the world, routine. However, he had no choice. Isidore had been named the surrogate guardian of his five nieces, which meant that he had the power to protect their rights and their estate, even against their father.

Isidore Guérin got to work immediately to find the home that his sister had dreamed of, big enough for everyone to be comfortable, with a bigger garden than the one at rue Saint-Blaise. On 10 September he found this dream residence, situated exactly 764 steps from his pharmacy and 700 from the church—one could not be more precise—in the Bissonnets district, which the Martin girls would distort into "Buissonnets," designating their house and the district with the same word.

So Thérèse prepared to leave Alençon, the house in which she was born, with its balcony from which she towered over the neighboring buildings; the prefecture; the Church of Notre Dame, where she had been baptized; and the Pavilion, which she loved visiting so much that she thought of each time as a reward, saying to her sister Céline: "We cannot have the *cheek* to think Papa will take us to the Pavilion every day."

All that was over now, and Thérèse was not sad about it: "I felt no sorrow in leaving Alençon; children like change and it was with pleasure that I came to Lisieux."

The post-Zélie began on 15 November 1877, when the five Martin girls arrived in Lisieux, taken there by their uncle, who frightened Thérèse a bit. On the sixteenth, they moved into Les Buissonnets, where their aunt Céline and their two cousins Jeanne and Marie welcomed them. Their father was detained in Alençon by various business matters, such as, among others, the liquidation of the lace business, which his wife had not been able to carry out. On the sixteenth, Marie wrote to her father to report on their moving in:

> It is a charming house, pleasant and cheerful, with a big garden where Céline and Thérèse will be able to frolic. Only the stairs

leave something to be desired, and also the access road, "Paradise Road," as you call it, for indeed it is narrow, it is not "the wide and spacious way." But what does it matter; all of that is nothing, for we are just camping on earth. Today we have our tents here, but our real home is in Heaven, where we will go one day to join our darling mother.

There was no need to go to heaven to join Zélie, who was omnipresent at Les Buissonnets. Photographs of her, her dresses, her cashmere shawl, and the Virgin's statue that she had revered, were so many proofs that Mme Martin was still here.

Mme Guérin, Marie, Pauline, and Léonie hastened to organize the house, where Louis was entertained like a king upon his arrival, on 30 November. He had just turned fifty-four years old and was completely bald. To Thérèse and her sisters, he was the most handsome man in the world, and the most beloved. Love, pure love, reigned at Les Buissonnets.

9

The Happy Island
of Les Buissonnets

(Winter 1877–Spring 1880)

Like Alençon, Lisieux counted some fifteen thousand inhabitants. Situated at the confluence of three rivers, the Orbiquet, the Cirieux, and the Touques, it was a city-museum, with its wooden houses dating from the fourteenth, fifteenth, and sixteenth centuries. These houses often fell prey to fire, and they would disappear forever during the bombings that preceded the Liberation, in the summer of 1944.

Aside from the houses that looked as if they had been made of wooden lace by a cabinetmaking Zélie, Lisieux boasted, justifiably, its Salamandre Hotel, adorned with sirens and monkeys; its Saint-Jacques Church; its Saint-Pierre Cathedral; its Chapel of the Virgin, rebuilt by Pierre Cauchon, the bishop who had persecuted Joan of Arc; and, finally, its Etoile Gardens.

Lisieux was not content to be a city of the past. It was also a city of the present, with its factories, its dyeing industries, its tanneries, which, alas, were decreasingly prosperous. This decline was of no concern to Louis Martin and his daughters. Thanks to Zélie's tireless labor and Louis's judicious investments, the Martins easily had enough to live on from their private means. The house at Les Buissonnets reflected this affluence.

The redbrick building comprised, on the ground floor, an oak-paneled dining room, a kitchen, a study, and a boudoir. On the second floor were four bedrooms and two bathrooms. Under the roof were three attic rooms, and over the middle one an observatory, a belvedere that overlooked the city of Lisieux. Louis made this his favorite nook, his retreat. Perched up high, his only companions the clouds and his bedside books, including *L'Imitation de Jésus-Christ* and *L'Histoire de la Trappe* [*The History of the Trappist Order*], he could at last become the hermit that he had dreamed of being, a brother of Simeon Stylites, who had lived perched on a pillar.

The furniture that decorated Les Buissonnets had been selected to last for generations. Hard-wearing mahagany and massive oak dominated. The canopy bed, spiral sideboard, and round table could have belonged to [Marcel Proust's characters] the Verdurins' cousins from the provinces.

Marie and Pauline shared a room in which the statue of the Virgin sat enthroned, now a part of the family. Céline and Thérèse occupied another room, with their dolls. Léonie, always a bit separate, was allowed to have her own room.

At Les Buissonnets, the Martins would live as if on an island lost in the ocean, an island well stocked with flowers, vegetables, trees, and birds.

Deep mourning spared them from either receiving or paying visits, and the Martins frequented only the Guérins and their two daughters, Jeanne, ten years old, and Marie, eight.

On 2 January 1878, Thérèse celebrated her fifth birthday. It was a modest party prepared by Marie and Pauline, guardian angels of Les Buissonnets, busy angels who oversaw everything, helped with the bigger tasks by Victoire Pasquer, the servant who took Louise Marais's place. Victoire would later attest to their good conduct: "These young ladies never went out alone, and when their father did not accompany them, it was I who accompanied them. I saw always that they were very reserved and like models of good manners. There are not many families like that one. I, who have been all over serving in society, have met only one other who even approached them."

Léonie and Céline went to school at the Benedictine Abbey of Lisieux, Léonie as a full boarder, Céline as a half-boarder. In the mornings, Marie gave Thérèse writing lessons, and Pauline took care of the rest—reading, arithmetic, grammar. Thérèse had trouble distinguishing between masculine and feminine nouns in her grammar. On the other hand, she had no difficulty with catechism and biblical history, which she learned with unconcealed joy. When she worked well, she earned an afternoon outing with her father. When she worked poorly, she was not allowed to go out. The entire household revolved around Thérèse and her education.

The walks with M. Martin were instructive. One at a time, they visited the churches in Lisieux. She learned about their history, their particularities, the convents, Carmel. The first time she walked into the Carmel chapel, Thérèse had no idea that she would enter it permanently nine years later!

Upon returning from these pious walks, Thérèse played in the garden. One of her favorite games was making teas from grains and peels. She presented these to her father, who pretended to drink them. She had, like [the fictional] Camille and Madeleine de Fleurville, a garden in which she cultivated her flowers. In the recesses of the walls, she erected altars, then rushed to get her father so he could admire them.

As in the Alençon garden, there was a swing in the Lisieux garden—"Higher Papa, higher." Louis Martin pushed his daughter higher, until she could see the neighboring garden and the white headdress of its owner. One cannot admire enough the inalterable patience of this father in his fifties faced with the demands of his five-year-old imp. But she was "the little queen" and he her "darling king." In the kingdom of Les Buissonnets, Louis and Thérèse reigned absolutely.

Sometimes this Robinson and Robinsonette Crusoe left their island for the bank of a river. Louis thought he could, without offending the proprieties that governed the mourning period in those days,
begin his fishing outings again. Pauline immortalized his best catches
in watercolors and drawings that ended up covering the walls of the
belvedere.

Thérèse did her best to imitate her father, and she fished for a
while. But before long she abandoned her rod, sitting by herself in a
spot of the meadow, watching the grasses undulate beneath the wind
and listening to the military music that emanated from Lisieux, a
garrison town.

Her daydreaming was interrupted by snack time—a beautiful slice
of bread with jam that any five-year-old child would be happy to
devour. But Thérèse was not just anyone. The beautiful slice of bread
with jam that had been prepared by her sisters had turned into a
mere rancid piece of bread. Faced with this transformation, she understood that "only in heaven would joy be without clouds." That,
at least, was what she wrote in *Histoire d'une âme*. A child who at
age five understood that all is ephemeral because of a slice of bread
with jam was decidedly not a child like any other!

In the evenings after dinner, the beloved king and his little queen
held court. Thérèse on his knees, Louis declaimed the verses of Victor Hugo or of Lamartine, then sang hymns to the airs of *Mignon*.
To his dazzled daughters, M. Martin embodied the theater and the
opera at home. What was more, this model father was skilled with
his hands. He made minuscule toys, figurines that they called "Tombi-
Carabi," which, ballasted with lead, always righted themselves. Louis
did not miss pointing out to his daughters the lessons of such a
recovery: "In the adversities and shocks of life, you must imitate the
Tombi-Carabi men and get up again after each fall."

The Martin girls contemplated these words, or commented on
the latest homily by Monseigneur Hugonin, the bishop of Bayeux,
which had been published in the *Annuaire des cinq départements de*

la Normandie [*Yearbook of the Five Departments of Normandy*] and ended with this statement: "A people without beliefs soon becomes a people without moral strength and without virtue, condemned to irremediable social dissolution." The Martins were completely in agreement with this opinion.

The evening ended with a communal prayer recited before the statue of the Virgin. Thérèse was sure to renew the offering that she had already made during the day: "Dear God, I give you my heart: take it, please, so that no creature may possess it, only you, good Jesus."

It was Pauline who came to tuck Thérèse into her bed and who had to answer the invariable question: "Pauline, was I a very good girl today? Will the little angels fly around me?" Even if angels did fly around Thérèse, these celestial presences were not enough to dissipate her fear of the dark, which she was learning, bit by bit, to overcome, again thanks to Pauline's reasoning and advice. Thérèse obeyed Pauline as she had obeyed Zélie.

When she was sick—most frequently colds of unusual violence, which sometimes worsened and became bronchitis—she slept, "incomparable favor," in Pauline's bed. One day, to distract her patient, Pauline gave her a little knife.

"Oh! Pauline, you must love me very much if you're giving up your pretty knife with the mother-of-pearl star. But since you love me so much, would you be willing to sacrifice your watch to keep me from dying?"

"Not only to keep you from dying would I give away my watch, but just to see you get better soon, I would sacrifice it immediately."

With these words, Thérèse felt almost cured.

It was once more Pauline who, on Sundays, and only that day, took Thérèse a cup of hot chocolate in bed. After drinking it, she got up, to be dressed by Pauline and have her hair curled by Marie. Then the little queen and her two attendants presented themselves to the king, who took them to mass at the Saint-Pierre Cathedral.

In April 1878, at five years and four months old, Thérèse finally understood a sermon delivered by Monseigneur Ducellier, having to do with passion. From that moment on, she would understand all sermons, especially those that included references to her patron saint, Teresa of Ávila.

In the cathedral, on the church sextons' bench, sat enthroned, notable among notables, her uncle, Isidore Guérin, at whose house, immutably, she spent Sunday evenings. Thérèse loved her uncle Isidore, of course, but she was a bit afraid of him, especially when he sang *"Barbe-Bleue"* [*"Bluebeard"*] in his formidable voice. When he had finished his vocalizations, he would tirelessly question Thérèse, who dreaded questions and answered in monosyllables. It was with relief, which she did her best to hide, that she saw her father arrive to take her back to Les Buissonnets.

During one of these nocturnal trips home, Thérèse, admiring the stars, saw a constellation forming a T. "Look, Papa, my name is written in the sky," she cried. The discovery did not completely console her for the sadness of seeing Sunday come to an end. Tomorrow, she would again have to start her homework, her lessons, and go down to the dining room to eat breakfast. Everything was happening too fast for Thérèse, who wished Sundays would never end, even when they were spent in the company of Uncle Isidore!

In August 1878, Louis Martin took his daughters to Trouville, where the Guérins were staying. "Never will I forget the impression that the sea made on me, I could not keep from looking at it ceaselessly; its majesty, the roar of its waves, everything spoke to my soul of the Greatness and the Power of the good Lord." Thérèse was pulled from her pious contemplation by a man and woman who asked Louis Martin if he was the father of this "very nice little girl." Louis responded affirmatively, and with a shake of his head made the intruders understand that they should not compliment his daughter, who might feel vanity. It was a feeling with which Thérèse had no experience and never would. To be sure, she did not hide her pleasure at being called "very nice" by strangers, but that was all.

On the island of Les Buissonnets, where she was more protected than legendary princesses locked up in their towers, the "little queen" grew both in sense and in beauty. With her lovely, moonlike oval face, her eyes like stars, her long hair like a golden comet, Thérèse was radiant. She was better than "nice." She was ravishing, as Zélie had predicted. This exterior beauty went hand in hand with her interior beauty. And one might well ask what on earth Thérèse could have been accusing herself of when, at age six, at the end of 1879 or the beginning of 1880, she went to confession for the first time, in the Saint-Pierre Cathedral. Unless, as happens with very pure and very scrupulous children, she accused herself of all the sins in the world!

All we know of this first confession is that Thérèse left the confessional "happy and light." But are not happiness and lightness the domain of "little imps"?

Sometimes, dark premonitions crossed this state of grace. During the summer of 1879 or 1880, Thérèse had a terrible vision concerning her father, who was in Alençon for a few days and whose imminent return was expected.

> It might have been two or three o'clock in the afternoon, the sun shone in a brilliant blaze and all of nature seemed to be celebrating. I was by myself at the window of an attic room overlooking the big garden; I was looking before me, my mind filled with pleasant thoughts, when I saw in front of the wash house right across from me a man dressed absolutely like Papa, of the same size, with the same walk, except he was much more curved over...His head was covered with a kind of apron of indistinct color, so that I could not see his face. He was wearing a hat like one of Papa's. I saw him moving forward in an even stride alongside my little garden... Immediately a feeling of supernatural fear invaded my soul, but for an instant I thought Papa was doubtless back and was hiding to surprise me; so I

called out very loudly, in a voice trembling with emotion: "Papa! Papa!" But the mysterious character, not seeming to hear me, continued his steady pace without even turning around; following him with my eyes, I saw him move toward the grove that cut the wide walkway in two. I expected to see him reappear on the other side of the big trees, but the prophetic vision had vanished! All this lasted only an instant, but it etched itself so deeply in my heart that today, after fifteen years…the memory of it is as present as if the vision were yet in front of my eyes.

When she heard the cry, "Papa! Papa!" Marie, in a neighboring room, rushed in and asked her sister why she was calling her father, since he was not home yet. Thérèse related her vision. To reassure her, Marie declared that it could only have been their servant, Victoire, who must have been passing by with her head hidden under an apron. Impossible: Victoire said she had not left her kitchen. Next the commotion attracted Pauline, who joined her sisters to try to find a trace of the mysterious visitor. All three visited the grove and walked around the big trees. A wasted effort—there was no one. They resigned themselves to accepting that Thérèse had had a nightmare such as the intense heat of a summer afternoon can sometimes bring on. The account of this episode allows us to better understand why Thérèse had little taste for visions and for visionaries.

The little queen forgot her "nightmare" to rejoice over Céline's first communion, on 13 May 1880. She said over and over again, "It's today! The big day has come." She felt "flooded with joy."

In *Histoire d'une âme,* she summarized the happy days of her privileged childhood thus: "My life went by tranquil and happy; the affection that I was surrounded by at Les Buissonnets made me grow, so to speak." Another reflection of this happiness is found in Thérèse's writing exercise of 5 June 1880, where she tells of her love for the Virgin, for cornflowers, for poppies, and of her dread of spiders. She also tells about what fun she had walking with her father in the countryside, and playing with her dolls at Les Buissonnets. Alas, she would soon have to give up spending entire days on her island of Les Buissonnets, which was worthy of being called one of the mythical happy islands.

10

Prayer at Age Nine

(Autumn 1881–Winter 1882)

On 3 October 1881 in the morning, Thérèse, who was eight years and ten months old, left Les Buissonnets to enter the Benedictine Abbey of Lisieux, where she was to be a half-boarder, as Céline already was. She went into a "green" class, so named because the pupils wore, over their black uniforms, a belt of that color.

Founded in the sixteenth century, the abbey was the oldest scholastic establishment in Lisieux. Its age did not prevent the Benedictine ladies from giving instruction intended to be modern, leading to the elementary and the upper-level diplomas. The subtleties of French, English, drawing, piano, violin, and even of the mandolin were studied there. The students learned all about needlework. A deportment class was usually provided by the teachers, and once a year by a specialist. At the request of the parents, this instructor could also give a few dance lessons.

It was exactly the same program that Anne-Marie Chassaigne followed with the Faithful Companions of Jesus in the Convent of Saint Anne d'Auray, from 1878 to 1885. Anne-Marie Chassaigne would become one of the most celebrated courtesans of her time, under the name Liane de Pougy. In 1881 the future saint and the future courtesan were in the convent, laboring over the same exercises and entertaining themselves in the same way, the first one roaming about a wooded hill, Mount Cassin, next to the abbey; the other frolicking about the bog. Which goes to show that two people can receive the same education and follow very different paths.

At the abbey, as with the Faithful Companions of Jesus, religious instruction took precedence over other lessons. In each classroom was a crucifix and a statue of the Virgin. Ten minutes before the end of recess, pupils could retire into the boarding school's oratory, to worship the Blessed Sacrament there. Thérèse never missed this and drew great comfort from the visits. The five years that she spent in the abbey would not be among the five best years of her existence: "The five years that I spent there were the saddest of my life; had I not had my beloved Céline with me, I could not have stayed there a single month without falling ill."

Accustomed to being the center of the family's world, in the abbey Thérèse was just a pupil like the others. Used to playing alone, she did not know how to participate in group games. She felt different. Her schoolmates immediately noticed this difference and did not fail to make fun of it. Céline spoke up in her favor every time she could, which immediately earned Thérèse the nickname "Céline's little girl."

Her intelligence, her winning ways, her pretty looks, aroused envy. Placed in a class of students older than she, the little queen had soon risen to the top of the class, for which she was not forgiven. She was hated especially by a fourteen-year-old harpy who made her "pay in a thousand ways" for her successes. Timid, Thérèse did not know how to defend herself. She knew only how to cry, thinking that her tears were her best weapon. But those who persecuted her delighted in her sobs. Thérèse did not complain, and she covered up for the bullying of which she was the object. When one of her teachers would ask, "Why are you crying?" she answered simply, "I'm crying for the sake of crying." She became an "excessive crier." She had to brave vulgarities, baseness, and intrigues of which she knew nothing. Every evening she greeted her father like a liberator and went home to Les Buissonnets with exhilaration.

The abbey's Benedictines, especially Sister Henriette, appreciated Thérèse. She worked well in class, where she felt protected. The drama developed during recess. Despite her efforts, she did not succeed in getting into the circle dances, the races, the games of hide-and-seek. Mortified at being not really like the others, she hid behind a tree and waited for the end of recess.

Since she liked to tell stories, she told them to the younger girls, who listened to her with delight. But this new success displeased the older girls, who would do anything to interrupt the storyteller. It also worried the supervising teacher, who scattered the flock with, "My children, I would rather see you running than chatting."

Poor Thérèse next discovered a gloomy pastime: She buried dead birds. The whole idea was to use up the time of the interminable recess while not attracting too much attention from her enemies. She would have liked to be invisible. Now more than ever, she took refuge in reading: "If I did not know how to play, I loved reading and could have spent my life doing it."

Thérèse loved tales of chivalry and dreamed of imitating Joan of Arc, who had not yet been canonized and was only "Venerable." She entertained herself with *Le Journal de la jeunesse* [*The Young People's Newspaper*] and *La Mosaïque* [*The Mosaic*], which succeeded the *Magasin pittoresque* [*Picturesque Shop*]. But her favorite reading was the Comtesse de Ségur and Cardinal Wiseman. Thérèse became the child of the Comtesse and the cardinal. She thought of Fabiola, Camille, and Madeleine de Fleurville as so many ideal friends, since she was not able to make friends with any of her schoolmates. Two of her attempts at friendship were crowned with failure, for they did not survive the separation of summertime: "When I saw my schoolmate again my joy was great, but alas! I got only an indifferent look...My love was not understood; I felt it and did not beg for an affection that was being refused me."

Her intransigence concerning the absoluteness of feelings saved Thérèse from the distractions that intimate friendships can engender. She sensed that no affection on earth could fulfill her. Since she had been abandoned by her mother, she could be abandoned as well by her father and sisters. She had to find someone who she could be sure would never deceive or abandon her. This someone could only be God, to whom she prayed more and more, all the while anxious to pray to Him better and better.

One day she asked Sister Henriette how a nun prayed. The sister answered, "I do not know how the others do it, but as for me, I imagine I do it a bit like you do, Thérèse, when you get home in the evening with your papa, whom you have not seen since the morning. You throw your arms around his neck, you show him your good marks, you tell him about all sorts of little things, everything is gone over—your joys and your sorrows. Well, I do the same with the good Lord; He is my Father. In my thoughts I put myself near Him, I adore Him, making myself very little, like you, I speak to Him; it is with my heart that I pray, and how the time goes by quickly!"

This very intimate way of praying, which was not provided for in the abbey's program, was certainly the most beneficial instruction that the pupil Thérèse Martin received while she was there. She would follow Sister Henriette's example and join, at age nine, those mystics who turn their hearts into prayer wheels!

11

The Miracle of Pentecost

(13 May 1883)

Weak in spelling and arithmetic, the pupil Thérèse Martin stood out in reading, religious history, and drawing. She did her homework and learned her lessons well, which earned her good marks, merit crosses, "honor seals" that she was proud to show her father. Her reputation as an industrious and pious student would not weaken during the five years she spent at the abbey.

Her hypersensitivity, her outbursts of tears when she got a bad mark, sometimes tried her teachers' patience. One of them, Mother Saint Léon, upon learning later that her former student was to be canonized, said, "When I think that I scolded a saint! But perhaps it is because I scolded her that she became a saint."

For it did happen that Thérèse whispered an answer to one of her schoolmates. Caught in the act, she was reprimanded right away with, "Thérèse, you have no conscience." Which provoked inexhaustible tears followed by an interminable repentance. "I have sinned, and I have caused another to sin," repeated Thérèse, who was aware that she had the most demanding, the most pitiless, of consciences.

Her conscience was also Pauline, to whom she confided everything, and who complemented the abbey's lessons. Since whatever Pauline said was gospel, Thérèse permitted herself to point out to Mother Saint Léon, "But Pauline does not say what you say, Pauline does not do what you do." Mother Saint Léon did not fail to reply,

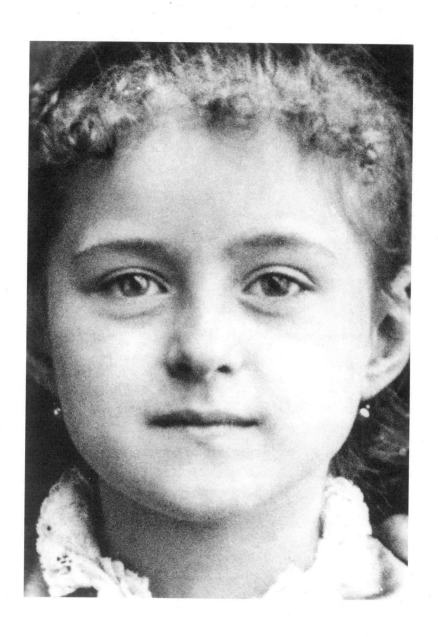

with as much firmness as spite: "Pauline is mistress at Les Buissonnets, whereas I am the mistress here." Which again brought tears to Thérèse's eyes; later she would acknowledge, "I really was unbearable because of my too-great sensitivity."

Admitted to various religious associations, such as L'Oeuvre de la Sainte Enfance (Works of the Holy Childhood), and received as a "Child of the Holy Angels," Thérèse redoubled her piety. Her devotion to the Virgin, who reigned over Les Buissonnets, grew greater still in the abbey, where the Benedictine nuns multiplied their acts of Marian devotion. A daily rosary recital and a weekly short service dedicated to the Blessed Virgin punctuated the passing of time and of the seasons, with the apotheosis of the month of May, which is Mary's month. Like Zélie, Thérèse wanted the most beautiful white flowers to adorn the altar of the one who had conceived without sin. This devotion was, of course, shared by her sisters, in particular Pauline.

On 7 September 1882, Pauline was twenty-one years old. She was of age, free to determine her actions. Less than a month later, on 2 October, she entered Carmel. Her decision dated from 16 February of that same year. On that day, during mass, she thought of a friend who had died the preceding year and who had planned to enter Carmel, taking the name Agnès de Jésus. Suddenly, she felt an irresistible vocation, which obtained the immediate approval of her father, her uncle, her confessor, and even of the Carmel's mother superior, Mother Marie de Gonzague.

In this concert of approval, there was one lone discordant note, Marie's; she asked Pauline if she was healthy enough to tolerate the Carmel austerity. Pauline the Intrepid reassured her sister.

God knows why—and the situation warrants this expression—Pauline did not consider it advisable to confide in her other sisters, Léonie, Céline, and Thérèse, about her sudden vocation. The latter learned of it by chance, during the summer of 1882, and it broke her heart. She felt once more betrayed, abandoned. "I shed very bitter tears, for I did not yet understand the joy of sacrifice; I was weak, so weak that I consider it a great gift that I was able to tolerate a test that seemed so far beyond my strength!...It was as if a sword had plunged into my heart."

Pauline tried as best she could to remove the "sword" that she had involuntarily plunged into the heart of her little queen, who cried out her pain. Very adeptly, she made her sister understand that this good-bye was not definitive; that one day they could meet again in Carmel, as, in earlier days, they had planned to go off together into a faraway desert. "I felt that Carmel was the desert where the good Lord wished that I also should go to hide."

After twenty-four hours of reflection, Thérèse announced her own vocation to Pauline, who approved of it, seeing in it "the will of Heaven." Thus, at age nine, Thérèse decided that she, too, would enter Carmel, the Carmel about which there was so much talk that summer, since the third centenary of the death of Saint Teresa of Ávila was being commemorated. And had not Teresa de Cepeda y Ahumada admitted to the Order one of her nieces, Teresita de Jesus, who at the time was as young as Thérèse Martin was now? Everything led the little queen to believe that she would enter the Carmel in Lisieux without delay, following in the footsteps of Saint Teresa of Ávila's niece. She daydreamed about it and wondered what name she would take:

> I wondered what name I would have in Carmel; I knew that there was a Sister Thérèse de Jésus, however my beautiful name of Thérèse could not be taken from me. All of a sudden I thought of little Jesus, whom I loved so, and I thought, "Oh! How happy I would be to call myself Thérèse of the Child Jesus!" I said nothing, in the parlor, of the dream I had had while completely awake, but when the good Mother Marie de Gonzague asked the sisters what name should be given to me, it came to her mind to call me by the name that I had dreamed.

For Pauline, imprudent for once, had taken Thérèse to Carmel, where the little queen had received the warmest of welcomes from Mother Marie de Gonzague and the other sisters, especially Sister Thérèse de Saint Augustin, who overwhelmed her with compliments. How was Thérèse not to take her dream for reality?

Reality, for the time being, was Pauline's entrance into Carmel, on 2 October. Thérèse received the last kiss from her sister, who, as soon as she had gone past the grille, was no longer Pauline but Sister Agnès de Jésus.

Sister Agnès de Jésus would understand, later, the suffering that she had inflicted on Thérèse, who had not been adequately prepared for her departure. Also, the visits in the parlor were frustrating. Mother Marie de Gonzague had authorized the Martins and the Guérins to come every Thursday. They had so many questions that Thérèse had to content herself with listening to the answers, with hearing that beloved voice. "Oh! How I suffered in that Carmel parlor....I said, in my heart of hearts, 'Pauline is lost for me!' "

Thérèse's precocious wisdom could do nothing about this excessive sorrow. She rebelled and confided to Mother Marie de Gonzague: "For some time, I have been answering back when Marie tells me to do something." This refusal to obey, this rebellion, did not last, and could not have filled the void caused by Pauline's absence. So Thérèse took refuge in illness. "Toward the end of the year, I was stricken with a continual headache."

One is alone when one suffers, Thérèse learned at her own expense. It is curious to note that no one at Les Buissonnets was worried about her migraines. They were so unconcerned about them that Louis Martin left for Paris with Marie and Léonie at the end of March 1883. Céline and Thérèse were entrusted to the Guérins during their absence, which for Thérèse seemed too much like a new abandonment. It was too much. She was stricken with a "strange trembling" that frightened her aunt and alarmed her uncle, who called Doctor Notta for a consultation. "The latter considered, as did my uncle, that I had a very serious illness with which such a young child had never before been stricken. Everyone was filled with consternation; my aunt had to keep me at her house and took care of me with a solicitude that was really maternal. When Papa came back from Paris with my big sisters, Aimée received them with such a sad face that Marie thought I was dead."

Thérèse was not dead, as suggested by the "sad face" of Aimée, the Guérins' cook. She was, however, in danger of death, and her father feared the worst. He was afraid that his little queen would take leave of her senses.

Neither Louis Martin, nor Isidore Guérin, nor Doctor Notta could imagine that the absence, and what she thought was the indifference, of Pauline, whose favorite she had considered herself to be and who now granted her only a few minutes of attention in the Carmel parlor, could make Thérèse mad with distress, ill to the point that she could not be moved to Les Buissonnets and had to prolong her stay at the Guérins'. Marie moved in as well and proved an excellent nurse, showing for Thérèse a solicitude that compensated somewhat for Pauline's abandonment.

On 6 April 1883, it was time for Sister Agnès de Jésus to receive the habit. The impossible took place: Thérèse was no longer ill, Thérèse no longer trembled. She thought she was cured. She wanted to attend, and she did attend, the ceremony. The Martins and the Guérins held themselves back from calling it a miracle.

Alas, the next day, Thérèse had a relapse at Les Buissonnets, where she had returned. Doctor Notta could not define, exactly, the disease from which his patient was suffering. He gave the impression that it could be some sort of St. Vitus's dance, but he ruled out all indications of hysteria. Modern doctors agree on a diagnosis of a neurosis provoked by six months of fear, "a behavior of infantile regression to cause herself to be pampered like a baby." Thérèse considered more simply that it was "the work of the Devil."

Faced with this strange disease that drove the family and doctors to despair, each did his best to try to heal the patient. Louis Martin multiplied his novenas. Céline deprived herself of her Sunday walks to remain with her sister, over whom Marie watched day and night. Léonie did her best to make herself useful and agreeable. But the best remedy was the weekly letter that Thérèse received from Pauline. Sister Agnès de Jésus sometimes sent a little present along with her letter, an hourglass or a doll dressed as a Carmelite. With each mailing, the patient almost fainted with joy.

Louis Martin, who no longer knew which doctor to consult or which way to turn, had had à novena of masses said in Paris, at Notre Dame des Victoires, in which Zélie had had absolute confidence. On Sunday, 13 May 1883, Pentecost Sunday, in the middle of this novena, Thérèse began to call out, *"Maman, maman..."* She was being looked after by Léonie, who, accustomed to the deliriums of her sister, paid no more attention than usual. Marie came to take over from Léonie. Thérèse continued her litany—*"Maman, maman..."* Faced with the persistence of the delirium, Marie called Léonie and Céline. All three fell to their knees before the Virgin's statue and prayed. Thérèse began to pray as well:

> Suddenly, the Blessed Virgin seemed to me so beautiful, so beautiful that never had I seen anything so beautiful; her face breathed an ineffable goodness and tenderness, but what penetrated deep into my soul was the *ravishing smile of the Blessed Virgin.* Then all my sorrows vanished....Oh! I thought, the Blessed Virgin smiled at me, how happy I am...but never will I tell anyone, for then my happiness would disappear.

Five weeks of delirium and suffering ended on that Pentecost Sunday, which commemorates the descent of the Holy Spirit on the apostles in the form of tongues of fire. No flames for Thérèse, who contented herself with the cooling smile of the Virgin, the statue that had already consoled Zélie after the death of her daughter Hélène at age five and a half. Because Zélie had feared that her daughter might be in purgatory, she had asked the statue, which had reassured her, "Hélène is here, with me." Since the statue spoke, why would she not smile? With the Martins, nothing should surprise us.

Thérèse was suddenly healed. The illness went away as it had come, leaving no after-effects. The little queen had gone up to the doors of death. She was just ten and a half years old; now all she had to do was to live again, with all the vigor of a well-fed Norman girl.

Faced with this resurrection, the Martins did not doubt for an instant the efficaciousness of their prayers and of the novena of masses at Notre Dame des Victoires. For the Martins, faith was better than science. Notre Dame des Victoires was stronger than Doctor Notta. Marie, who adhered completely to this opinion, wanted, just the same, to know more. She asked Thérèse questions "so tender and so urgent" that she who had been miraculously cured confessed the secret that she had wanted to keep deep in her heart. Yes, she had seen the Virgin smile; yes, she had been cured upon seeing this smile.

Grace immediately turned into disgrace, which would last for four years. Marie, with Thérèse's permission, told Mother Marie de Gonzague of the miracle, and she communicated the news to the other nuns. When she went back to Carmel to visit Pauline, Thérèse was assailed with questions. Deprived of her secret, stripped naked, she saw it as an extreme humiliation. "For four years, the memory of the ineffable grace that I had received was for me real unhappiness of the soul." She began to wonder if she had not lied, she who, as her mother had remarked, "would not lie for all the gold in the world."

12

The Strength to Suffer

(14 June 1884)

This "unhappiness of the soul," this fear that she had simulated the illness and lied about a cure brought on by a "smile from the queen of the Heavens," did not stop Thérèse from taking full advantage of the vacation provided by Louis Martin, who took his daughters to Alençon from 20 August to 30 September 1883.

It was the first time that the young Martin ladies had returned to Alençon since the death of their mother in 1877. Their first visit was, of course, to the cemetery, where they gathered around Zélie's grave. Thérèse asked her mother to "protect [her] forever." This sad duty accomplished, the little queen made her "debut in society."

In Alençon, the daughter of Louis Martin and Zélie Guérin was celebrated, spoiled, admired—"I admit that this life had its charms for me." In short, the vacation was a success, even if, from the prominence of her ten years, she judged severely the excesses of society life and the needless bustle.

Luckily, in Alençon Thérèse had a good encounter. On 22 August, she was introduced to Father Pichon, a Jesuit and Marie's spiritual guide. She immediately felt confidence in this priest, who had the gift of putting his interlocutors at ease, no matter who they were. At her father's request, Thérèse kissed him unaffectedly. This kiss given to the Jesuit was a pious counterpoint to the frivolous embraces of Alençon reunions.

Father Pichon left a valuable portrait of Thérèse at this time: "What struck me strongly about this child was her simplicity, her ingenuity, and her innocence. She was very much loved by her father and by her sisters, without my having seen any weakness on their parts. But what is particularly remarkable in a child of that age is that she related nothing to herself and forgot herself entirely, using none of her advantages to her benefit. She was timid and reserved, never putting herself forward."

The vacation ended, Thérèse returned to the abbey on 1 October. To the usual classes were added catechism, since she was to make her first Communion the following year. She seemed to have difficulties in learning word for word the catechism that Abbot Domin taught. Therefore, she asked permission to continue studying during recesses. Permission granted. Thérèse had finally found the way to escape the persecutions of the bigger girls and the sterile games of the children of her own age. She had decorated her catechism with images that Sister Agnès de Jésus had given her, and she meditated upon these. She became attached especially to one entitled "the Little Flower of the Divine Prisoner."

Another gift from Sister Agnès de Jésus was a "ravishing little book," a notebook bound in blue velvet that the Carmelite had made herself. It was a manual that suggested sacrifices and short prayers for each day, symbolized by flowers and scents. Thérèse, who often referred to herself as "a little flower" and who loved flowers, could only multiply the sacrifices that turned into roses, violets, and daisies.

With her letters and gifts, Pauline was attempting to repair the harm that her absence had caused. But little by little, Marie had taken her place, and it was on her knees that Thérèse learned of the struggles of life, of the immortal riches that must be placed in storage, and of "the way to be holy by faithfulness to the little things." Thérèse was convinced that if the greatest sinners could listen to Marie, they would immediately repent!

From 4 to 8 May 1884, the little queen went on retreat at the abbey. She slept there. If bedtime did not present too many problems, the same did not apply to getting-up time. At the age of eleven, Thérèse, who had never before been separated from her sisters, was incapable of washing and dressing by herself, or of doing her hair. She held out her comb to the mistress of the rest room, which provoked laughter and mockery. To emphasize her difference, she wore a big crucifix around her waistband. The Benedictines thought she was trying to imitate her Carmelite sister who was also in retreat; 8 May was not only the day of Thérèse's first Communion, it was also that of Pauline's profession of faith.

At the beginning of the retreat, Thérèse listened very attentively to Abbot Domin's instructions. Her attention dwindled abruptly when she learned that it was the abbot's niece who on 8 May was to deliver the Act of Consecration to the Blessed Virgin. She choked at this news, and with good reason. The only orphan among her schoolmates, she thought that the honor of this consecration should go to her. She choked so much that she had to be taken to the infirmary.

Informed of their little queen's trouble, and upon learning what had caused it, the Martins and the Guérins intervened immediately with Abbot Domin, who promptly sacrificed his niece. What priest in Lisieux would dare refuse something to Louis Martin and Isidore Guérin, the firmest supports of Catholicism? It was Thérèse who said the consecration and who, as a result, recovered her breath!

She received the host like "a kiss of love." She felt loved and said to Jesus, "I love you, I give myself to you forever." Such a gift could not fail to bring on tears, which could not help but intrigue her schoolmates, who questioned her about the reasons for such sadness. None could understand that she was crying with happiness, believing that her exile on earth was ending and that she was really in heaven.

On the evening of 8 May, Thérèse's father took her to Carmel, where she met Pauline, who, like her, was dressed in white and crowned with white roses. The communicant and Carmelite joined their emotions. Mother Marie de Gonzague gave the communicant a holy image with these lines: "From Mother Marie de Gonzague to her cherished child, her Thérésita! Remembrance of a day doubly dear to the heart of the mother of her beloved children! Her Thérèse receives her Jesus for the first time. Her Agnès is united with the Husband of virgins! With the King of kings! Happy day for her heart!" In reading these lines, Thérèse felt as if she had found a new mother in the mother superior.

The next day, she suffered the sadness that unfailingly follows excesses of joy. She realized that only Jesus could fill her heart, and she yearned to take Communion a second time. She took Communion on Ascension, repeating the words of Saint Paul: "It is no longer I who live, it is Jesus who lives in me." Thérèse could no longer do without this presence and obtained from her confessor the permission to take Communion at each major feast.

The day before each Communion, Marie tried to persuade her that she would not walk along the road of suffering and that she would be carried by God. Was this argumentativeness? Thérèse felt a curious desire: "I felt the birth in my heart of a great desire for suffering and at the same time the deep conviction that Jesus was saving a great number of crosses for me; I felt inundated with consolations so great that I see them as one of the greatest graces of my life. Suffering became my attraction, it had charms that enraptured me without my knowing them well. Until then I had suffered without loving suffering; after that day, I felt a real love for it."

Then Thérèse repeated these words of the *Imitation*: "O Jesus! Ineffable gentleness, change into bitterness for me all of the consolations of the earth." In drawing from the *Imitation* and from Saint Paul what would from then on constitute one of her rules of life, she was delighted that she had devoted so much time to reading the holy books, which she preferred to the amusements of her abbey schoolmates.

The fourteenth of June was the day of her confirmation. Thérèse found in it above all an affirmation of her "strength to suffer." For once, she did not shed one tear. Her confirmation godmother, Léonie, cried in her place. The unpredictable, inexplicable tears of the Martin young ladies must have fed the conversations of devout Lisieux citizens....

13

Interlude at Saint-Ouen-les-Pins and Trouville

(August 1884—May 1885)

For most children, first Communion and confirmation are just occasions to show off in the family, to get a maximum of presents, and to discover that the host has a very bland taste. Rare are the children of eleven years of age who decide, thanks to the two ceremonies, to unite themselves to Christ forever, as Thérèse did. But it can never be said enough that Thérèse Martin was not a child like others!

Reserved despite her confidences and confessions, solitary despite the vigilance of her entourage, a recluse who was bored in society, Thérèse lived in the wrong century and in the wrong country. She should have been born in Spain, at the time of Saint Teresa of Ávila and Saint John of the Cross.

This daughter of fire, who found no peacefulness in the green paradise of her Normandy, could perfectly well have made her way through the heat waves of Castille and the flames of Saint John's dark night in Andalusia. The austerity of Ávila and Almería would have suited Thérèse better than the opulence of Alençon and Lisieux.

The object of all of her family's attentions, the little queen could have let herself be content with being dressed, led about, and pampered. She gave in at times to the temptation of being like others, of no longer being different, "poor Thérèse," just as they said "poor Léonie." She did what she could to conform to her image of a good little girl, to that photograph showing her holding a jump rope, she who hated playing and preferred the company of books to all else. Nevertheless, she neglected these at the end of June 1884 to welcome a white spaniel, Tom.

Like any eleven-year-old child, she found herself romping about with Tom, who proved to be a joyous companion. With Tom, she could believe that she was as ordinary as the most ordinary of little Lisieux girls. It was but a momentary confirmation of her ordinariness: Thérèse caught whooping cough in July. She coughed so much it was heartbreaking. A change of air became necessary. Louis Martin took Thérèse, with Marie, Léonie, Céline, and Tom, to Saint-Ouen-les-Pins, where he had rented a house—a small main house that adjoined a farm.

On 8 August, in a rush of inspiration, Thérèse drew this farm. "The farm's ponds and little stream interested her very much, and, beyond the pastures, a minuscule little wood, often the goal of our walks," related Céline. One cannot help but notice that Céline, like Thérèse, used and abused the adjective *little*.

At Saint-Ouen, "Thérèse's face is always shining with happiness." And how could she not be happy, when she was rediscovering her first impressions as an infant in Sémallé? She inhaled with delight the odors of hay, of honeysuckle; she listened to the birds' songs and chased butterflies....She was profoundly a country girl. Surrounded by nature, she came back to life with unique strength and avidity. She wanted to breathe in every flower, taste every fruit.

Another little girl comes to mind, her exact contemporary, since she was born in the same month of the same year—on 28 January 1873—in Saint-Sauveur-en-Puisaye: Colette. In August 1884, in her mother's garden, Colette showed the same avidity as did Thérèse toward the vegetative and animal world. The Burgundian and the Norman, the pagan and the saint, would never meet and yet would have, without knowing it, a friend in common, Notre Dame des Victoires, whom at the end of her life the pagan—less pagan than it has been said—would implore.

During the month of August 1884, Thérèse was a young sovereign to whom all of nature seemed to belong. She had a perfect inner holiday, an interlude from her private torments. Louis Martin, Marie, Léonie, and Céline were there, always ready to respond to her slightest call. Her terror of being abandoned abated. The whooping cough was no more than a bad memory. Thérèse was able to continue at the abbey, where, in October, she was admitted into the orange class.

While her father and Marie went to Le Havre to see off Father Pichon, who was leaving for Canada, Thérèse joined the Confraternity of the Holy Rosary and was named adviser to the Association of Blessed Angels at the abbey. Signing up with several pious confraternities was in fashion, and for once the little queen, atypically, followed fashion.

Another style that started at that time and has not stopped since was the style of vacationing in Deauville and Trouville, where the Guérins rented the Chalet of Roses in May 1885. They invited Thérèse to join them, and she spent a week there. From Rose Taillé to the roses of the chalet, roses were predestined in the life of Thérèse Martin!

Just as she had drawn the farm at Saint-Ouen-les-Pins, Thérèse drew the Chalet of Roses. It seemed as if she wanted to fix firmly in her memory the decor of her interludes and her ephemeral happy times. "My aunt procured for us every possible pleasure: donkey ride, fishing, etc....I remember my delight in wearing the pretty sky-blue ribbons that my aunt had given me for my hair; I also remember confessing in Trouville about even this childlike pleasure, which seemed to me to be a sin."

Everything was a sin for Thérèse, who would soon fall prey to the terrible affliction of scruples.

14

"The Most Unhappy Creature in the World"

(May 1885–September 1886)

Upon their return from the holiday in Trouville, from 15 to 21 May 1885, under the direction of Abbot Domin, Thérèse went on a retreat in preparation for her second Communion. "It was during my second-Communion retreat that I saw myself assailed with the terrible affliction of scruples…"

Thérèse had only too much of a tendency toward excessive scruples, as we have just seen. And as if that predisposition were not enough, Abbot Domin added to Thérèse's torments by painting an appalling picture of mortal sin. But Abbot Domin should not be blamed too much for darkening the scene. He was only reflecting the color of his times. At the end of the last century and the beginning of ours, the rigor of Catholicism was pitilessly, rigidly confining: Everything was evil, everything was sin. If it was easy, and almost inevitable, to fall into the flames of hell, it was nearly impossible to get to heaven. Numerous were the confessors, the preachers, who caused terror to reign in churches and in minds.

In reading the notes that Thérèse took during this retreat, one feels her fear at the thought of committing a mortal sin. Since a disaster never comes alone, two others followed. Céline, now sixteen, left the abbey, leaving "poor Thérèse" there with no defense.

This abandonment was followed by that of Louis Martin, who, had he not been held back by his family, would have surpassed Pierre Loti in his love of traveling. He went off to visit Constantinople and a few other cities. He left at the end of August and came back only in mid-October.

This model father separated himself from his five daughters for seven weeks. The most affected was, of course, Thérèse, who, in a writing exercise—a fictitious letter that she would not send to the addressee—expressed her fears and poured out her feelings thus: "My beloved little father, you are going to tell me that I am not being reasonable, that I am making up chimeras."

Stricken with the affliction of scruples, which Marie tried in vain to allay, distressed by her isolation at the abbey, tortured by the absence of her father, whom she imagined prey to a thousand dangers, Thérèse suffered as one suffers at her age.

Louis Martin came home safe and sound from his trip, which he related to his bedazzled daughters—Vienna, Constantinople, Athens, and Rome, where, since the invasion of the Papal States in October 1870, popes considered themselves prisoners of the Vatican. The whole Martin family began to pray for the liberation of Leo XIII.

Barely recovered from the anxiety caused by the faraway traveling of her "beloved king," Thérèse realized that without Céline, the abbey was unbearable. She had increasingly painful headaches, which forced her to take frequent absences. She could no longer stand it, and in February 1886 her father allowed her to leave the Benedictine ladies. She was thirteen, and to employ the modest language of her days, it was certainly at this time that she must have become a young woman, with the aggravation of headaches that this includes. We do not know what was her reaction to menstrual blood, which, for the severe minds of 1885, made woman an inferior creature, "eternally injured." In all likelihood, it only added to the shame that she felt about her body, and this, it will be recalled, from her earliest childhood.

To clearly show that she had reached grown-up status, this young woman converted one of the Buissonenets' attic rooms into a study. But it was at Mme Papinau's home that she continued her education. This respectable lady, in her fifties, was as distinguished as she was learned, and she received all of Lisieux. Her lessons were often interrupted by visits, ladies who asked who this pretty student was. It was Mlle Martin, who did not try to hide her "feeling of pleasure" in hearing them, a pleasure that she immediately regretted.

At Mme Papinau's home, Thérèse got a glimpse of the world and its vanities, which she fled as soon as she could, finding refuge in her attic room, which she described as "a real bazaar." And it was a real bazaar, with its black wood cross, its baskets of dried flowers, a statue of the Virgin, statuettes of saints, a portrait of Pauline, souvenirs of Trouville in the form of baskets of shells, a bird cage, a window box....

Thérèse could stay for hours in this place where she had chosen each object, settled on each detail. "Really this poor attic room was a world for me."

It was with regret that in July 1886 she abandoned her bazaar to go on vacation in Trouville at the Guérins', with whom she felt less and less at ease. And with good reason. Uncle Isidore and Aunt Céline held the youngest of their nieces in low esteem. They considered her to be "a little ignoramus, good and gentle, of sound judgment, but incapable and awkward." A prophet is without honor in her own family. The Guérins overlooked nothing in Thérèse, criticizing even her "indecipherable handwriting" and weak spelling. They tried in vain to change this Martin demoiselle into a Guérin demoiselle who would be a credit to the clan.

Wounded by their remarks, which their customary little treats failed to counterbalance, Thérèse, after two or three days, asked to be sent home to Lisieux. She longed too much for Les Buissonnets and her attic room, and especially for Marie, who, she learned upon her return, wanted to join Pauline in Carmel. Thérèse was, as we

can imagine, astonished. "My room lost all its charms for me; I did not want to desert for a single instant the beloved sister who was soon to vanish."

A new departure was another catastrophe for Thérèse, who now embarked upon the path of renunciation: "As soon as I learned of Marie's resolution, I resolved to no longer take any pleasure on earth."

To whom would she confide about her scruples when Marie was no longer there? Marie would attest to the terrible affliction that had stricken her sister: "It was especially the day before her confessions that her scruples redoubled. She came to tell me about all her supposed sins. I tried to cure her by telling her that I took her sins upon myself—they were not even imperfections—and I allowed her to accuse herself of only two or three of them, which I indicated to her."

Marie was twenty-six years old. She had taken Zélie Martin's place since 1877. She had the leading role. Nothing is more tiring than to play a leading role, without faltering, for nine years. She wanted to devote herself a bit to her own self, and a great deal to God. She believed that she had carried out her duty to her family and wanted to fly with her own wings. Encouraged by Father Pichon, Marie told her father and her uncle of her resolution, and they approved it.

Louis Martin, without trying to conceal his sorrow, submitted to what he considered to be the will of God. Thérèse, who had not yet reached such a degree of self-denial, complained to Marie: "You can't imagine what it is like to be separated from a person you love as I love you."

To create a diversion, Louis took Marie, Léonie, Céline, and Thérèse off to Alençon. They gathered around Zélie's grave. "I cannot even tell how I cried on Maman's grave...I was really upset about everything." In yet another painful episode, Léonie took advantage of the brief sojourn at Alençon to enter the Poor Clares convent, without asking anyone's advice. She had always been a bit bizarre, but this time she went too far, unleashing Marie's furor. Marie, who had been counting on Léonie to take her place at Les Buissonnets!

Unpredictable Léonie, twenty-three years old, remained just two months in the Alençon convent and came back to Les Buissonnets on 1 December. No one could have foreseen this premature return. And it was at the peak of distress that Thérèse came home to Lisieux to attend, on 15 October, at Marie's entrance into Carmel, where she took the name Sister Marie du Sacré-Cœur.

At Les Buissonnets, Thérèse remained alone with Céline, who took the place, after a fashion, of her older sisters. She was in charge of the tidiness and cleanliness of the room that she shared with Thérèse. The latter did no housework. She remained the "baby of the family" who was spared the slightest effort. When she tried to show that she was willing to help and made her bed, the result must have been less than outstanding, since Céline showed no satisfaction. Thérèse cried in exasperation. With these little upsets of communal life added to the great sorrow caused by Marie's departure and the torments provoked by her affliction of scruples, Thérèse thought of herself as "the most unhappy creature in the world."

15

The Miracle of Christmas

(25 December 1886)

A t the end of October 1886, having reached what she believed to be the peak of despair, thinking she would no longer find help or consolation among the living, Thérèse turned to the dead, to her two brothers and her two sisters who had gone to heaven prematurely, angels among angels. "Their departure for heaven did not seem to me a reason to forget myself; on the contrary, finding themselves in a position to draw from among the heavenly treasures, they were supposed to select peace for me, and thus show me that in heaven, there was still love!"

To be loved in heaven and on earth, such was, in the end, one of Thérèse's dearest wishes; she had remained the child who had said, "I choose everything." She was increasingly convinced that life on earth was an exile that ended only with death. And death was just a transition leading to the other life, to the other world, where all was eternal peace. At the beginning of her adolescence, Thérèse already wished for that peace known only by those who, having reached the end of their days, understand the vanity of existence and its agitations.

After the graces she said she received from her four angels, Thérèse, at once lucid and insatiable, wished for something else. Lucid, she realized that her perpetual crying was beginning to make her unbearable for those around her. Insatiable, she wanted to grow up and no longer be attached to the kingdom of her childhood. With this demanding, extraordinary simplicity, she awaited a miracle from God. She had already received one from the Virgin, during Pentecost 1883. Why, then, would not God in turn perform one as well? She seemed to find this sort of intervention normal; moreover, the marvel did occur, during the night of 24–25 December 1886, at Les Buissonnets. "The good Lord had to perform a little miracle to make me grow up in an instant, and he achieved this miracle one unforgettable Christmas Day....It was on 25 December 1886 that I received the grace of coming out of childhood, in a word the grace of my complete conversion."

On that Christmas night (during which, by a strange coincidence, Paul Claudel's conversion also took place), Louis Martin, Léonie, back from the Alençon convent, Céline, and Thérèse went to hear the midnight mass. They took Communion. Back at Les Buissonnets, Thérèse, who would be fourteen years old eight days later, was delighted to find the presents set out in the shoes that she had left by the fireplace, as was the custom—"this ancient custom had brought us so much joy during our childhood that Céline wanted to continue treating me like a baby, since I was the littlest in the family." This detail shows to what degree Thérèse was still kept, whether or not she realized it, in a state of puerility that could have turned her into a child-woman, still playing with dolls on her twentieth birthday.

Louis Martin, until that Christmas of 1886, had been enchanted to hear his big child's cries of joy. But on that 25 December, tired after the midnight mass, he did not try to conceal his bad mood when faced with the "ancient custom" that had gone on only too long, that was nothing more than childishness unworthy of a young lady. Sighing, he said, "Oh well, thank goodness it's the last year." Thérèse, on her way upstairs to her room to take off her hat, heard this sigh and these words. Céline, who was following her and who also heard, feared some torrent of tears and implored, "Oh, Thérèse!

Don't go downstairs, it would be too upsetting for you to look in your shoes right away." But Thérèse was no longer the same. The miracle had just taken place, at the exact instant when she had heard the words that had broken the spell of her childlike gullibility.

The fragile Thérèse had metamorphosed into a Thérèse strong enough to force back her tears, calm the beating of her heart, take the shoes, and put them down in front of her father. She took the gifts from them with such infectious delight that Louis forgot his fatigue and bad mood, and he smiled with the others. Céline thought she was dreaming. "Fortunately, it was a pleasant truth, little Thérèse had recovered the strength of soul that she had lost at age four and a half, and it was forever!"

On that Christmas night, Thérèse passed through, like Alice, to the other side of the mirror, but in the opposite direction. Whereas Alice had gone from reality into a dream, Thérèse went from a dream into reality. It was none too soon!

16

A Memorable Month of May

(May 1887)

Having gotten past the crisis of puberty, Thérèse, as she herself noted in all modesty, "grew large in size and especially in grace." She had gotten over the marvel of that Christmas night; she was not one to linger in ecstasy or try to prolong it. Thus, in 1887 she entered her fourteenth year with a fine optimism and good resolutions: "Freed from its scruples, from its excessive sensitivity, my spirit developed. I had always loved the great and the beautiful; I was seized with a strong desire to learn."

A shocking desire for her time, which reserved for men the exclusive use of knowledge. Any feminine incursion into this domain provoked scandal and its immediate penalty: One did not marry a learned woman. The concern of finding a husband having never crossed Thérèse's mind, she could devote herself in peace to history and science, subjects that Mme Papinau considered with circumspection and taught with parsimony. Initiated to some of the mysteries of history and science, a young lady ceased to be a young lady worthy of the name.

For history, Thérèse turned to her father, whom she asked for advice about reading. For science, she spoke to her uncle, who would not have failed to caution her against the drawbacks of too much knowledge. It was one thing to have a female mystic in the family, but a female scientist, never! Defying this reluctance, Thérèse read history and science books written for the edification of Christian families.

But her desire to learn did not stop there. She took drawing lessons from Céline. Between the fourteen-year-old pupil and the eighteen-year-old teacher, one can imagine these lessons and the giggles they provoked. On 31 March, Thérèse drew a fish in red, green, and purple ink, crowning it with a comb that she gave to Céline the next day, as a gift for the first of April. Under the fish she wrote:

> I will keep my Diadem until Tomorrow morning
> But after that, onto your head will pass my Destiny
> April Fool's!

Renewed giggles. Thérèse and Céline agreed that the life they led at Les Buissonnets constituted an "ideal of happiness," which was briefly interrupted on 1 May 1887: Louis Martin, who would be sixty-four in August, fell victim to an attack that caused a partial hemiplegia, which did not last. The stroke seemed to have no aftereffects, and everything got back to the order of the "ideal of happiness" at Les Buissonnets.

Thérèse could devote herself to her beloved studies, and during that month of May she forgot the torments caused by the illness that had befallen her father, reading *La Fin du monde présent et les mystères de la vie future* [*The End of the Present World and the Mysteries of the Future Life*], by Abbot Arminjon. This covered nine lectures that Arminjon, formerly a professor at a major seminary, had given in the Chambéry Cathedral, and that he had collected in a volume that was read with fervor in Carmels of France and Navarre. It was the Carmelites of Lisieux who loaned the book to Louis Martin. Tempted by the title, Thérèse obtained permission to read it. "This reading was yet another of the greatest graces of my life; I read it at the window of my study room, and the impression that I felt from it is too private and too pleasurable for me to be able to render it."

There is, in certain existences, a book that comes at the right moment, like a sign, like a road to follow. And for Thérèse, this book was *La Fin du monde présent et les mystères de la vie future*. In *Le Génie de Thérèse de Lisieux* (Editions de l'Emmanuel), Jean Guitton presented Arminjon as "an almost modern author. He does not speak of the atomic bomb, but he speaks of the possible destruction of the universe by fire. He introduces the prospect of an end of the material world, reassuring us with the view that this is not going to happen tomorrow. He seems to foresee the discoveries of astronomy, multiplying by the infinite the multitude and dimensions of stars; he predicts interstellar voyages." It is not hard to see how Thérèse would have been exhilarated by such celestial perspectives. "After this elating lecture," concludes Guitton, "Thérèse must have conceived of the glory of beatitude as a glory that was shared, communicated, multiplied by the mutual love of the elect."

She immediately shared her discoveries with Céline. Céline had become the "intimate confidante" of her thoughts, taking up the role previously held by Pauline and then by Marie. To pour out her feelings, Thérèse needed a sister soul. This was, moreover, the expression that she found to define the harmony reigning between them. They were "sisters of the soul," united by "bonds stronger than those of blood." The slight age difference separating them was abolished. They treated each other as equals and talked, talked, talked.

During these endless conversations, Thérèse could not for long hide from Céline what she had already revealed to Marie and Pauline: Like them, she wanted to become a Carmelite. Marie thought Thérèse was too young, Pauline that she was too impatient. But neither Marie's reservations nor Pauline's appeals for calmness could slow down this race to Carmel that, day by day, accelerated.

As for Céline, she completely approved of Thérèse's decision to become, as soon as possible, Jesus' wife. Why frequent the world and its temptations any longer? What was the use of losing time? They talked more than ever: "How pleasant were those conversations we had every evening in the belvedere!...I feel that the outpouring of our souls resembled that of Saint Monica with her son when, at the Port of Ostia, they stayed lost in ecstacy at the sight of the Creator's wonders!"

To compare the ecstasies that had united Saint Monica and Saint Augustine to the outpourings that she shared with Céline was quite bold on Thérèse's part! But she was no longer the timid girl who used to whimper; she no longer had any reason to be jealous of the strong women whom Saint Teresa of Ávila held up as examples. And Thérèse would need strength and courage now; after having discussed it at length with Céline, she decided to announce to her father her irrevocable decision to enter Carmel in her fifteenth year.

On Sunday, 29 May 1887, the Feast of Pentecost, Thérèse spoke to her father and obtained, without too much difficulty, his consent. To mark the moment of his sacrifice, Louis Martin picked a white flower that had grown in a wall, a saxifrage that he gave to his daughter and that she put in her *Imitation,* in the chapter "That You Must Love Jesus Above All Things."

Two days later, on 31 May, Thérèse went to the abbey to declare her Act of Consecration of the Children of Mary:

> O Mary, conceived without sin,
> I, Marie Françoise Thérèse Martin,...
> I want from now on to profess
> to belong to you without reserve,
> to walk in your glorious steps
> and to imitate your virtues,
> especially your angelic purity,
> your blind obedience
> and your incomparable charity.

It is superflous to specify that this child of Mary did not declare her act lightly and that she would put into practice each word of her commitment. Thus ended the memorable month of May 1887, in which Thérèse read Arminjon and reached the decision to enter Carmel at age fifteen.

17

Thérèse's First "Child"

(August 1887)

During that same year, 1887, Thérèse would experience two other unforgettable months: July and August. One Sunday in July, while meditating on an image representing Christ on the cross, she was struck by a vision of blood falling on the ground without anyone thinking to collect it. She decided to place herself, in spirit, at the foot of the cross, "to receive the divine dew that dripped from it, understanding that I would then have to spread it out over souls."

Since Christmas night 1886, Thérèse had been haunted by the souls that were lost, like the blood of Christ, and by the necessity of saving them. She wanted to work on the conversion of sinners. She knew that her wish followed precisely that of Jesus, "who made of me a fisher of souls." She interpreted Jesus' cry on the cross, "I am thirsty," as "I am thirsty for souls." A thirst that devoured her as well, completely. She burned to wrest the souls of great sinners from the eternal flames.

While in this state of mind, she heard of a trial that was widely talked about in Paris and the echoes of which disturbed the most outlying provinces. It was the Pranzini trial, which lasted from 9 to 13 July 1887. It was a case that fascinated the public, since blood, voluptuousness, and death were its protagonists. In it, evidence was seen of the "*fin de siècle*" decadence that had been brought by foreigners, stateless persons, "cosmopolitans." What was becoming of this country where three women could be savagely assassinated in the middle of the night, and by a "wog," moreover? Was it really France?

Here are the facts. In the night of 19–20 March 1887, a demimondaine, Marie Regnault—whose nom de guerre was Mme de Montille—her maid, and the latter's daughter had their throats slit in their Paris apartment. Theft (of jewels, principally) seemed to be the motive of the crime. Two days later, the presumed assassin, Henri Pranzini, was arrested in Marseille. In the eyes of the world, Pranzini was guilty. For the public and for the judges, everything pointed to it. At age thirty, he was handsome, seductive, and lived on his charm, which was not in the least surprising since he had been born in the most voluptuous city of Egypt, Alexandria, where Europe's debauchees arranged to meet, and where the poet Constantine Cavafy was living the adventures from which he would draw the inspiration for his best poems.

Pranzini was capable of doing anything with anybody, on condition that he be paid. He was what would be called today "a good buy." In Paris, his clientèle, very posh, counted actresses, countesses, the wife of a fabulously wealthy industrialist, and a few marquesses, who extolled the power of his mysterious seductiveness. All of this can be read between the lines of countless articles that the newspapers published on Pranzini. "A peculiar fellow, this Levanter; one must have traveled to have come across anything like him. He is not at all the lackey of good families who has been described. With his little raised mustache, his frizzy, carefully combed beard, his lithe, insinuating appearance, his self-complacent air, his elegant clothing—white piqué waistcoat, impeccable linen, handkerchief corner showing in the side pocket—Pranzini completely carries off the hotel interpreter in Austria or Italy, half cicerone, half procurer, who by day shows the city's curiosities and who, when evening comes, guides the romantic wanderings of generous travelers," reported *Le Journal illustré*. Pranzini was the foreigner who had to be slain to make an example and frighten others like him. On 13 July 1887, even though he had always denied the charges and protested his innocence, he was condemned to death.

As soon as she learned of this, Thérèse wanted to save Pranzini's soul; she was certainly the only one in France to show some compassion for the one who was being presented as the worst of criminals. It is true that for Thérèse, the words *debauchery* and *depravaty* had no meaning at all and evoked nothing precise.

For the Lisieux demoiselle, the man from Alexandria incarnated all bad thieves, past, present, and future. She had to save this soul at all costs, and she began her fishing for souls with a truly miraculous catch. "I heard about a great criminal who had just been condemned to death for horrible crimes, everything suggested the belief that he would die in impenitence. I wanted at any cost to stop him from falling into hell, and to achieve this I used every imaginable means."

Despite the fact that her father had forbidden her to read the newspapers—a prohibition that had nothing extraordinary about it and was imposed on young ladies from good families to protect their innocence until their wedding day—Thérèse considered that she was not disobeying by reading the parts about Henri Pranzini in *La Croix* [*The Cross*], to which Louis Martin subscribed, especially the account of the last session, when the members of the jury retired to deliberate, and the accused, protesting one last time his innocence, clamored, "Death or freedom."

Then Thérèse addressed the good Lord directly: "I was certain that He would forgive the poor unfortunate Pranzini...I would believe it even if he did not confess and showed no mark of repentance, so much did I have faith in Jesus' infinite mercy, but...I asked him for just *one sign* of repentance, just for my consolation."

Pranzini's execution took place in Paris on 31 August, and provoked ignoble swarms of people. The next day Thérèse opened *La Croix*, her heart racing, and learned that, impenitent until the end, Pranzini had refused to confess. But when he arrived on the scaffold, right at the moment when they pulled him toward the guillotine, he turned to the priest who had insisted on accompanying him and kissed the cross that the priest held in his hand. Thérèse saw in this last gesture the sign that she had asked from God. God had granted her wish, and so she concluded that Pranzini's soul would "receive the merciful sentence of He who says that in Heaven there will be more joy over a single sinner who repents than over ninety-nine just men who have no need of repentance."

She immediately began calling Henri Pranzini her "first child." At fourteen years and nine months, Thérèse was a virgin and a mother. Like all mothers, she would retain a particular tenderness for this first child, for whom she would continue, until the end of her days, to ask for prayers and masses from those who wanted to follow her in her fishing for souls.

In the life of love that Thérèse led, the Pranzini episode was one of the most amazing, the most disturbing, and also the most secret. Céline had been her only confidante. "Quite far from making fun of me, [she] asked to help me convert *my sinner.* I accepted with gratitude, for I would have wanted all creatures to unite with me to plead for grace for the culprit." Love, which makes us ingenious, gave Thérèse a sense of the universal, since she dreamed of the union of all creatures to save just one of them.

18

An Obstacle Course

(October 1887)

A t fourteen years and nine months, Thérèse had already seen a statue of the Virgin smile, received a resplendent Christmas grace, and obtained from God Himself the sign that closed the Pranzini case. She boasted of none of it. She now knew that the Almighty Himself would not hold out against her Norman will, capable of demonstrating a stubbornness that was worthy of a Breton! Whatever Thérèse wanted, her Father in heaven and her father on earth eventually wanted it as well.

The speed with which she obtained Louis Martin's consent to enter Carmel—a brief conversation had sufficed—was miraculous. It was true that, at sixty-four, Louis could have been his Thérèse's grandfather. He had the weakness that grandparents are alleged to have for their grandchildren, to which was added the weariness caused by his recent attack. He recovered from it, to be sure, but he wanted to live in peace. He knew what a refusal would subject him to: He would have been drowned in torrents of tears. To those torrents, he preferred rivers, where he abandoned himself tranquilly to the pleasure of fishing, the product of which he brought to Carmel. He aspired only to finish out his days in the calmness of Les Buissonnets.

Louis could not foresee the storms that this precocious vocation would arouse. Thérèse had kept her habits of a little queen accustomed to the obedience of her subjects. She still had to convince the most rebellious among them: Uncle Isidore, who was her legal guardian and from whom she had to get authorization, since she was a minor.

A sharp customer, she had carefully avoided admitting to her uncle her inclination for Pranzini. She knew only too well the exacerbated provincialism of the pharmacist, who was thrilled that Normandy still belonged to the Normans. No cosmopolitanism in Lisieux!

A fervent supporter of the monarchist, Catholic-leaning newspaper *Le Normand,* to which he would contribute from 1891 to 1896, he did not forget for one instant that he was a first-class pharmacist, numbering among Lisieux's notables. He had founded l'Oeuvre de l'Adoration Nocturne (The Society of Nocturnal Adoration), and, at the Corpus Christi procession, he held one of the canopy cords. Faced with this living monument of Lisieux, Thérèse continued to be divided between admiration and fear, fear getting the better of admiration. She knew that her tears had no effect on her uncle, who wondered at times what he had done to heaven to have nieces as bizarre as "poor Léonie" and "poor Thérèse."

On 8 October 1887, Thérèse Martin finally dared to approach Isidore Guérin and tell him of her decision. "It was only in trembling that I could confide to my uncle the resolution I had taken…he did not give me the permission to leave; on the contrary, he forbade me to speak to him of my vocation before the age of seventeen. It was against human prudence, he said, for a child of fifteen to enter Carmel. Carmelite life being, in the eyes of the world, the life of a philosopher, it would be doing a great wrong to religious life to let a child with no experience embrace it.…Everyone would talk about it, etc. He even told me that to convince him to let me go, it would take a *miracle.*"

Poor Monsieur Guérin, who had the imprudence to speak of a miracle to his niece, she who lived a miracle of love every day and who obtained, when she wanted to, a smile from the Virgin or a sign from God! So, Uncle Isidore wanted a miracle? Well, he would have one. And this miracle took the form of a letter sent by Pauline.

On 21 October, Sister Agnès de Jésus came up with the argument that changed Isidore Guérin's refusal into consent. This argument seemed rather like blackmail: Thérèse might well die of grief if her uncle persisted in his refusal. Between two scandals, death and entrance into Carmel, M. Guérin chose the lesser. Of course, this premature entrance would set tongues wagging in all of Lisieux, but not as much as would the death of a young lady in her fifteenth year.

To die of grief, and because of her uncle's refusal—Thérèse was indeed capable of it! Isidore Guérin shuddered at the idea, and on 22 October he gave his consent. Thérèse did not attempt to conceal her joy, all the more intense because the refusal had set off "a very painful martyrdom that lasted three days." Luckily, during those three days of waiting, it rained. "Nature seemed to take part in my bitter sadness; during those three days the sun did not let a single one of its rays shine, and the rain fell in torrents. I have noticed that in all the grave circumstances of my life, nature has been the image of my soul. On days of tears, heaven cried with me, on days of joy, the Sun sent its cheerful rays in profusion and the sky was darkened with no cloud."

One can see in this coincidence a certain egocentrism projected onto the elements. When Thérèse was sad, it rained. When she was happy, it was beautiful. Like Saint Francis of Assisi, she could have considered the sun a brother and the rain a sister. It was with the sun in her heart, and over her head, that Thérèse rushed to Carmel to announce the good news to Pauline, whose epistolary intervention had been of capital importance. Alas, she learned from the latter that Carmel's prior, Canon Jean-Baptiste Delatroëtte, absolutely opposed her admission, which he, like Uncle Isidore, judged to be premature, and about which he wanted to hear no more until the young lady's coming of age. According to the prior, Thérèse would be admitted only in her twenty-first year, like most of the applicants. Six more years to wait—it seemed impossible!

An intervention by the mother superior, Mother Marie de Gonzague, only made his opposition grow. And another by Mother Geneviève de Sainte Thérèse, founder in 1838 of the Lisieux Carmel as attendant prior, succeeded only in provoking his anger. If Carmelites were dismayed by this refusal, Thérèse was even more so!

Her admission to Carmel became an obstacle course that she would have to get through one hurdle at a time. Thérèse, her father, and Céline tried to sway the prior. The canon received the trio coldly, declaring that there was no peril in the home and that Thérèse could lead a Carmelite life at Les Buissonnets, if she chose to. He finished his speech by pointing out, ironically, that he was, after all, only a delegate of the bishop of Bayeux, Monseigneur Hugonin, and that if Monseigneur accepted, he also would accept. Then he dismissed the trio as coldly as he had received them.

Thérèse left the presbytery in tears. She was glad that the rain was pouring down, enabling her to hide her tears under her umbrella. When the rain and the crying ceased, she was rooted more firmly than ever in her decision. "I was determined to achieve my goals, I even said that I would go all the way to the Holy Father, if Monseigneur did not want to permit me to enter Carmel at age fifteen."

Before going all the way to the pope, Thérèse followed the ironic advice of Canon Delatroëtte. She rushed to Bayeux to plead with the bishop on 31 October 1887. She gathered her hair up into a bun so she would look older. She put on a "nice outfit." She overlooked nothing to win her case.

When she got to Bayeux, accompanied by her father, it was raining. A bad omen! Monseigneur Hugonin and all his clergy were attending at a funeral in the cathedral. The appearance of the demoiselle from Lisieux in a light-colored dress and white hat caused a stir among the women dressed, rigorously in black.

At the bishop's palace, the vicar general, Maurice Révérony, who had set the date for the Martins' visit, was absent. Distraught and under ceaselessly falling rain, Thérèse and her father wandered about Bayeux, lunched without appetite in a good restaurant, and returned to the bishop's palace, where Fr. Révérony had at last arrived and inquired about the purpose of this visit. When he learned it, he made no attempt to conceal his astonishment, then said: "I am going to introduce you to Monseigneur, would you be so kind as to follow me?" Faced with the imminence of such a meeting, Thérèse's eyes filled with tears. Révérony noticed this and exclaimed gallantly: "Ah! I see diamonds…you must not show them to Monseigneur!" There followed the crossing of immense sitting rooms, which gave Thérèse the impression of being "a poor little ant." At last she was admitted into the office of the Great One.

"Monseigneur asked me if I had wanted to enter Carmel for a long time. 'Oh yes! Your Excellency, for a very long time…' 'Come now,' Fr. Révérony corrected, laughing, 'You can surely not say that you have had this desire for fifteen years.' 'That is true,' I answered, also smiling, 'but there are not many years to subtract, as I have wanted to become a nun since the awakening of my reason and I wanted Carmel as soon as I knew it well, because I thought that all my soul's aspirations would be fulfilled in that order.' "

These explanations did not at all affect Monseigneur Hugonin, who, thinking that he would please Louis Martin, pointed out that Thérèse could stay with him for a few more years. To his stupefaction, this father pleaded in favor of his daughter. Decidedly, this monsieur and demoiselle Martin were out of the ordinary!

Louis's plea was as useless as Thérèse's. Monseigneur Hugonin said he could not reach a decision without having had a prior conversation with Canon Delatroëtte. All was lost for Thérèse, who resorted to her supreme weapon, tears, despite Fr. Révérony's prohibition. She did more than show her "diamonds" to Monseigneur— it was rivers of diamonds that ran from her eyes. Faced with such an inundation and such sorrow, the bishop, moved, bestowed some consolation upon the despairing young lady: "He told me that all was not lost, that he would be very happy for me to make the trip to Rome to strengthen my vocation and that instead of crying, I should rejoice...and that I would certainly receive my answer in Italy."

Thérèse no longer knew whether to cry or to rejoice. But she knew that she would go to the end of her obstacle course. She was more resolved than ever to throw herself at the pope's feet to obtain the grace of entering Carmel at age fifteen. The bishop and the vicar general could not hide their amazement in front of such obstinacy. Fr. Révérony said that never before had such a thing been seen, "a father as eager to give his child to the good Lord as this child is to offer herself!" The clergy does not like for anyone to be conspicuous, even for a good cause. And it was certain that in the domain of conspicuousness, Thérèse and her father particularly stood out.

19

The Trip to Italy

(November 1887)

T hree days after the disastrous Bayeux interview, three days spent
in the vain hope of a sign, a reversal, a miracle, Thérèse rushed
to Rome to try to obtain from the pope that which she had been
unable to obtain from her bishop. The obstacles, the difficulties,
stimulated her and dried up the source of her tears.

With a dry eye and a racing heart, Thérèse left Lisieux on Friday,
4 November, at three in the morning. She was going out into the
unknown, with the feeling that great things awaited her out there.
Louis Martin and Céline, who accompanied her, shared her hopes.

When the train began to move, Louis hummed an old refrain,
"Roll, roll, my carriage, we're on the road." He was all happiness
because he was engaging in one of his favorite passions, traveling,
and because he wanted to introduce his two daughters to the beauties of Paris, which they could then compare to those of Rome. From
Friday the fourth to Sunday the sixth of November, Louis showed
his little queen and her attendant the Paris of his youth, the Champs-
Élysées, the Palais Royal, the Louvre.

Thérèse was not in the least dazzled by the capital: "The beautiful things of Paris do not at all captivate my heart," she wrote to
Marie and Pauline. Faced with the density of the traffic, she was
afraid of being run over at any moment. She found herself at peace
only in the churches, and especially in Our Lady of Victories. In a

burst of fervor intensified by her fear of the unknown, Thérèse begged Our Lady of Victories to keep anything that could tarnish her purity away from her. "I was not unaware that on a trip like the one to Italy, we could come across many things that could disturb me, especially because not knowing evil, I feared discovering it, not having experienced that all is pure to the pure."

Indeed, all is pure to the pure, but one cannot take too many precautions! After having pleaded with Our Lady of Victories, Thérèse invoked Saint Joseph, the "father and protector of virgins."

Certain that she had obtained the benevolence of the Virgin and her husband, Thérèse could throw herself with a lighter step into the conquest of Rome, adapting easily to the demands of a pilgrimage. For if the Martin trio visited Paris without anyone's help, it was out of the question to leap into Italy with no guide. Nothing had been left to chance, for Louis Martin had chosen a solution that involved no risk, that of a pilgrimage, and not just any one; he chose the official pilgrimage of Coutances, organized by a renowned agency, the Lubin Agency, which had promised to reconcile comfort and mysticism, luxury and artistic emotion.

For the occasion of Leo XIII's golden sacerdotal anniversary, the diocese of Coutances, incited by its bishop, Monseigneur Germain, was sponsoring this pilgrimage, joined by a delegation of the Bayeux diocese, led by the vicar general, Fr. Révérony, who had introduced Thérèse to Monseigneur Hugonin. The pilgrims, who numbered 195, intended to make of this journey "a shining manifestation of ultramontane faith." The pope was still a prisoner in the Vatican, and the pilgrims felt in themselves the souls of crusaders going off to deliver the holy sepulchre from Jerusalem.

The biggest names of Normandy were represented: the viscount of Lorgeril, the marquess of Bellefond, the viscountess of Berenger, the countess of Chivré, and a few noble demoiselles such as Jeanne de La Roque, Antoinette de Larminat, Yvonne de Banneville, Marguerite d'Annoville, and Edmée de Grainville.

The Martins were practically the only ones who did not have a
title. This inconvenience was disposed of immediately by the group's
ennobling Louis, whom they would call M. de Saint-Martin, since
he and his daughters were to travel in the compartment placed under Saint Martin's protection, each compartment carrying the name
of a saint.

This fine company met on Sunday morning, 6 November, in the
crypt of the Sacré Cœur Basilica, which was under construction.
They looked at one another, examined one another, looked one another up and down. They were to spend about twenty days together;
they might as well pray ardently to the Sacred Heart that they would
be able to stand one another! It was Monseigneur Germain who
presided, in this crypt, over the pilgrimage's opening ceremony, followed by a mass in the church of Saint-Pierre-de-Montmartre.

On Monday, 7 November, the train for Rome left the Gare de
l'Est. The compartments quickly turned into the latest in salons,
where they talked—where they prayed, too, though not enough for
Thérèse's liking; nevertheless, like her father and sister, she found
herself at ease among such an aristocratic assembly. "I, so timid that
normally I hardly dared to speak, I found myself completely re-
lieved of this embarrassing fault; to my great surprise I spoke freely
with all the great ladies, the priests, and even with Monseigneur de
Coutances. I felt as if I had always lived in that world."

It was true that the marquesses, the viscountesses, and the noble
demoiselles were as friendly as could be with the Martins. There
was only one shadow in the picture: the presence of Fr. Révérony,
who carefully examined the trio, especially Thérèse, whose gestures
he observed and whose words he noted. The vicar general was no-
where near forgetting about the crying, the "diamonds" that this
hothead had shed in the presence of Monseigneur Hugonin, who
was little accustomed to such demonstrations. He was on the defensive and wondered if this Martin demoiselle would not, by some
display, throw discredit upon the Bayeux delegation, to the secret

delight of the Coutances delegation. Pilgrims are not always motivated by Christian charity. But Thérèse quickly forgot about Fr. Révérony's presence. She was completely absorbed in the joy of what she considered her "honeymoon trip," as she wrote to Pauline. Was she not, when she entered Carmel, going to become the wife of Jesus? Always original, she was going on her trip before the wedding! And in the country that at the time was considered ideal for a honeymoon: Italy. The first days, and the first nights, of conjugal life were spent in Rome, Florence, Naples, and the Borromean Islands.

Thérèse's knowledge of the world was limited to Alençon, Lisieux, Trouville, and Deauville. In a few hours on the train, she saw more scenery than she had ever looked upon until that day. The crossing of Switzerland enchanted her. The mountains, the cascades, the deep valleys "filled with gigantic ferns and pink heather," intoxicated her. She wanted to be on both sides of the car so that she would not miss anything of the beauty of the scenery that bore witness to the greatness of their Creator. Everything brought Thérèse back to God.

First stop in Italy: Milan. Thérèse and Céline visited every nook of the cathedral. Intrepid, they climbed up to the top of the bell tower.

Louis Martin, who had remained below, did not know which to admire more, the splendor of the cathedral or the intrepidity of his daughters. The incessant wonder of the Martin trio exasperated a grumpy old pilgrim, who muttered: "Ah! The French are so enthusiastic." It was a remark that failed to please Thérèse, who thought, "That old gentleman would have done better to have stayed home."

Unlike the old gentleman who was happy with nothing, the Martins were enchanted and did not try to hide it. The hotels, the restaurants, the service, were perfect. The only people who inspired their reserve were the priests who were part of the pilgrimage. The deans, such as Victor Turgot and Louis Fossard; the parish priests, such as Achille Paquet and Théodore Potel; the vicars, such as Adrien Bouillon and Jules Delarue, were not all saints. Thérèse discovered that, priests though they were, "they were none the less weak and fragile men." She immediately decided to pray as much for preachers like Révérony as for sinners like Pranzini. That was the way Thérèse was: She prayed to save; she would love before she would condemn.

The trip went on, bringing the Lisieux demoiselle her share of various sensations and observations. After Milan it was Venice, which she found unbearably dreary. She preferred Padua to Venice; there she became engaged in intense devotions to Saint Anthony. She did not at all like Bologna, where, upon her arrival at the station, a student had the audacity to take her in his arms, pouring out gallant remarks, which he stopped abruptly when he saw the glacial look they were provoking.

In the streets of Bologna, it was worse. Students formed an honor guard when the two Martin sisters passed by. It was true that Thérèse and Céline were ravishing, especially Thérèse, who wore a black dress, a buff-colored coat, the large grain of which imitated fur, and a matching furlike hat from which her blond curls escaped. Her modesty was severely tested. Our Lady of Victories and Saint Joseph must have had some distraction in the exercise of their protection, to have permitted such license. But they took up their vigilance again quickly, and after Bologna, Thérèse and Céline were no longer bothered by overeager seducers.

In Loreto, Thérèse almost fainted with happiness when she visited the Holy Family's house. Like the Catholics of her time, she believed that Joseph and Mary's house had been carried by angels from Palestine to Italy in the thirteenth century. She took Communion under the roof that, it was said, had sheltered Jesus' childhood. "It was a celestial happiness that words are powerless to translate."

During this trip in Italy, Thérèse knew that she was storing up memories for the rest of her days. "Later, during test time, when, a prisoner in Carmel, I will be able to gaze at only a small corner of the starry sky, I will remember what I am seeing today."

On 13 November in the evening, the pilgrims arrived in Rome and went to the Hotel du Sud, on Via Capo le Case. It was raining.

It would not stop raining for almost their entire stay. For once the rain was not in concurrence with Thérèse's feelings; she jubilantly walked upon this sacred earth, trod upon this soil that was impregnated with the blood of martyrs. She had read *Fabiola* too often not to see standing at every street corner the ghosts of Saint Sebastian or Saint Agnes. In Rome, reality and fiction intermingled for Thérèse, increasing still more her jubilation, which the pilgrims shared. They were at last in the papal city. So what did the rain matter?

Thérèse shuddered when she saw the Colosseum. But what a disappointment when she entered it: The center, where so many Christians had met death, was no more than a pile of rubble that was off limits to tourists and protected by a barrier. Thérèse had only one desire: to go down into the arena, like the first martyrs. She succeeded, pulling Céline along in her wake. Louis Martin pleaded in vain with his daughters to retrace their steps. Upon reaching the center of the arena, Thérèse and Céline fell to their knees and kissed the ground, from which they gathered a few pebbles in remembrance. This was accomplished in so little time that the pilgrims did not notice the absence of the Martin girls, whom their father did not have the heart to scold.

Thérèse rejoined the tour as the guide was pointing out the magnificent arcades with "the little *cornichons* ["pickles"—the guide meant to say *corniches*, "cornices"], and the *cupides* ["greedy ones," rather than *chérubins*, "cherubs"] set on top of them." Thérèse smiled mockingly; she would always be assured a laugh when, later, she would imitate the guide's accent and malapropisms.

After the Colosseum came the catacombs, where Thérèse took a little earth from the bottom of Saint Cecilia's grave. The earth of the catacombs joined the pebbles of the Colosseum in a cloth sack, as Thérèse increased the number of pious thieves. In the Church of Saint Agnes, she picked up a little red stone that was opportunely, as she passed by, coming loose from a mosaic, and she carried it off for Sister Agnès de Jésus.

For six days, the troop of pilgrims, often with Thérèse and Céline in the lead, were shown the wonders of Rome. The Castel Sant' Angelo, the Farnese Palace, the Trevi Fountain, the Medici Villa, the Borghese Palace, the Saint John Lateran Basilica...the Lubin Agency spared its pilgrims none of the sights. Enchanted but exhausted, they asked for mercy. Thérèse summed up thus her sojourn in the Eternal City: "Six days were spent visiting the principal wonders of Rome, and it was on the seventh that I saw the greatest of them all: Leo XIII."

20

Jesus' Plaything

(20 November 1887)

For Thérèse, Leo XIII surpassed all the sights of Rome. Excessively conscious of her smallness, she felt smaller than ever before such greatness. Faced with the bishop of Bayeux, she had shrunk until she had believed herself to be an ant. In front of the pope, she thought she would be a mere speck of dust.

Leo XIII, who had never accepted the loss of Rome or temporal power, had made the Vatican the symbol of his resistance. He had been pope since 1878, and he was seventy-seven years old. Thérèse had placed her last hope in this tired man in his seventies, all the more so because the news from Lisieux was bad.

Monseigneur Hugonin appeared to be increasingly reticent concerning Thérèse's project. A girl of fifteen entering Carmel would be plenty to provoke exclamations of horror from the anticlericals, who continued to look upon nuns with the eyes of Diderot and his *Religieuse* [*The Nun*], and who depicted convents as branches of Lesbos!

To overcome this hesitation, defy public opinion, and quiet the gossiping of all Lisieux, just one word from His Holiness would suffice. Thérèse knew this when she wrote to Pauline: "Since Monseigneur is not willing, the last means that I still have available is to speak to the pope." She signed her letter, "Jesus' little plaything." She pictured herself as a ball that rolled wherever Jesus wanted it to; He was having fun with it. She who hated playing thought of herself as Christ's plaything. But would Christ deign to throw His ball into the Vatican? Would the divine will bend the papal will? Would Leo XIII deign to imitate the Lord? Nothing was less certain!

The Lisieux Carmel prayed for the success of Thérèse's visit to the pope. Initially hostile to a petition addressed directly to the Holy Father, Pauline-Sister Agnès de Jésus, on the advice of her mother superior, Mother Marie de Gonzague, and of Mother Genviève de Sainte Thérèse, had changed her mind. She went as far as envisaging the wording of the request. Which did not keep Thérèse from being plunged into extreme perplexity: "I do not know how I will go about speaking to the pope."

The audience was set for Sunday 20 November. The day before the big day, Thérèse wrote to her cousin Marie Guérin: "It is tomorrow that I will speak to the pope...if you only knew how fast my heart beats when I think of tomorrow." To understand her agitation, one must realize that the pope was likened at the time to a living god, not touching the earth, walking on clouds of incense, offered for the veneration of the faithful from the heights of an inaccessible palanquin carried by guards.

In Emile Zola's novel *Rome,* which would appear in 1895 and one of the protagonists of which is in fact Leo XIII, the hero, Abbot Pierre Froment, thought of the master of the Vatican in this way: "And now that his terrestrial monarchy had reached its end, into what spiritual sovereignty had risen this thin old man, so pale, before whom he had seen women faint as if stricken down by the formidable divinity that emanated from his person. It was not only the resounding glories, the triumphs dominating history that unfolded behind him, it was heaven that opened."

Faced with such majesty, was Thérèse going to faint? She feared the worst. There was no doubt that the 254th successor of Saint Peter was imposing. The loss of his earthly power did not stop him from carrying himself like an absolute monarch, the supreme pontiff before whom the king of Italy felt like a little boy. What to say, then, of Thérèse? Even the noble ladies of Coutances and Bayeux were impressed.

As the supreme instant approached, the countess of Chivré, the viscountess of Berenger, Jeanne de La Roque, Antoinette de Larminat, Yvonne de Banneville, Marguerite d'Annoville, Edmée de Grainville, and the others lost their fine self-confidence with the thought that they would soon have to kneel before the pope, kiss his hand and foot, then get up afterward with all of the requisite dignity, without stumbling. A stumble, a slip, on the Vatican's marble floor was always possible. There was plenty to shudder about, in anticipated horror! And these ladies did not hold back! But no one was as upset as "poor Thérèse."

On Sunday, 20 November, dressed in black and wearing a black mantilla, according to protocol, Mlle Martin went through the doors of the Vatican. She clung to her father's arm, Iphigenia going to the sacrifice. She had, like all young Catholics of her day, studied Racine's only two tragedies that were authorized in the convents: *Esther* and *Athalie*. Like Esther before Ahasuerus, the little queen could have said to the pope:

> One word from your mouth, by putting an end to my sorrows
> Can make Esther the happiest of queens.

But Thérèse was not Esther, she was just an unknown, impressed by the pomp of the Vatican. She was completely lost among the ladies of Coutances and Bayeux who nervously patted their mantillas while waiting to be introduced to His Holiness. On the absence of the bishop of Coutances, it was Fr. Révérony who was in charge of the line. Ladies first, then priests, then gentlemen. He reminded his pilgrims that it was formally forbidden to speak to the Holy Father. He set the example by speaking as little as possible, limiting himself to indicating important people to His Holiness. Thus it was that

Louis Martin would be allowed this distinction, introduced as the "father of two Carmelites."

Thérèse was allowed no favor and was not presented as the "sister of two Carmelites" or as aspiring to enter Carmel. She knew she had to defy Fr. Révérony's interdiction; she hesitated, imploring Céline's opinion with her eyes. Céline whispered an imperial "Speak." Thérèse obeyed. Kneeling before Leo XIII, she joined her hands and found the strength to articulate: "Most Holy Father, I have a great favor to ask of you."

Surprised, the pope leaned over to examine she who dared to take the floor in his presence, and who persisted by continuing: "Most Holy Father, in honor of your Jubilee, permit me to enter Carmel at age fifteen."

The Most Holy Father, more and more surprised, murmured, "I do not really understand." He turned toward Fr. Révérony, who, expecting the worst with this Martin demoiselle—well, the worst had happened—did not conceal his annoyance and explained, "Most Holy Father, it is a child who wishes to enter Carmel at age fifteen; however, the superiors are examining the question at this moment."

Reassured, the pope contented himself with suggesting to Thérèse: "My child, do as the superiors tell you to." A dilatory answer, which provoked this immediate reply: "Oh, Most Holy Father, if you said yes, everyone would be willing."

Thérèse's insistence threatened to cause an incident, which the pope avoided with an irrefutable, "Come now, come now, you will enter if the good Lord wishes it."

This was politely but firmly dismissing Thérèse, who would have liked to talk more and convince Leo XIII. But two guards, helped by Fr. Révérony, intervened to put a stop to this conversation that had gone on too long already. They picked Thérèse up and quickly carried her away—"at the moment where I was taken away like this, the Holy Father placed his hand on my lips, then he raised it to bless me, and then my eyes filled with tears and Fr. Révérony could gaze upon as many diamonds as he had seen in Bayeux."

Louis Martin and Céline tried, in vain, to console Thérèse, who noticed at last that it was raining in Rome. "On that day...the sky...did not cease crying with me." She had wanted to be Jesus' plaything. That plaything was broken. In the evening of that 20 November, Thérèse wrote to Sister Agnès de Jésus: "The good Pope is so old that you would think he is dead, I would never have imagined him like that, he can say almost nothing...Oh! Pauline, I cannot tell you what I felt, I was as if destroyed, I felt abandoned."

The picture that Thérèse would paint of the pope in her *Histoire d'une âme* would not have as much spontaneity. She would evoke not his extreme age, but his extreme splendor.

The trip to Italy no longer had any appeal in Thérèse's eyes. Its purpose had failed. She would not enter Carmel at age fifteen—she had even envisioned entering for Christmas, just before her fifteenth birthday. So what did she care for Naples and Pompeii, which she visited on 21 November? What did Vesuvius matter, which, in her honor, seemed to shoot off canonballs? In Pompeii, she would have liked to walk alone to meditate about her failure, about the fragility of human endeavors. Impossible—there were too many pilgrims, too many tourists. She hastened back to her hotel, which was as luxurious as all the others where she had stayed. How burdensome this luxury seemed to her! The gilded paneling, the marble, the rugs, only reminded her again of the magnificence of the Vatican. And there were elevators, which Thérèse discovered and which she would not forget, as shall be seen.

She hoped that her papal escapade had gone unnoticed. Alas, the pilgrims spoke only of that. The vicar general of Coutances, Monseigneur Legoux, came up to her with a smile, saying, "How is our little Carmelite?" The little Carmelite was not well and suffered in silence. Even the newspapers echoed her incredible audacity. In *L'Univers* of 24 November, in the "Roman Correspondence" column, one could read: "Among the pilgrims was a young lady of fifteen who asked the Holy Father for permission to enter the convent right away, to become a nun."

The trip continued. After Naples and Pompeii came Assisi, where, during an excursion, Thérèse providentially lost her sash, looked for it, and found herself alone near the Monastery of Saint Agnes. All the carriages had left except one, which was occupied by distinguished gentlemen, among whom was Fr. Révérony. Thérèse found herself facing the fearsome Révérony, who showed an unforeseeable friendliness and went so far as to pay for her seat. Thérèse was extremely grateful, and she thanked God for the temporary loss of her sash, which had brought about this promising face-to-face meeting.

Another time, in an omnibus, she was again seated next to Fr. Révérony, who was even friendlier and promised that he would favor her admission into Carmel. Thérèse could not believe her ears. Decidedly, during this trip to Italy, Jesus had had a good time with his plaything!

But Fr. Révérony's transformation had not been due to a miracle. Louis Martin had succeeded in speaking at length, in a tête-à-tête, with the vicar general of Bayeux, and had persuaded him that his Thérèse's vocation was not the fantasy of a spoiled child or a whim like those of Léonie, who entered a convent only to leave it two months later. Louis Martin vouched for the authenticity of this vocation with a sincerity that, in the end, convinced Fr. Révérony.

After having visited Pisa and Genoa, the pilgrims went back to France. The Lubin Agency had seen to it that the trip would end with an apotheosis of scenery: The train went along the Italian Riviera and then the French Riviera. The orange trees, palm trees, olive trees, which seemed to tumble down the hills, the ports that lit up as evening fell, the waves that came up to break right at the edge of the tracks—all of this delighted Thérèse, who nevertheless remarked that Lisieux drew her "like a magnet." The magnet had a name, Carmel, where she rushed upon her return, on 2 December.

21

An Incomprehensible Delay

(1 January 1888)

On 2 December 1887, Louis Martin and Céline, following Thérèse's example, did not try to hide their happiness at being back in Lisieux at Les Buissonnets, with their tranquillity, which they had elevated to an art of living.

The good citizens were certain that M. Martin had given Thérèse the trip only to dissuade her from entering Carmel. This was obviously not the case, since, as we have seen, Louis had personally intervened with Fr. Révérony. The vicar general of Bayeux was not the ogre that Thérèse imagined: He simply wanted to assure himself of the depth of such a precocious vocation.

Thérèse's secret was now out in the open. The echo that *L'Univers* had published on 24 November now resonated throughout all of Lisieux, which had recognized, in the young lady of fifteen whose name had not been cited, Thérèse Martin. The pilgrims of Coutances and Bayeux had hurried to tell all about how Mlle Martin had had the audacity to speak to the pope. The viscountess of Berenger, the countess of Chivré, Antoinette de Larminat, Edmée de Grainville, and the others even spoke of a "scandal at the Vatican."

During the trip, Thérèse had discovered not only the splendor of the scenery and of the sights, but also the limitations of priests, the power of gossip, and the uselessness of luxury. "What a trip that was! It alone taught me more than long years of study," she sighed.

She had even discovered, with amazement, in what contempt the feminine condition was held in Italy. "I still cannot understand why women are so easily excommunicated in Italy; all the time we were told: 'Do not enter here...Do not enter there, you would be excommunicated!' Ah! Poor women, how they are scorned!"

She had endured this scorn with a spirited cheerfulness. Even so, she was happy that it was over! And when her father proposed a more distant journey to broaden her horizons, a pilgrimage to the Holy Land, Thérèse refused without hesitation. She had had more than enough of the earth's beauties; she no longer aspired to any but the beauties of heaven.

In her absence, the intransigence and irritation of the prior, Fr. Delatroëtte, had only grown. Sister Agnès de Jésus did not try to hide her discouragement and advised her sister to write to Monseigneur Hugonin, reminding him of his promise of a rapid response. To enter Carmel for Christmas had become an obsession with the applicant, and she had succeeded in sharing it with those who were close to her.

Thérèse followed Pauline's advice and wrote to the bishop of Bayeux, letting her heart speak: "Your Excellency, I am writing to ask Your Greatness to be kind enough to give me the answer that I have been wanting for so long." Thus began her petition. She showed it to her uncle, who deleted the heartfelt outbursts and gave the missive a more official tone, perhaps less imperious. Corrected by M. Guérin, the letter began this way: "Your Excellency, I am writing to remind Your Greatness of the authorization request that I had the honor of addressing to him." The rest was in keeping with that tone. Thérèse asked for nothing more; she restricted herself to "waiting with confidence" and hoping for "this notable favor." The letter was mailed on 18 December.

She did not fail to write as well to Fr. Révérony, reminding him, also humbly, of the promise that he had made to speak in her favor to Monseigneur Hugonin, and pointing out to him "that there are only eight days from now until Christmas." An affirmative response from the bishop of Bayeux would have been a magnificent Christmas present for the aspirant.

The two letters had hardly been sent when Thérèse began to await the responses. She no longer knew what to expect. From 19 to 24 December, accompanied by her father—a young lady never went out alone—she went to the post office each morning. And each morning it was the same disappointment: no response.

Christmas arrived. Thérèse had been counting on attending midnight mass behind Carmel's grille. She had to content herself with going to the cathedral. Like Moses, she looked upon the Promised Land without being able to get into it.

On Christmas Day, in her room, she found a present from Céline, a ship holding a sleeping baby Jesus, who held a ball. On the white sail, Céline had written these words: "I am sleeping, but my heart is vigilant," and on the ship's stern, *Surrender.* Surrender to the will of the Lord. This produced an entire afternoon of Thérèse's tears.

Toward the evening, full of sorrow, she went to Carmel, where she received a gift that was almost identical to Céline's—a baby Jesus holding a ball, upon which her name was inscribed. The coincidence succeeded in forcing a smile from her.

On 28 December, Mother Marie de Gonzague received the response from Monseigneur Hugonin: She was authorized to admit Thérèse Martin to Carmel without further delay. Thérèse was not informed of this until 1 January. An inexplicable delay. Worse, in an even more incomprehensible about-face, Sister Agnès de Jésus, who had moved heaven and earth to get her sister into Carmel as quickly as possible, prevailed upon the mother superior to push this entry back to Easter, under the pretext of sparing Thérèse the rigors of Lent. Thérèse would have found them quite gentle compared with the torture of an endless wait, which was now renewing itself in an unpredictable way. "I could not hold back my tears at the thought of such a long delay."

One is never betrayed except by one's own people. Thérèse could have considered herself betrayed by Pauline and lost herself in conjectures about the motives behind this adjournment. Had Sister Agnès de Jésus wanted to impose upon her sister an ultimate test, which she could well have done without? But Thérèse passed no judgment on the decision. Courageously, she decided to row on the ship *Surrender* and arrive in port at all costs, at Easter or on Trinity Sunday. The most important thing was His Excellency's acceptance, and it was the most beautiful gift that she could have received for her fifteenth birthday.

22

The Death of the Little Lamb

(15 February 1888)

Indeed, what difference did the delay imposed by Pauline's excessive forethought make? Rather than being upset about it, could
not Thérèse consider this three months' delay a reprieve of freedom,
during which she could live as she pleased? To this question, she
gave an unequivocal answer: "At first it came to my mind not to
bother with living as well-ordered a life as I was accustomed to, but
soon I understood the value of the time that was being given to me,
and I resolved to absorb myself more than ever in a serious and
mortified life."

She specified that by *mortification* she did not mean penance,
and that she tended to let Céline pamper her. Her mortifications
consisted of breaking her own will, of not answering back, of doing
little good turns without drawing attention to them, of not leaning
back when she was sitting—in short, of practicing those thousand
little nothings that seem like nothing, but that, when one practices
them daily, tirelessly, cost a great deal. "It was in practicing these
nothings that I prepared myself to become Jesus' fiancée."

Thus, during those three months that could have been arid and
that she succeeded in making fertile, Thérèse made her first steps
along the "little way" that would lead to sainthood. She applied
herself to meditating, to learning a lesson from each event, as insig-
nificant as it might be. What she called "the value of the time" also

107

included an understanding of each instant that must not be allowed to be lost. One drop of time is as precious as one drop of blood. At the age of fifteen, Thérèse knew what it takes most people an entire life to learn, or that is learned when it is already too late.

On Ash Wednesday, 15 February 1888, Louis Martin, who no longer knew what to come up with to please his little queen, gave her a one-day-old lamb, who would live for just one day. This lamb had the destiny of Thérèse's favorite flower, the rose. Born in the morning, it died in the late afternoon.

Dead, it lost nothing of a prettiness that inspired Céline: She promptly drew it. Then the Martins carried out the innocent creature's burial, with the requisite solemnity. Thérèse told her sister Marie—Sister Marie du Sacré-Cœur—about it, with surprising gravity: "You do not know, my beloved godmother, how much the death of this little animal gave me to think about, oh yes! On earth we must become attached to nothing, not even to the most innocent things, for you miss them when you are thinking about them the least. Only that which is eternal can satisfy us."

A Tibetan hermit living in a Himalayan cave, a Hindu ascetic meditating on the banks of the Ganges, would not express himself differently.

And they were not just words: Thérèse lived every word that she wrote. She tried to forget her thirst for eternity by taking up once more her lessons with Mme Papinau, who continued obstinately to mix up teaching with society life. But Valentine Papinau's salon, with its useless chatter and frivolous observations, confirmed the need that Thérèse felt for silence, for isolation and desert. This was where she hoped as well to become a saint, as she wrote to Pauline on 27 March, thus following the wishes of her mother, Zélie Martin, who had wanted all of her daughters to become saints.

Thérèse's entry into Carmel had been scheduled for 9 April, the Feast of the Annunciation. The day before, at Les Buissonnets, a dinner brought the Martins and the Guérins together. Louis spoke

almost not at all, his eyes fixed on his little queen. Uncle Isidore and
Aunt Céline did not try to hide their emotion and showed their
niece an affection that until then they had tended to hide under
reprimands, at times unjust ones. The cousins, Jeanne and Marie,
vied with each other in kindness, especially Marie, who asked Thérèse
to forgive her for any sorrow that she might have caused her. The
unstable Léonie, who again, this time for health reasons, had left
the Visitation, showered her sister "with kisses and caresses." And
then there was Céline, who surpassed them all in sensitivity and
affection, Céline whose bed Thérèse shared for her last night in Les
Buissonnets.

On 9 April in the morning, Thérèse walked all around Les
Buissonnets, where she knew she would never return. The flowers,
the trees, Tom the spaniel, each got its display of affection. Then she
left on her father's arm, as she had so many times before, exactly as
if she were going for a walk through Lisieux or in the surrounding
countryside: "I left on my beloved king's arm to climb the mountain
of Carmel." There the Martins and the Guérins had gathered to
hear mass and take Communion. Before disappearing inside the
convent, Thérèse received her father's blessing: "He also got down
onto his knees and blessed me while crying....A few instants later,
the doors of the holy arch closed on me."

But first Carmel's prior, Jean-Baptiste Delatroëtte, suddenly appeared like a devil leaping from holy water. Insensitive to the moving scene before him, he called out loudly and intelligibly, under the
guise of a welcome: "So, my reverend mothers, you can sing a *Te
Deum*! As the delegate of His Excellency the bishop, I present to
you this child of fifteen years whose entry you have desired. I hope
she does not disappoint you, but I remind you that if it is otherwise,
you alone will bear the responsibility."

Sister Marie de Jésus, who related this angry outburst, added,
"The entire community was frozen by these words." The door closed.
Thérèse was at last in Carmel. She forgot what she had just heard,

allowing herself to be overcome "with an inexpressible peace," which she refrained, wisely, from expressing.

23

The Thorns of Carmel

(Spring 1888)

On 9 April 1888, at the Carmel's door, the party in attendance was in tears, all except Thérèse. She had cried so much for this day to arrive that she was not going to shed one more tear, not even a tear of joy. She said again and again, ecstatically, "It is forever that I am here." Fifteen is generally the age of departures. For Thérèse, it was the age of arrival. For she believed that she had definitively arrived in Carmel, where her immobile voyage was nevertheless just beginning.

Like all postulants, she was led to the choir immediately after her entrance. In the shadow shone the Blessed Sacrament and the eyes of Mother Geneviève de Sainte Thérèse, then eighty-two years old, founder of Carmel of Lisieux in 1838 as the attendant prior. She was now crippled. Her reputation for saintliness had gone beyond the walls of the convent. Thérèse threw herself at her feet, "thanking the good Lord for the grace He granted me to know a saint." Mother Geneviève kindly helped her back up.

Next, the mother superior, Mother Marie de Gonzague, showed the postulant around the principal places of the community. In Carmel, Thérèse knew only the chapel, the parlor, and the exterior—dark redbrick buildings crowned with slate roofs. She now discovered the oratory, the refectory, the kitchen, the heated room, the cloisters, and then the garden, with its ornamental pond and its grounds, its walkway bordered with chestnut trees, its Hermitage of the Holy Face and its Grotto of the Magdalen. Along the garden were the washhouse, the laundry, and a shed.

"Everything seemed delightful to me," wrote Thérèse, whose delight increased at the end of the tour, when she found herself facing her cell, and its penury. In this room with its whitewashed walls, there was only the strictly necessary: a simple straw mattress on the bare floor, a little bench, a writing table, a kerosene lamp. No water, no heat, no horizon other than the slate roofing, and above the roofs, the sky.

The penury of this cell was worth more for Thérèse than the queen of Sheba's wealth and palaces. "I thought I had been transported into a desert; our little cell charmed me especially." Imitating the hermits of the desert who flee from the world to meet God, Thérèse wanted nothing to distract her from this celestial face-to-face. Not a painting, not a mirror, not a flower, not a bird. The little queen had abandoned her teeming bazaar for a room so bare that it seemed like an antechamber to nothingness.

Thérèse was enchanted. It was exactly what she had wished for. She received no special habit: She wore a black cape over her blue dress and the traditional little bonnet on her head. She read the schedule that regulated the community, and she followed it strictly starting on 10 April.

Like her companions, Thérèse got up at 4:45. From 5:00 to 7:00, there were various prayers. Mass was at 7:00, then thanksgiving. At 8:00 it was breakfast, consisting of soup, after which came work. The first examination of conscience took place at 9:50, and at 10:00 there was a meal. At 11:00, recreation.

At noon, there was silence, or free time. At 1:00, work. At 2:00, vespers. At 2:30, spiritual reading. At 3:00, work. At 5:00, prayer. At 6:00, supper. At 6:45, recreation. The last service was at 7:40, with recital of the Canticle of Simeon and Antiphon to the Virgin. At 8:00, silence or free time, as at noon. Prayers were at 9:00, along with the second examination of conscience. Finally, at 10:30 or 11:00, bedtime.

The rigor of such a timetable did not surprise Thérèse. "I found religious life as I expected it to be; no sacrifice surprised me." Such submission would certainly have surprised all of Lisieux, which claimed, wrongly, that the youngest of the Martin demoiselles had entered the convent only to join her two sisters Pauline and Marie. In fact, she was there to become Jesus' wife. If she had not been sustained by such a lofty ambition, she would never have tolerated so much constraint!

After having familiarized herself with the surroundings and schedules, Thérèse approached a more difficult task: to learn to know her companions, and to love them, if possible. It was a hard task for a beginner who had lived the first fifteen years of her life being adulated by her family, and who was not ready for communal life. Which she willingly admitted: "My first steps encountered more thorns than roses."

The main thorn was the mother superior, Mother Marie de Gonzague, whom Thérèse had become accustomed to calling "beloved mother" when she wrote to her. Such familiarity was now out of the question. Mother Marie de Gonzague would be "Our Mother" for Thérèse, as for her companions.

Born in 1834, in Caen, Marie de Virville had entered the Carmel of Lisieux in 1860. Never forgetting that she belonged to the ancient family Davy des Harpes, proud of her coat of arms, "azure with a band of gold accompanied by three harps of the same; placed two at the top facing each other and to a point," Mother Marie de Gonzague was impressive. She was a convent Galigaï who wanted to assert the power of her strong soul over the weak souls with which she believed herself to be surrounded.

Elected mother superior almost without interruption from 1874 to 1892, it seemed as if she would hold the position for life. She tended to think herself as a shrine. In favor of the Martin sisters' arrival, despite Saint Teresa of Ávila's interdiction—Teresa had strongly recommended not admitting more than two members of the same family into a community—she was perhaps not insensitive to the substantial dowry that these demoiselles brought. Eight thousand francs for Pauline, the same for Marie, and ten thousand francs for Thérèse. These were tidy sums, when we consider, for example, that a cook earned a hundred francs per month at the time.

Mother Marie de Gonzague had two weaknesses: her family and her cat, Mira. She had remained attached to the Virvilles more than was allowed by Carmel rules. She tended to consider her Carmelites as much the Virvilles' servants as God's. When one of her relatives came to visit, it caused a commotion in the convent, which had to see to her well-being, as it had to ensure also—all the time—the comfort of the cat. Mira was entitled to special considerations, medium-cooked calf's liver, carefully plucked little birds, and the rat that had just been caught. Whoever wanted to attract the favor of the mother superior had first to please Mira.

Despite her weaknesses, Mother Marie de Gonzague was a capable woman who knew how to administer, to manage a budget. Her personality sparkled with the attraction given by power. Thérèse's fifteen springs were fascinated by Mother Marie de Gonzague's fifty-four autumns.

The second thorn of Carmel was Sister Marie des Anges, a forty-five-year-old nun, the novice mistress. She could claim a birth as noble as Marie de Virville's, since she was born Jeanne de Chaumontel. She showed a disconcerting naiveté. One fourteenth of July holiday, she thought a soccer ball was an apparition of the devil. There were many other, similar occurrences.

Sister Marie des Anges was more distracted than a novice mistress should be. Accustomed to the good bourgeois food of Les Buissonnets, Thérèse had difficulty getting used to the Spartan food of Carmel. The result of this was stomachaches, of which she complained to Sister Marie des Anges, who promptly ordered her to let her know each time she had these pains. Then she forgot her order and soon found Thérèse's frequent complaints intolerable. Thérèse digested poorly soups that her spaniel, Tom, would not have wanted.

The third thorn...but one could go on forever, enumerating the thorns that pricked or wounded Thérèse. At age fifteen, she was the convent's youngest recruit. She had to share the life of women who, for the most part, were entering their dangerous fifties; the others were approaching their forties. Withered by the austerities of monastic life, they were a bit irritated by Thérèse's extreme youth, and by her beauty. In Carmel, she felt as different from others as she had in the abbey. She was, once again, apart, and her companions made her feel her difference.

And her arrival had not been desired unanimously. "What foolishness, to allow such a young child into Carmel," whispered some who, in their heart of hearts, approved of the attitude of their prior, Canon Delatroëtte. Among those opposing Thérèse, Sister Aimée de Jésus must be included. Of rural origin, she found the Martin sisters "too artistic." This expression had a clearly pejorative sense and was synonymous with laziness, marginality.

Sister Marie de Jésus and Sister Marie de Saint Joseph would give Thérèse the opportunity to explore the infinite resources of her patience. Sister Saint Jean Baptiste represented "the severity of the good Lord" for the beginner, who also had to suffer the incessant cutting remarks of Sister Saint Vincent de Paul. As for Sister Thérèse de Saint Augustin, she overflowed with affection for Thérèse, who, for her part, could not stand her, but would manage nevertheless to hide her antipathy.

For someone as reclusive, as solitary, as Thérèse, communal life indeed offered more thorns than roses. Among the roses, her two blood sisters must be included, Sister Agnès de Jésus and Sister Marie du Sacré-Cœur, as well as Mother Geneviève de Sainte Thérèse, who, having reached the end of her life, was all indulgence and gentleness.

The Lisieux Carmel, where Thérèse was preparing to live, resembled certain marriages that are just the union of two solitudes. There were some twenty-five different solitudes in this convent, and everything separated them—birth, education, temperament. It took Mother Marie de Gonzague's authority to manage everyone's susceptibilities and obtain the calm necessary for the respect of the rules, for prayer, and for contemplation. Indeed, a Carmel is a women's prison with God as guard.

However much Thérèse claimed to be without illusions about the exigencies of convent life, she would be nonetheless tortured by her daily asperities. "Jesus made me understand that it was by the cross that He wanted to give me souls, and my attraction to suffering grew as the suffering increased. For five years this path was mine, but on the outside, nothing translated my suffering, which was more painful because I was alone in knowing of it. Ah! What a surprise we will have at the end of the world in reading the story of souls!...How many people are amazed when they see the path by which mine was led!"

To Jesus' celestial teachings were added those, more practical, of Sister Marie des Anges. In charge of the linen room, the novice mistress initiated Thérèse in sewing and ironing. She soon noticed that the novice was not particularly talented at this sort of labor. At Les Buissonnets, it had been the servant who had taken care of all that.

On top of her activities at the laundry, Thérèse had to sweep out a dormitory, she who had never held a broom in her life! Sewing, ironing, sweeping, were so many thorns that she would learn, with Jesus' help, to turn into roses.

24

"You Have Never Committed a Single Mortal Sin"

(28 May 1888)

In Carmel, Thérèse felt sheltered. She no longer ran the risk of being run over by cars, as in Paris, or of being subjected to a romantic assault, as in Bologna. Cars and men entered only rarely here.

Thérèse scrupulously adhered to the timetables that punctuated her daily life, and to the exigencies of the novitiate. She joined her sister Marie, who was still a novice, and two others, Sister Marie-Philomène and Sister Marthe de Jésus. She was the fourth of the novices who, every day, gathered around Sister Marie des Anges to benefit from her teaching. Curiously, when she taught, the novice mistress forgot to be naïve or distracted, and she explained perfectly the Order's Rule, constitutions, and customs. She found in Thérèse a docile student, as she would later attest: "Sister Thérèse of the Child Jesus had such an intuition for religious virtue and perfection that the only reason to teach her these things was so that she could, so to speak, immediately carry them out to perfection."

Thérèse learned to walk slowly, to make the fewest gestures possible. To lower her eyes. To address Marie and Pauline with the formal "you"—*vous*—when she had always addressed them with the informal *tu*. Each time she encountered her mother superior, she kissed the ground as a sign of humility and submission. "Our Mother, often ill, had little time to look after me. I know that she loved me very much and spoke as highly as she could of me, however the good Lord allowed that without knowing it she was very severe."

And it was true that, if she was severe with Thérèse, Mother Marie de Gonzague esteemed her. "Not a word to say, everything is perfect," she wrote to Mme Guérin, who worried about her niece's behavior in Carmel. Mme Guérin would have been very surprised to see how Thérèse mended, swept, gardened, as best she could, putting into these activities more willingness than know-how.

Louis Martin hid as best he could the pain he felt at no longer seeing his little queen except in the parlor. He showered Carmel with gifts for the sole purpose of receiving thank-you letters from Thérèse. Feeling, perhaps, a bit guilty about having abandoned her father, she increased her demonstrations of affection: "Yes, I will always be your little queen and I will try to bring you glory by becoming a great saint." Thérèse wrote to Céline as well, to assure her of the endurance of her feelings: "Tomorrow it will be one month that I have been away from you, but I feel that we are not separated, no matter where we are...if the Ocean separated us we would still stay united, for our desires are the same and our hearts beat together." And she signed it, "Your little Thérèse of the Child Jesus." Thérèse of the Child Jesus did not forget those whom Thérèse Martin had loved, and still loved.

The more she wrote, the more Thérèse felt a growing vocation for letter writing. Withdrawn in her cell, she took pleasure in writing page after page, interrupting a sentence when the bell rang, calling her to prayers. She even wrote to Sister Agnès de Jésus and Sister Marie du Sacré-Cœur, expressing in her missives that which she had not been able, or had not dared, to say during recreation.

On 20 May 1888, she composed a veritable declaration of love for Sister Marie du Sacré-Cœur: "If you only knew how much I love you. When I encounter you, I feel like you are an angel...You who are an eagle destined to soar on the heights and stare at the sun, pray for the little reed, so weak, that is at the bottom of the valley; the least breeze makes it bend. Oh! Pray for it on the day of your profession!"

On 22 May 1888, Sister Marie du Sacré-Cœur made her profession, which meant that she professed her perpetual vows. Thérèse crowned her sister with roses.

The next day, Sister Marie du Sacré-Cœur received the black veil. The convent celebrated. On that day, the nuns also commemorated the fiftieth anniversary of the founding of their Carmel. For this exceptional event, Fr. Pichon, back from Canada, gave an exceptional sermon. Thérèse had a long conversation with him, followed by her confession, which she relates in this way: "At the end, the Father said these words to me, the most consoling that had ever rung in the ear of my soul: 'In the presence of the good Lord, of the Holy Virgin, and of all the saints, I declare that never have you committed a single mortal sin.' Then he added: 'Thank the good Lord for what He has done for you, for if He abandoned you, instead of being a little angel, you would become a little demon.'" Ah! I had no difficulty believing it, I felt how weak and imperfect I was, but gratitude filled my soul.

Thus the "radiant celebrations of the month of May," Marie's profession, and the commemoration of the fiftieth anniversary ended with a quiet apotheosis for Thérèse. God and Father Pichon be praised! Over, really over, were the scruples, the turmoil, the worries, the fears, that had martyrized the young devotee. In Carmel, Thérèse felt sheltered from cars, from men, and from mortal sin.

25

A Father's Misfortunes

(23 June 1888)

From the beginning of April to the end of June, Thérèse did her best to blend the various ingredients of her life: Mother Marie de Gonzague's severity, Sister Marie des Anges's teachings, Fr. Pichon's revelation. For indeed it was a revelation, and a major one for this scrupulous person, to know that she was free of all mortal sin. Even so, despite this assurance, she did not succeed in opening her soul completely.

Sister Fébronie de la Sainte Enfance, who was one of the convent's elders—she was seventy-nine years old—and who knew well the torments that afflicted beginners, said to Thérèse, during a recreation:

"My little girl, I feel that you must not have much to say to your superiors."

"Why, my Mother, do you say that?"

"Because your soul is extremely simple, but when you are perfect, you will be even simpler; the closer we get to the good Lord, the more we are simplified."

Thérèse recognized the soundness of this observation, upon which she had to meditate. Could saintliness be an extreme simplification of the person, who, detached from everything, could at last merge with God, no longer blocking His light? Yes, Thérèse had to meditate for a long time on this theme.

Attentive to the elders' words, she was not, as they believed in Lisieux, "the community's plaything." She continued to be only Jesus' plaything. Jesus, whom she took as her spiritual director, since the one she had chosen, Fr. Pichon, was returning to Canada. Thérèse addressing Divinity directly, here was a fine example of simplicity to propose for Sister Fébronie de la Sainte Enfance's meditation. It was with the same simplicity that Thérèse interpreted the role of Saint Agnes in a play, a "recreation" written by Sister Agnès de Jésus for the name-day feast of their mother superior. She achieved a great success, recalling that she had visited the saint's tomb during the trip to Italy, of which she reminded her father on 17 May 1888: "The memory of this wonderful trip taken with my beloved little father will always remain with me."

During that month of May, the "beloved little father" had gone to Alençon to reflect at his wife's grave and pray in the church of Notre Dame. He came back agitated, confessing to his three daughters who were gathered in Carmel: "My children, I just came from Alençon, where in the Church of Notre Dame I received such great graces, such consolations that I said this prayer: 'My God, it is too much, yes, I am too happy, it is not possible to go to heaven like this, I want to suffer something for you!' And I offered myself."

God would hear this offer of sacrifice only too well! To Louis's three daughters who had already given themselves to the Lord, the request was nothing extraordinary. But it was for Louis, who, having reached the final years of his life, noticed that his health was inexorably declining. He felt an immense lassitude, and he was affected by frequent memory losses. He was sixty-five years old and feared that he would regress into a second childhood.

If Léonie was too unstable for him to lean on, Louis knew that he could count on Céline to guide his last steps. To reward his daughter for her devotion and encourage her talent for painting, during a trip to Paris he rented a villa in Auteuil, where they would live and from where Céline could broaden her horizons and frequent artists' studios. Céline flatly refused this arrangement and gave her reason: "I do not seek celebrity, I prefer my innocence to all other advantages and I do not want to lose it in the studios. I want to be a nun."

The brutality of this admission, made on 16 June, overwhelmed M. Martin. On 23 June he vanished. Where was he? Was he hurt? Held prisoner? Dead? The five Martin girls, mad with fear, lost themselves in speculations.

On 27 June, thanks to a telegram requesting a response in care of general delivery, M. Guérin and Céline found Louis in Le Havre, somewhat confused about his flight. Since a disaster never comes alone, during his absence a fire had destroyed a house near Les Buissonnets, and now a terrified Léonie, already seeing herself the prey of flames, fell ill.

M. Martin's inexplicable disappearance, which was impossible to conceal, caused a great stir in Lisieux. The origin of his mental troubles, and the strange conduct they engendered, were attributed straightaway to Thérèse. No one was unaware of Louis's preference for his youngest child.

The rumor in Lisieux spread to Carmel, where Marie, Pauline, and Thérèse, who prided themselves in having the best of fathers, had to see his reputation tarnished by malicious gossip. They had to face indiscreet questions and insulting assertions: "One day in the parlor, we heard the harshest things about our father; in speaking of him, scornful terms were used." Only Mother Geneviève de Sainte Thérèse understood the Martin girls' helplessness. As Pauline would relate, "Many people held us responsible for this trouble."

Had not Marie, Pauline, and Thérèse exhibited, without realizing it, egoism? Before serving their Father in heaven, would they not have done better to devote themselves to their earthly father? Admittedly, all three had received Louis Martin's permission and blessing when they had entered the order. But these three departures had been so many blows for this aging and sick man. The announcement of a fourth departure finished him.

After his flight, Louis Martin regained his reason and was delighted to learn of the considerable inheritance that was to come to his brother-in-law, to whom one of his wife's cousins, M. David, had left securities, property, houses, and the Château de la Musse. A few months later, Isidore was able to retire and live magnificently from his private means, devoting himself to journalism, to his family, and especially to the Martins, who needed it the most. Louis's health continued to deteriorate. Céline and Léonie agreed to give up, temporarily, their religious vocations to devote themselves to their father. They resigned themselves to being mere home attendants.

After this family turmoil, Thérèse, who often compared herself to a reed, again stood up straight and faced the inevitable disadvantages of communal life. "Sometimes little gusts of wind are more unbearable for the reed than great storms," she confided to Sister Agnès de Jésus.

In her letters to her father, she never made allusion to the squall that had shaken them, contenting herself with intensifying her affection: "The longer I live, my little beloved father, the more I love you; I do not know how that can be, but it is the truth. I wonder what it will be at the end of my life."

Lost in the abysses of his sacrifice, Louis Martin knew that he could count, no matter what, on Thérèse's love. He would always be her king, even if he became a mad king.

26

A Fighting Reed

(December 1888)

During the summer and fall of 1888, Thérèse forgot about herself, thinking only of her father, and of Céline, who also needed support in a test such as this. Céline knew, as did Louis Martin, that she could count on Thérèse's inalienable love and understanding. "Your Thérèse understands your entire soul…there is between our souls something so sensitive, so much alike. Always we have been together; our joys, our pains, everything was shared. Ah! I feel that it continues in Carmel; never, no never, will we be separated from it."

Thus everyone in the Martin family relied on the youngest, who showed a surprising maturity for her fifteen and a half years. Thérèse's age must be kept in mind to realize fully that she was, no matter what she thought, an exceptional creature.

No more tears, no more complaints, no more headaches; Thérèse was facing the situation, both for herself and for the others. She grew accustomed, as best she could, to the rigors of convent life, the burdens of lack of privacy. The community was satisfied with her habituation to the inevitable, and at the end of October it was decided that she was worthy of receiving Carmelite habit, according to the custom requiring that after six months of postulancy, the candidate should don the religious habit. The decision was reached despite the prior, Canon Delatroëtte, who was unrelenting. He had seen in Thérèse's premature admission an insupportable attack on his authority. He saw now, in her success, a refutation of his 9 April prediction. He refused to join his approval to that of the community. Once again, the intervention of the bishop of Bayeux, Monseigneur Hugonin, was needed for this controversial receiving of the habit to be scheduled for 10 January 1890.

In November, Louis Martin's mental state worsened, just after he had suffered a second attack. He was seized once more by his contradictory obsessions with being a hermit withdrawn in some cave and a voyager who traveled all over the world. He indulged in giving alms incessantly, as well as generous gifts, which worried Isidore Guérin, who was concerned about preserving his nieces' property; he was still their legal guardian.

In December, Louis gave ten thousand francs toward a new altar for the Cathedral of Saint-Pierre, which had called upon the generosity of its faithful. After such a gift, added, the same year, to the ten thousand francs of Thérèse's dowry, and in order to prevent other rash expenditures, M. Guérin considered having an administrator appointed for M. Martin's fortune. His daughters energetically opposed this, especially Thérèse, who thought the expense incurred for the altar was perfectly fair, and justifiable: "After having given us all to the good Lord, it is perfectly natural that he should give himself an altar upon which to immolate us and himself." Isidore Guérin, who, thanks to the David inheritance, had attained the haute bourgeoisie, could not bear to hear such language, that of renouncing the riches of this world. Not wishing to get into a conflict with his nieces, he preferred to wait for his brother-in-law's next extravagance before carrying out his project.

On 31 December 1888, Thérèse reviewed the year that had just passed and that had seen her enter Carmel: "Yes, suffering held out its arms to me and I threw myself into them with love." A thinking reed, suffering reed, and especially a fighting reed, as proven by her ability to defend her father, Thérèse was a reed that was metamorphosing into an oak, of which it was acquiring, little by little, the strength.

27

A Mirror of Snow

(10 January 1889)

On 5 January 1889 in the evening, Thérèse, who was entering her sixteenth year, began the retreat that preceded her receiving the habit. For four days, she stayed alone with herself, alone with the immensities that one carries in oneself and that one never explores for fear of losing oneself in them....It is enough to frighten the most confirmed sages, and the most valiant warriors of God!

For four days, she traveled without respite or rest across her interior deserts, with the tireless impetuosity of her youth. She could speak only to the mother superior and to the novice mistress. She was allowed to correspond with her two sisters, Sister Agnès de Jésus and Sister Marie du Sacré-Cœur. She did not deny herself this. On 6 January, the first day of her retreat and the Feast of the Epiphany, she wrote to Sister Agnès de Jésus: "Nothing near Jesus, dryness! Sleep! But at least it is silence! Silence is good for the soul. But creatures, oh! Creatures!...Those who surround me are good indeed, but there is something, I do know not what, that repels me!...My only desire is to do always the will of Jesus....Oh! I do not want Jesus to have any distress on the day of my commitment, I would like to convert all sinners of the earth and save all souls from purgatory."

Dryness, sleep, and silence were Thérèse's companions during this retreat of which she had hoped so much. Dryness of the soul while awaiting the Savior who did not come, sleep of the body, exhausted by the rigors of life in Carmel, silence received as beatitude. The silence followed the chattering of her companions during the recreation periods. For if she accepted the convent's constraint, Thérèse could not bear her companions, who, misled by her perpetual smile, were convinced of the contrary. Only Mother Marie de Gonzague, Mother Geneviève de Sainte Thérèse, Sister Fébronie, Sister Agnès de Jésus, and Sister Marie du Sacré-Cœur found favor in her eyes and a place in her heart, which extended its need for love to the sinners of the earth and to the souls in purgatory whom she wanted to save. Thérèse would have been ready to refuse paradise if she knew that someone was suffering in purgatory, or in hell.

On 7 January, after a rebuff from Sister Saint Vincent de Paul, Thérèse had a very heavy heart and again poured out her feelings in a note to sister Agnès de Jésus: "Since I can find no creature who makes me happy, I want to give everything to Jesus." This reasoning had a divine simplicity: Since she was not fulfilled by creatures, she would be by the Creator, or more exactly, by His Son. And she added: "May Jesus always make me understand that He alone is perfect happiness, even when He Himself seems absent!"

This absence of Jesus, or this appearance of absence, wounded Thérèse, who was still somewhat the spoiled child who had seen her wishes granted quickly. She called Jesus. Jesus did not come. She said she was "denied all consolation." The interior desert turned into an opaque night, the one that mystics cross before reaching the light.

On 8 January, again to Sister Agnès de Jésus, she confided: "I believe that the work of Jesus during this retreat has been to detach me from everything that was not Him." That same day, she showed her impatience to Sister Marie du Sacré-Cœur: "Just one more day and I will be Jesus' fiancée, what a grace." Sustained by the hope of receiving this grace, she awaited the departure from the desert, the end of the tunnel.

These four days of retreat were a test from which she would emerge victorious. It was then that Sister Agnès de Jésus showed Thérèse the treasures that were hidden in the Holy Face of Christ, "the mysteries of love hidden in the face of our Husband...I understood that it was true glory. He whose kingdom is not of this world showed me that true wisdom consists of wanting to be unknown and counted for nothing." She decided to add to her religious name this extra mention: "and of the Holy Face."

Thus, on 10 January 1889, Thérèse Martin became Sister Thérèse of the Child Jesus and of the Holy Face. To celebrate the event, her father sent champagne to Carmel, along with a surprise package that, when a wick on top was lighted, exploded into a shower of candies.

On 10 January in Carmel, the bishop of Bayeux, Monseigneur Hugonin, presided over the ceremony of the receiving of the habit. The Guérins and the Martins were there, poorly controlling emotions that intensified when Thérèse came out of the enclosure. She wore a dress given by her father, white velvet trimmed with swansdown and Alençon lace, that Alençon lace on which her mother had spent so many days and nights. Crowned with white lilies, haloed by her blond curls, she looked, according to the witnesses, like a madonna walking on clouds. Louis Martin welcomed his daughter with an "Ah! There she is, my little queen."

The little queen took her king's arm, and they entered the chapel followed by the other family members, who walked two by two, as for a wedding. They attended mass. Then the retinue formed again to walk to the sacristy, where Thérèse took leave of her family. The embraces over, she went past the gate behind which the nuns awaited her, each carrying a lighted candle. The mother superior led Thérèse to the choir where the receiving of the habit took place, which the Martins and the Guérins could watch through the grille. Monseigneur Hugonin pronounced the ritual words while Mother Marie de Gonzague dressed Thérèse in the homespun dress and white cloak.

Thérèse Martin was thereafter Sister Thérèse of the Child Jesus and of the Holy Face. And she was so with so much splendor that Monseigneur Hugonin struck up the *"Te Deum,"* forgetting the ritual, for this hymn should be sung only during the profession of faith.

This incident is generally presented as absent-mindedness, but perhaps it was just teasing on the bishop's part, aimed at his representative, Canon Delatroëtte, who was also present and who, on 9 April 1888, had ironically urged Carmelites to sing a *"Te Deum"* to celebrate Thérèse's admission. Not even one year later, Carmelites, led by Monseigneur Hugonin, sang the *"Te Deum"* that, for once, reverberated disagreeably in Canon Delatroëtte's ears.

The ceremony over, Monseigneur Hugonin displayed his predilection for this Carmelite who was so young—"He showed a kindness toward me that was all paternal. I truly believe that he was proud to see that I had succeeded. He told everyone that I was his little girl." But Thérèse was none the less her father's "little girl," and she joined him in the parlor. It was a moment of perfect happiness. As a symbol of this perfection, it had snowed over Lisieux as she had hoped.

This unexpected snow surprised everyone except Thérèse: "How sensitive Jesus is! Providing for the wishes of His fiancée, He gave her snow...where is the mortal, as powerful as he may be, who can make snow fall from heaven for the delight of his beloved? Perhaps those in the outside world asked themselves this question; what is certain is that the snow of my receiving of the habit seemed like a small miracle to them, and that the entire city was surprised by it. They thought I had strange taste, to love snow."

She loved snow like a mirror in which she recognized herself, immaculate.

28

A Roughly Handled Treasure

(Spring 1889)

Thérèse saw in that day of 10 January 1889 her father's "triumph." But this triumph did not last long. On 12 February, after being seized by delusions that were stronger than all the others had been, during which he brandished a revolver, Louis Martin was hospitalized at Caen, at the Bon Sauveur, an institution that specialized in mental illnesses. He would remain there for three years.

Léonie and Céline immediately found lodging near the Bon Sauveur so that they could attend their father, visiting him frequently thanks to special authorization.

For Thérèse, it was shattering. Her father, her beloved king, in a madhouse! Her father locked up in an asylum in Caen, and she, imprisoned in Carmel! Impossible to help him other than by prayers.

In June 1888, during Louis Martin's flight, she had said: "I am suffering very much, but I feel that I can stand greater tests." What greater test was there than the one she endured now? When she learned the news of the confinement, Thérèse did not believe that she could suffer anymore. She believed that she had drained the chalice of suffering down to the dregs. Yet, in the very bosom of this desolation, she declared herself "the happiest of creatures." To explain this strange happiness, she said: "Yes, the three years of Papa's martyrdom seem to me the kindest, the most fruitful of our entire lives; I would not give them up for all the ecstacies and revelations of the saints, my heart is overflowing with gratitude in thinking of this inestimable treasure, which is enough to cause the angels of the celestial court a saintly jealousy."

Thérèse thought of suffering as a treasure that engendered redemption. Suffering was her fifth sister, a sister more difficult than the others and whom she cherished, perhaps, more than the others. She firmly believed that suffering led to perfection on earth and then to the eternal joys of paradise. It was a belief shared by Pauline, Marie, Léonie, Céline, and some other devout individuals of their time. On 28 February, Thérèse wrote to Céline:

> Ah! Beloved little sister, far from complaining to Jesus about the cross that He sends us, I cannot understand the infinite love that brought Him to treat us this way…our darling father must be well loved by Jesus to have to suffer so, but do you not think that the trouble that afflicts him is altogether the complement of his beautiful life?

Thérèse suffered with an elation that may surprise the immense majority of mortals, who do not at all wish to achieve sainthood at such a price! She thought of the test that she was undergoing as a gold mine to work. Now Thérèse was a miner for mystical gold, the only kind that knows nothing of devaluations. She no longer hoped for anything from earth. She expected everything from heaven. She was sixteen years and three months old.

Her rejection of the earth was a theme that reappeared often in the letters she addressed, during this period, to Céline. "I need to forget earth…down here, everything tires me, everything burdens me." She felt like a prisoner on this earth of exile, a prisoner of Carmel, where everything wounded and bothered her. There was nothing elevating about sweeping, ironing, and gardening.

After receiving her habit, Thérèse was put under the command of Sister Agnès de Jésus; she had to sweep out the refectory and place

the water and beer on the tables. This work earned her only criticism and reproaches. She was too slow, too careless. If Pauline had once been a second mother for Thérèse, Sister Agnès de Jésus was a cruel mother. She treated her sister with a severity that she would later regret: "In the two years that she was, with me, responsible for the refectory, I supervised her closely and scolded her over nothing. One day I reproached her so harshly...that she could not keep herself from crying....I was as if excited by her tears and by her gentleness itself, and the more she cried, the more I attacked her."

As soon as she was, symbolically, slapped, Thérèse, following the evangelical precept, turned the other cheek. She became the "whipping boy" of the convent. She was not Carmel's "plaything," as was believed at the time in Lisieux, but its scapegoat. She was what the others were not. "Her exterior, always so calm, annoyed the imperfect ones and the assiduous ones like me," acknowledged Sister Agnès de Jésus. And the others, exasperated, took their revenge, increasing the vexations—all in good faith, since it was for the good of a novice who did not know how to make herself useful. This incompetent was spared nothing. For example, if Thérèse had an undisguised phobia about spiders, she was sent to sweep out the spiderwebs right away!

Confronted with such fury, Thérèse was alone. She could expect help from no one, not even from the novice mistress, even less from the mother superior. From the attendant prioress, whom she could have loved and whom she would have liked so much to visit in her cell, Thérèse received no consolation. In the end, she saw her with no joy at all.

Mother Marie de Gonzague, who had known Thérèse as a child and who had done so much for her to be accepted into Carmel as soon as possible, wanted her novice to be perfect. Unfortunately, Mother Marie de Gonzague and Sister Thérèse of the Child Jesus did not have the same concept of perfection. Certainly, the mother superior appreciated the novice. "She is a treasure for Carmel," she confided. But she kept herself from showing the slightest benevolence, thinking that severity was the only path to preserve this treasure, which in the spring of 1889 was a very roughly handled treasure!

Rejected by Sister Agnès de Jésus, overwhelmed by Mother Marie de Gonzague, annoyed by the chattering of Sister Marie des Anges, and despairing about the confinement of her father, Thérèse took refuge in silence, which she broke to pour out her feelings in letters to Céline: "Life...ah! It is true that for us it has no more charm...we still have reality, yes, life is a treasure, every instant is an eternity, an eternity of joy for heaven, an eternity to see God face to face, to be but one with Him! There is only Jesus that is; all the rest is not."

All the "rest"—assistant prioress, novice mistress, sisters—was only a dream, illusion. This truth, Thérèse learned it at her own expense.

29

The Discovery of the Holy Face

(July–December 1889)

On 18 June 1889, the Lisieux court appointed an administrator to manage Louis Martin's affairs. This represented complete degeneration for Louis, and horror for Thérèse, who thought of the words of Ecclesiastes: "Sustain your father in his weakness. Is his spirit weakening? Be indulgent." How she would have liked to sustain—physically—her beloved king, and how she suffered not to be able to. As if that were not enough, a new sorrow afflicted her: The lease on Les Buissonnets was to terminate in December. Les Buissonnets, symbol of happiness on earth. The Martin tribe was now dispersed. Léonie and Céline would live at the Guérins. Thérèse no longer had anything but her straw mattress on which to rest her head.

The news that she received from Caen was not of a nature to lessen her distress: "I cannot get used to seeing our beloved little father ill like this," wrote Céline, who added, "Oh! How the good Lord must love us to afflict us so much."

Léonie, "poor Léonie," also got in tune with the atmosphere of great suffering: "The best thing is to curl up in Jesus' heart….Only there will we find once more the courage to bear the sufferings of life, which, indeed, we do not lack….Let us make ourselves worthy of such a father!"

Sister Marie du Sacré-Cœur compared Louis to Job on his dung-hill, continuing to praise the Lord despite the trials with which he was overwhelmed. And Sister Agnès de Jésus summarized the situation with a peremptory "Let us be saints, Jesus is asking this of us."

In Thérèse's path to sainthood, it is undeniable that her father's decline helped a great deal. By her will, and with God's help, she was able to change this decline into an ascension.

The summer of 1889 marked for all of France the commemoration of the centenary of the French Revolution and the beginning of the World's Fair in Paris. But for Thérèse, July '89 was above all a week of respite.

One evening while praying in the garden in front of the Grotto of the Magdalen, she received the grace of a feeling of quietude, as if an invisible hand had erased her suffering. For eight days her tortures ceased. Her body and her spirit, at last reconciled, rested. "It was as if a veil had been thrown for me over all things of the earth…I did things as if not doing them. I stayed that way for an entire week."

July '89 also saw the deepening of Thérèse's devotion to the Holy Face. Mother Marie de Gonzague gave her novice an image representing this Holy Face of Christ.

We recall that Jesus, during his climb to Mount Calvary, fell. One of the holy women, Veronica, took advantage of this collapse to dry the face of the master, dirtied with blood and sweat, with her veil. On this veil, preserved at Saint Peter's Basilica in Rome, Jesus' face was marked forever. In the nineteenth century, the venerable M. Dupont, from Tours, spread the worship of this Holy Face, likenesses of which Carmels distributed generously.

For Thérèse, this image constituted a revelation. She who in January 1889 had chosen to call herself Sister Thérèse of the Child Jesus and of the Holy Face suddenly understood, seven months later, all that this represented. Even better, she recognized, through that martyred face, her father's face, and the faces of those who suffered moral or physical tortures. She found in the prophet Isaiah truths that comforted her in this recognition: "His face was as if hidden! He looked wretched and we did not recognize Him." Thérèse recognized Him and venerated Him. In her eyes, the face of Jesus shone and would always be with her, as Sister Agnès de Jésus testified: "That Holy Face was the book of meditation from which she drew the science of love."

On 21 October, lost in her meditations and in her study of the "science of love," Thérèse forgot to wish Céline a happy birthday. On the twenty-second, she repaired the oversight by excusing herself as best she could: "The life of Carmel is so reclusive that the poor little solitary never knows what date it is." She sent as a gift an image of the Holy Face, recommending that Céline become another Veronica.

During the autumn of 1889, she continued her quest for the Beloved. One day, overcome with love, she knelt before the altar, knocked on the door of the tabernacle, and asked; "Are you there, Jesus? Answer me, I beg you." Sister Marthe, who told of this scene, which she witnessed, did not report, alas, Jesus' response.

Louis Martin still lived, but his mental state prevented all communication with his daughters. On 31 December Thérèse ended the year in Céline's company, writing to her: "It is with a heart full of memories that I am going to stay up and await midnight. I remember everything...now we are orphans."

Louis was prey to hallucinations. The mad king was lost to his little queen, who had to remind herself of one of the nicknames her father had given her: "the orphan of Berezina."

On the last day of the year 1889, the orphan contemplated the image of the Holy Face with even greater fervor.

30

An Interminable Engagement

(Summer 1890)

One year after receiving the habit, a novice could make her profession, which meant professing her perpetual vows, on condition that she be older than seventeen years old. Thus, in January 1890 Thérèse could hope to make hers. She learned that Canon Delatroëtte, unrelenting, had decided to delay her profession. Was this how he was taking his revenge for the *"Te Deum"* intoned by the bishop of Bayeux during Thérèse's receiving of the habit? Did he hope to exhaust the patience of the undesirable novice? Lessen the pride of the girl who had caused a scandal in the Vatican? Even though she had not yet made her vow of obedience, Thérèse submitted herself blindly to the decision of her prior.

To console herself over this delay, she read the Song of Songs and Saint John of the Cross, from which she recopied passages celebrating the radiance of the Beloved that made her forget her disappointment, "and I surrendered, leaving all my concerns lost in the middle of the lilies!" She wrote to Sister Agnès de Jésus: "Is our family not a virginal family, a family of lilies?"

After the lilies came the night. The dark night of the soul that Saint John of the Cross endured Thérèse knew only too well. How many times had she evoked "the black night," "the night of the

139

soul," "the night deeper than the night of nothingness"? She found, however, a bit of light, and comfort, with Sister Geneviève de Sainte Thérèse, "a saint sanctified by hidden and ordinary virtues." One Sunday, Sister Geneviève said to Thérèse: "You ask me to give you a spiritual bouquet. Well then, today I am going to give you this one: Serve God with peace and with joy; remember, my child, that our God is the God of peace."

These words restored Thérèse's confidence; she had been so sad that she had doubted God's love.

And then a new killjoy suddenly appeared, Father Blino, a Jesuit like Fr. Pichon. As beneficial as Fr. Pichon had been for Thérèse, so Fr. Blino was all incomprehension. He came, in May 1890, to preach a retreat at Carmel. With a spontaneity that she soon regretted, the novice admitted: "My father, I want to become a saint, I want to love the good Lord as much as Saint Teresa of Ávila."

The Jesuit saw in these words only unbearable pretention and sharply rebuffed the nun who had dared to speak them: "What pride and what presumption; confine yourself to correcting your mistakes, to no longer offending the good Lord, and to making a little progress each day and moderating your reckless desires." Thérèse, who did not consider herself beaten, replied, "But, my father, I do not find these to be reckless desires, since Our Lord said, 'Be perfect as your heavenly Father is perfect.'"

It was a dialogue of the deaf, between the Jesuit and Carmelite. One cannot fail to admire, in passing, the audacity of the seventeen-year-old novice who stood up to the eminent sixty-one-year-old Jesuit! Thérèse was in agreement with Father Blino on only one point: to make a little progress each day. She called this "practicing the little virtues." She folded the coats that were forgotten by the sisters, did every little favor for them that she could, accepted, in the refectory, food that no one else wanted. She had stopped counting the reheated omelettes, dry as worn-out old shoes, that she had had to swallow.

When Sister Marie des Anges accused her of having broken a vase, she lowered her head and promised not to do it again, even though she had not been the one who had done it. She continued not to lean against the back of the chair upon which she was sitting, thus continuing a mortification that she had begun in the outside world. Alas, this mortification was soon precluded because her spine began to curve, this spine to which she administered the discipline three times per week, according to the Rule. In other words, she was flagellating herself, a torture that her beloved Comtesse de Ségur, so quick to castigate the world, had spared her characters.

Thérèse acknowledged that the mortifications suffered by her self-esteem did her "much more good than the corporal penances." To be a Carmelite involved a great deal of constraint, and it was not as easy as Marie Guérin thought; she, too, wanted to be a nun, and she imagined that her cousin Thérèse did not feel the blows, triumphed over all obstacles, and inhaled only roses with no thorns. "You are mistaken, my darling, if you think that your little Thérèse walks always with ardor along the path of virtue; she is weak, very weak, and every day she experiences something new."

A new experience, and sometimes a new image. Ever since the image of the Holy Face had entered her life the preceding summer, she was aware of the power that these representations of divinity can have. During the summer of 1890, another image came to the novice's aid. It was a variation on the Holy Face, painted by Sister Agnès de Jésus for Céline, a miniature on parchment representing Veronica's veil held up by nine lilies. This caused another revelation for Thérèse, who understood that "divine blood waters our corollas": The blood of Jesus bathed the nine lilies, the nine Martin children—four in heaven, five still on earth.

This image made Thérèse more impatient to profess her perpetual vows and see the end of this interminable engagement: "The time of the engagement...it was very long for poor little Thérèse."

Canon Delatroëtte continued, meanwhile, to consider that the novice was "too young to profess her perpetual vows." It was necessary, once again, to submit the matter to Monseigneur Hugonin, who set the date for Thérèse's profession of faith for 8 September. Once again, Canon Delatroëtte had to admit defeat. Thérèse now had only to count the days separating her from 8 September.

31

The Wedding of the Child Jesus and the Child Thérèse

(8 September 1890)

Thérèse prepared herself for her profession of faith with a ten-day retreat that began on 28 August. She expected everything from this retreat, and she received nothing from it. "The most absolute aridity and almost abandonment were my lot." She attributed the dryness to what she believed to be her small amount of fervor. She fell asleep during prayers and thanksgivings. But she believed that her sleep pleased God as the sleep of children pleases their parents. She also thought that "the Lord sees our fragility, and He remembers that we are only dust."

These fine thoughts did not suffice to make her retreat blossom; it was a nocturnal, interior desert. On 31 August, Thérèse wrote to Sister Marie du Sacré-Cœur, referring to herself in the third-person singular, as she had become accustomed to doing: "Her wedding trip is very arid, her fiancé takes her, it is true, across fertile and magnificent countries, but the night prevents her from admiring anything and above all from enjoying all these marvels." She energetically underlined the word *night,* which she had encountered so many times in Saint John of the Cross and which was now her lot. She would say, on the first of September: "I am in a very dark underground."

Thérèse was worried about Céline's health—she was suffering from cardiac trouble—and even more about her father's health. Against all reason, she hoped that he would come for her "wedding." Louis Martin was incapable of traveling. All he was able to do was to bless the crown of roses that she was to wear that day.

On 2 September, an official luminary threw some light into the underground: The pope gave his benediction, obtained thanks to the intervention of Brother Siméon, of the Christian schools. He taught in the French College of Rome, where he willingly welcomed his compatriots. M. Martin had been one of them during his two sojourns in Rome.

On this same 2 September, Thérèse took the canonical exam in the convent's chapel, and to the question "Why did you come to Carmel?" she answered: "I came to save souls, and above all to pray for priests."

And then, the day before her profession of faith, horror and mental chaos struck: Thérèse doubted her vocation. "My darkness was so great that I saw and understood only one thing: I did not have a vocation! Ah, how to depict the anguish of my soul?"

The novice mistress, Sister Marie des Anges, succeeded in calming this anguish and in reassuring Thérèse, who, after the confession of her doubt, felt as if delivered. She felt the need to confirm her deliverance by making the same confession to Mother Marie de Gonzague, who contented herself with laughing about it. This novice was decidedly not like the others!

Reassured of her vocation and "inundated with a river of peace," Thérèse made her three vows—obedience, chastity, and poverty—on 8 September 1890, the Feast of the Nativity of the Virgin. She also prayed for favors, among which was her father's recovery. "My God, I beg of You, may it be Your will that Papa recovers!"

Thérèse asked her heavenly Husband as well for a few favors for herself: "May creatures be nothing for me and may I be nothing for them, but you, Jesus, be everything."

On 24 September, the taking of the veil completed the profession of faith. The black veil that Thérèse received and in which she shrouded herself was a veil of tears. Disappointments had accumulated for the young wife: She had hoped that a temporary improvement of her father's condition would have allowed him to attend at her taking of the veil. Isidore Guérin had been against it, fearing the shock that would inevitably result. Monseigneur Hugonin, who had promised to be there, was sick. He sent his brother, Canon Jean-Baptiste Hugonin.

Thérèse could take no more. She cried as she had not cried for a long time. The congregation lost themselves in conjectures and attributed her tears to the incredible bizarreness of the Martin girls. Only one person understood, her cousin Marie Guérin, who decided that day that she would become a Carmelite to drink, in turn, the chalice to the dregs.

Eight days after her sad receiving of the veil, Thérèse found an occasion for a little fun—one time did not make it a habit. She had received the wedding announcement of Marie's sister, Jeanne Guérin, to Doctor Francis La Néele, and so she amused herself by composing an announcement of her wedding to Jesus, which she entitled *Letter of Invitation to the Wedding of Sister Thérèse of the Child Jesus of the Holy Face.* It was a puerile amusement. This wedding really was that of the Child Jesus and the child Thérèse.

32

Thérèse's Three Obsessions

(Autumn 1890—Summer 1891)

In conformity with her vows, Thérèse applied herself to living each day on the summits of obedience, poverty, and chastity. She was so happy on these heights that she wanted to attract Céline to them as well, and she began to constantly laud the powerful charms of virginity to her. She was possessed by it, but this was one of the major obsessions of her time, when virginity was considered a woman's most precious asset.

Every social class agreed on the importance, the integrality, of virginal purity, which was symbolized on the wedding day by the white dress, and which so many poems and songs celebrated. Few were those who took the chance of "erring," as it was called at the time. They knew that nothing could erase this stain, which threw discredit upon their family and upon their descendants. The daughter or the son of a woman who had "erred" had a hard time finding a spouse.

Thérèse was aware that Céline was well liked and was receiving offers of marriage, which she rejected from the eminence of her twenty-one springs. Always quick to become alarmed, Thérèse feared an intruder, an abductor. A rival to Jesus? Impossible. She wanted to persuade Céline that virginity was too precious to offer to a man, and that God alone was worthy of it. Marriage with the Divine Son allowed virtue to remain intact.

Had Thérèse been entrusted with the secrets of married cousins about the "horrors" of their wedding night? After a visit from one of Mme Guérin's nieces, Marguerite-Marie Maudelonde, who had married a magistrate, Thérèse exclaimed, "Ah! Céline, how fortunate we are to have been chosen by the Husband of virgins! Marguerite confided intimate secrets to us that she tells no one."

To this obsession with virginity was added the one that she shared with Saint John of Cross, whom she read, reread, and commented upon as she felt the need. Saint John of the Cross said: "I no longer have any other function, because now my entire purpose is to love." Sister Thérèse of the Child Jesus and of the Holy Face went further: "Love, which knows how to benefit from everything, has very quickly consumed everything that could displease Jesus, leaving only a humble and profound peace deep down in my heart." Through the centuries, John the Castilian and Thérèse the Norman conversed, understood each other, and discovered in the other a brother and sister in Jesus.

The warmth of this duo would have surprised Carmel's sisters, who shivered during that winter of 1890–91. Thérèse suffered from what she called "the hell of cold." It is enough to wonder if one actually burns in hell, or if one does not, rather, suffer the torture of an eternal frigidity! On her eighteenth birthday, Thérèse's teeth chattered.

In February 1891, she was appointed attendant sacristan under Sister Saint Stanislas des Sacrés-Cœurs. Among her functions was accompanying Carmel's chaplain, Abbot Youf—who was also her regular confessor—when he brought the Eucharist to Mother Geneviève, who could no longer move about. "When I see your sister so close to me under the cloister, when I am carrying the Holy Sacrament, she always makes me think of the votive candles that burn in the churches; just the sight of them inclines one to prayer and contemplation," Abbot Youf would later confide to Sister Agnès de Jesus.

Luminous Thérèse. Luminous for others, when she was often plunged into that darkness where she encountered Saint John of the Cross and Saint Teresa of Ávila, whose creed she persistently repeated, the creed of Carmelites:

> Let nothing trouble you,
> Let nothing frighten you,
> Everything is fleeting,
> God alone is unchanging.
> Patience attains everything.
> Who possesses God wants for nothing.
> God alone is enough.

The contemplative state in which Thérèse lived was not enough to distance her completely from the rumors and news of the world. Thus, in the beginning of summer 1891, she learned of the Hyacinthe Loyson affair, which became her third obsession.

Like Henri Pranzini, Hyacinthe Loyson was an exemplary sinner, rejected by all. Everything about him pleased Thérèse, who saw in this man, whom God-fearing people considered a human wreck, a brother to save.

On 8 July 1891, she got Céline involved in this salvation as well when she quoted her Jesus' words to the blessed Marguerite-Marie: "A just soul has so much power over my heart that it can win the pardon of a thousand criminals." Hyacinthe Loyson could not have been any more of a criminal in the eyes of his contemporaries, since he was a priest and married.

Born in 1827, Loyson had been ordained a priest in 1851. In 1864, he preached at Notre-Dame de Paris, with success. He went on to preach in Rome, where he met an American widow, Mrs. Émily Meriman. She had "crises of the soul." He had them, too. Their crises united so much that in the end they were married, in 1872. They had a son in 1873. Father Loyson founded a Gallican Catholic Church, rejected papal infallibility, demanded that mass

be said in French and no longer in Latin, and asked for freedom of marriage for priests. The scandal was immense. There was talk of a new Luther, of an Antichrist heralding the end of time. Loyson died in 1912, murmuring "my sweet Jesus." These last words suggest that Thérèse's prayers were not in vain; concerning him, she said repeatedly, "We do not tire of praying; confidence makes miracles." Of Thérèse's three obsessions—Céline's virginity, reading the works of Saint John of the Cross, and saving Father Loyson—the latter was the most enduring, since Sister Thérèse of the Child Jesus' last Communion, on 19 August 1897, would be offered for this sinner.

33

A Flower of Suffering

(Autumn 1891)

In the implacable monotony that governed Carmel life, the slightest incident was looked upon as an event. Thus, in the garden, the asters flowered one month ahead of time. No one noticed this precocious flowering except Thérèse, who drew surprising conclusions from it that she passed on to Céline: "Winter is suffering, misunderstood suffering, misjudged, regarded as useless by profane eyes, but fertile and powerful in the eyes of Jesus and of the angels who, like vigilant bees, know how to gather the honey contained in the mysterious and multiple calyxes that represent the souls or rather the children of the virginal little flower. Céline, I would need volumes to write all that I think about my little flower."

Thérèse would not write these volumes, this new language of flowers. But how could she not suffer from everything when just the sight of an aster flower released such thoughts in her mind? A flower of suffering, Thérèse suffered with special intensity during the retreats that the priests came to preach regularly at Carmel. Each one revealed the risks of committing a mortal sin, "even by simple thought." Each one made such terror reign that Thérèse stopped sleeping because of it, hardly ate, and would have fallen ill if the retreat had gone on. Sin, sin, everything was sin and damnation, this is what the preachers taught to the nuns, just as to their other audiences.

It was with commendable resignation that Thérèse prepared to suffer, once more, during Father Prou's retreat, from 8 to 15 October 1891. She even applied her efforts to a preparatory novena, so that she would nevertheless be able to benefit from it.

A recollect Franciscan, Father Alexis Prou, at the time fifty-three years old, was accustomed to great sinners, and not to little Carmelites. During the fall of 1891, Thérèse of the Child Jesus was going through "all kinds of interior tests," to the point of doubting the existence of heaven! She did not know how to express her doubts, her fears, her obsessions. In the confessional, after having said "few words," she was suddenly understood, her soul discerned without having to spell it out: "My soul was like a book that the father read better than I did."

For Thérèse, Father Alexis Prou was truly sent from God. He gave her back her confidence with this simple message: "Go out into the middle of the ocean and throw your nets." It was exactly what this fisher of souls wished to hear. Her joy was so great that it worried her mother superior, who forbade the penitent to see her confessor again. This distressed Thérèse, whom Father Prou had told to come back. She confided her helplessness to Sister Marie des Anges, who, moved, advised her to try again with "Our Mother." An order from the mother superior was sacred to Thérèse, who, true to her vow of obedience, obeyed and relinquished another interview with Father Prou, whom she would never see again but would also never forget. Yes, Thérèse preferred to obey, then to remember, suffering in silence.

Her navigation on the river of Suffering stopped on 24 November 1891, when, to celebrate the tricentenary of the death of Saint John of the Cross, Monseigneur Hugonin came into the cloister and showed for Sister Thérèse of the Child Jesus, who was snubbed and humiliated, a thousand signs of esteem. The bishop of Bayeux's kindness joined the good words of the Franciscan, and Thérèse felt herself come alive again and regain her strength.

On 5 December, Mother Geneviève de Sainte Thérèse died. It was the first death that Thérèse had ever witnessed. She found the sight "enchanting," since it marked the end of exile on earth.

At the foot of the dying woman's bed, she watched every movement of the death throes. Thérèse remembered saying to Mother Geneviève: "You will not go to purgatory."

"I hope not," the octogenarian had answered.

Her death gave rise to an altercation that showed that the class struggle, so energetic at the end of the nineteenth century, did not spare Carmel, where the Martin daughters were considered rich girls by most of their companions, who were daughters of poor peasants or of the petite bourgeoisie.

While Thérèse was placing sprays of flowers near the casket, she was verbally attacked by a Carmelite who said to her: "It is easy to see that those big bouquets were given by your family; those of the poor people will again be hidden."

Thérèse, remembering her vow of poverty, did not answer and took refuge, as was her habit, in her friend silence. She collected her thoughts while contemplating Mother Geneviève. She noticed that at one of the dead woman's eyelids, a tear glistened. Reverently, she collected it on a cloth and wrapped it in a little sack that never left her. This relic, the tear of a saint and perhaps the tear of the soul, was for Thérèse a source of secret joy, reinforced by the dream she had shortly thereafter. She saw Mother Geneviève in a dream, writing her will and giving something to each Carmelite. When there was nothing left, Thérèse approached, expecting to receive nothing. Then Mother Geneviève repeated three times: "To you, I give my heart."

Thérèse was completely penetrated with the symbolic significance of this dream, she who generally attached but little importance to her dreams, which were populated exclusively with children, butterflies, and birds, and which had as scenery the woods, flowers, streams, the sea. She seemed to enjoy the blessed sleep of innocence, which only made her waking that much more tedious. About twenty days after the death of Mother Geneviève, on 28 December 1891 precisely, began an influenza epidemic that would ravage the Lisieux Carmel.

34

The Beneficial Effects of an Epidemic

(January–February 1892)

If, thanks to Father Prou, Thérèse could believe that she made God happy, she knew that she did not satisfy her companions in Carmel. But the servant of God who could not assert herself in the everyday would blossom in the exceptional, in adversity: during the epidemic that had already taken seventy thousand victims in France the year before.

Sister Saint Joseph de Jésus, who was eighty-three years old, died from it on 2 January, the same day as Thérèse's nineteenth birthday. On the fourth, Sister Fébronie de la Sainte Enfance departed; she was seventy-three years old and had been assistant prioress three times. On the seventh, it was the turn of Sister Madeleine du Saint Sacrement, the seventy-five-year-old sister who did manual labor, to succumb. Those who did not die lay listless on their straw mattresses.

Thérèse kept her wits about her and managed to be everywhere at once: She made the funeral preparations, brewed herbal teas, opened the choir grilles for mass....She showed herself to be very efficient, attributing her efficiency to graces from God: "The good Lord gave me many graces of strength at that time, I wonder now I was able to do all that I did without fear."

Thérèse's deep humility can never be sufficiently stressed; she attributed her tireless courage to the Lord, not to her own worth. And courage was certainly needed, to go into a dark cell where a nun had just died and carry out the funeral rites. When she had finished, Thérèse went, wasting no time, to wash the dirty linen, rushing to wherever she was called. Day and night, she was at the disposal of her companions, except during morning mass, when she took Communion. She was practically the only one who was able to receive the host, the others being too sick to welcome the Body of Christ. This favor increased her fervor tenfold. Since the sacristan was confined to her bed, it was Therese, as assistant sacristan, who placed the sacred objects on the altar. She recalled the words that had been spoken to a deacon: "Be holy, you who touch the vessels of the Lord." At that moment, her desire to be a saint grew stronger.

Alone with two other able-bodied companions—her own sister, Sister Marie du Sacré-Cœur, and Sister Marthe—the servant of God showed "a calm, a presence of spirit and an intelligence that are not at all ordinary." Carmel's prior, Canon Delatroëtte, was forced to acknowledge that the "recruit" was not as bad as he had announced her to be. The young girl's dedication, her sangfroid, finally softened this rock, who deigned to say with a sigh: "Sister Thérèse of the Child Jesus is a great hope for the community."

The epidemic had an unpredictable consequence. Carmelites were to elect a new mother superior in February. Most of them being ill, or not completely recovered, the election was delayed for one year. Mother Marie de Gonzague remained "Our Mother" for another year. The haughty Virville must have blessed this opportunity, which satisfied her inextinguishable thirst for power. Another consequence, equally unexpected, was that Thérèse at last was able to assert her capabilities and convince her companions that she was not a dreamer and a good-for-nothing.

35

A Time of Grace

(Summer–Fall 1892)

Thérèse was destined to be deprived of the calm and tranquillity that a Carmelite should normally enjoy. Barely recovered from the trauma of the influenza epidemic, the servant of God was again filled with anxiety when she learned that Céline, on the occasion of the marriage of Henry Maudelonde, Mme Guérin's nephew, was going to dance, perhaps even the most dangerous dance of all, the waltz, which was so much in fashion!

Thérèse became so alarmed that she called Céline to the parlor and shed one of the "torrents of tears" that had once been normal for her. Although affected, even saddened, by this deluge, Céline explained to her sister that she could not "make herself look ridiculous" by refusing to dance at the ball that would follow the marriage. Thérèse replied heatedly, citing the example of the three Hebrews who preferred to be thrown into a furnace rather than adore the golden calf. Céline protested that she had no intention of adoring that calf, or of abandoning herself to dangerous pleasures that could incite her to break the vow of chastity that she had taken. This confrontation destroyed, temporarily, the harmony that reigned between the two sisters.

During the dance, Céline refused several partners, even offending some of them. Then, at the end of the evening, she was "literally carried off by a young dance partner." But, oh surprise, they were not able to take even one dance step. Confused, the partner vanished. When she learned of the defeat of this bold young man, Thérèse, exultant, wrote to her sister on 26 April 1892: "Céline, you alone can understand my language; in the eyes of creatures, our life seems very different, very separate, but as for me, I know that Jesus has united our hearts in such a marvelous way that what makes one beat also makes the other flutter."

Harmony reigned once more between Thérèse and Céline, who indeed did speak the same language. Why lose time waltzing, when there were so many souls to save? "Our mission as Carmelites is to form evangelic workers who will save thousands of souls, whose mothers we will be....I think our role is very beautiful; for what reason would we envy priests?" said Thérèse to Céline, who was now completely convinced that it was better to give in to the vertigo of souls than to the whirl of the waltz.

Céline, twenty-three years old at the time, listened to and benefited from the lessons of nineteen-year-old Thérèse, who seemed to have collected all of Mother Geneviève's knowledge and experience along with that last tear. Clearly, Thérèse knew more about divine things than the other nuns of the Lisieux Carmel. And it was perhaps for that reason that she continued, after the influenza epidemic was no more than a bad memory, to be criticized, even persecuted. But what did that matter to Thérèse, who had Jesus as a husband and Saint John of the Cross as a holy companion! She went her own way, she climbed one by one the steps leading to sainthood, her *idée*, which overwhelmed her other obsessions, including the health of her father.

Poor Louis was by now completely paralyzed. Flights and gesticulations during his attacks were no longer to be feared. There was no longer any reason for the supervision that he was under at the Bon Sauveur of Caen. Léonie and Céline, whose visiting rights had been reduced to one meeting per week, from then on intended to care for their father in a permanent way. Giving in to their appeals, M. Guérin consented to bring the incurable Louis back to Lisieux on 10 May. When she learned of this, Thérèse could not deny herself an outburst of joy. She was not as detached from earthly feelings as she had thought.

On 12 May, Louis was brought to Carmel. It had been three long years since the little queen and her "beloved king" had seen each other. Not one word was exchanged. Louis could no longer speak. Only his eyes retained some expression. His three daughters, Sister Agnès de Jésus, Sister Marie du Sacré-Cœur, and Sister Thérèse of the Child Jesus, who did not know how to prove to their unfortunate father how much they cherished him, increased their signs of affection without obtaining the slightest reaction. When the moment came to leave them, he pointed to the sky, as in days past at Les Buissonnets, when they had gazed at the stars together and Thérèse had seen the initial of her name in a constellation. At last Louis managed to articulate: "In heaven." It was the last word—a celestial rendezvous?—that the three Carmelites ever heard from the mouth of their father.

From then on, Louis was perfectly cared for by Léonie and Céline, which gave Thérèse peace of mind; they had moved him into a house next to M. Guérin's, on rue Labbey. If at times Louis regained the use of speech, it was to say, "My daughters, pray well for me." The message was immediately transmitted to the three Carmelites, who redoubled their prayers for the person who had given them life. Thérèse had headed the announcement of her wedding to Jesus with: "Monsieur Louis Martin, proprietor and Master of the Lordships of Suffering and Humiliation." The suffering had been attenuated; the humiliation had become bearable.

For the procession of Corpus Christi, the archpriest of the Cathedral of Saint-Pierre took care to show special honors to the invalid, who did not try to hide his emotion. He was also clearly pleased with the wheelchair in which he was made comfortable, for the summer months, under the trees in the Guérins' garden.

For Thérèse, who recognized it herself, it was "a time of grace." In the fall, she went on her private retreat, taking advantage of this time to meditate on the words of Saint John of the Cross: "Everything is mine, everything is for me, the earth is mine, the heavens are mine. God is mine and the mother of my God is mine."

During this retreat, she had the simplicity, or the boldness, to say to the mother of her God: "My good Blessed Virgin, I think that I am more fortunate than you, for I have you as a mother, and you do not have a Blessed Virgin to pray to." This was admirably self-evident, when it was expressed. Yes, but it took Sister Thérèse of the Child Jesus to feel it, and to say it!

At this end of 1892, Thérèse felt as if she had wings. She no longer walked, she flew. In her limitless generosity, she wished it could be this way for everyone. Noticing that Sister Marthe de Jésus was stuck in too intense an admiration for Mother Marie de Gonzague, whose grand airs were seductive to some of her humble companions, Thérèse decided to act. She wanted to open the eyes of her companion, who was attached to the mother superior "like the dog to his master."

Informed of this plan that she judged to be too bold, Sister Agnès de Jésus tried to point out to Thérèse the dangers of such an intervention. If the mother superior should come to learn of it, one dared not imagine the violence of her reaction! "I am very aware of that, but since I am certain now that it is my duty to speak, I must not be concerned with the consequences," answered Thérèse obstinately to Sister Agnès's protestations. She spoke to Sister Marthe, found the words that enlightened her, and turned her away from a too-particular affection, all without Mother Marie de Gonzague's noticing the change.

Thérèse had not yet formulated her famous "Everything is grace," but she was currently living "Everything is grace." Even the flowers joined in. In making herself a prisoner at age fifteen, the servant of God knew that she was giving up all earthly happiness, including that of running in the fields and picking her favorite flowers. Now it was the flowers of the fields which came to her. Because it was known that it was her job to adorn the statue of the Child Jesus, bouquets were constantly brought to her. One day she found in one of them, oh joy, the lychnis she had picked as a child in the Alençon country-side. God knew how much the Carmelite wished to see this flower of her childhood again. "It was in Carmel that it came to smile at me, showing me that in the smallest things as in the greatest, the good Lord gives a hundredfold, starting in this life, to the souls that have left everything for His love."

Thérèse had left everything to enter the kingdom of God that Saint John of the Cross said is within us. It was a belief that she shared and thought of as a supplementary grace.

36

A Euphoric Election

(20 February 1893)

Exactly one month after her twentieth birthday, on 2 February 1893, and at the request of Sister Thérèse de Saint Augustin, Thérèse wrote her first poem, which was titled "The Divine Dew" and subtitled *The Virginal Milk of Mary*. In it, she compared the Child Jesus drinking his mother's milk to the fully open rose drinking dew. She saw in the rose that blossoms on the cross divine blood that is virginal milk. *Rose* and *dew, milk* and *blood,* were the four words that appeared most often in this poem of six stanzas, which could be sung to the melody of *"Minuit Chrétien"* ("O Holy Night"). There was no false elegance here, in this vision of the metamorphosis of milk into blood. Thérèse did not at all appreciate visions and would not have wanted to be called a visionary.

Beginning with these first stanzas, Thérèse revealed herself to be a poet, which is to say that she saw beyond appearances. She saw what the common mortal does not perceive.

Too modest to boast of the success of some of her poems or to be saddened that others were less successful, she wrote to obey the request, as part of her vow of obedience. She remained, in her work, the servant of the Lord. She wrote only to serve God and her beloved Jesus. When she felt inspired, she contented herself with stringing the words together and then making alterations, until she considered her task to be finished.

The year 1893 was the year of beginnings for two of the Martin sisters. Thérèse started writing poetry, and Sister Agnès de Jésus became Carmel's mother superior. On 20 February, Sister Agnès was elected mother superior, replacing Mother Marie de Gonzague. She immediately named the former mother superior novice mistress, as was the custom.

Mother Marie de Gonzague had to have an attendant. Mother Agnès de Jésus remembered intervening on one occasion with the former mother superior to spare Thérèse what she considered to be harassment. She had received this refusal: "You would no doubt like Sister Thérèse to be moved ahead; but it is the exact opposite that I must do. She is much more prideful than you think, she needs to be constantly humiliated." It was time for Mother Agnès to have her retaliation and to move Thérèse ahead. Thus she appointed Sister Thérèse of the Child Jesus as Mother Marie de Gonzague's attendant. In this euphoric election of Mother Agnès de Jésus, some have seen the apotheosis of the Martin clan. But this is an exaggeration; it was above all the triumph of the Guérin tribe, exultant at having a relative as mother superior of Carmel of their good city of Lisieux.

The prior, who was still Fr. Delatroëtte and who did not miss an occasion to play the killjoy, tempered this joy by solemnly reminding Mother Agnès de Jésus that her election owed much to the memory of the recently deceased Mother Geneviève, of whom she must "imitate the valuable example." This was exactly what the Carmelites hoped for; they were somewhat tired of the despotism of Mother Marie de Gonzague, who had often behaved like an absolute monarch. They wished for an easing, a renewal. For her part, Mother Marie de Gonzague hoped to reign through Mother Agnès de Jésus, retaining first place, and retaining as well her cat's privileges. In short, everyone was pleased in Carmel, including and especially Thérèse. She was going to be able to publicly call "Our Mother" the person she considered to be her second mother. That same 20

February, Sister Thérèse of the Child Jesus addressed this letter to Mother Agnès de Jésus:

> My darling mother,
>
> How sweet it is to be able to call you that name! For a long time already you had been my mother, but it was in the secret of my heart that I gave this sweet name to the one who was my guardian angel and at the same time my sister; today the good Lord has consecrated you....You are truly my mother and you will be for all eternity....Oh! What a beautiful day it is for your child!...Now you are going to penetrate the sanctuary of souls, you are going to lavish upon them the treasures of graces that Jesus has filled you with. No doubt you will suffer....

It is undeniable that Thérèse could not abandon herself entirely to a joy without foreseeing the suffering that would inevitably follow. In the budding rose, she saw the faded flower.

37

Thérèse's Four Jobs

(Spring–Summer 1893)

Shortly after Thérèse's admission to Carmel, Sister Agnès de Jésus had written to Sister Marie du Sacré-Cœur: "We must not in the least look after Thérèse of the Child Jesus. For myself, I am going to leave her entirely to her own devices....It is more than enough to look after ourselves." This was Carmelite version of "Charity begins at home."

Was Mother Agnès de Jésus sorry that Sister Agnès de Jésus had been so unconcerned? Did the new mother superior want to erase the humiliations inflicted by the former mother superior on the servant of God? It was possible. To Thérèse's functions as assistant novice mistress was added a new job that fulfilled her secret aspiration: She would be a painter. She would paint holy images, religious subjects, she would paint like Céline, who had received lessons that she would have liked to share.

If Thérèse and Céline, who, whether or not Marie liked it, had obvious talents for painting, had remained in the outside world, they would certainly have been among the women painters of their time, like, for example, Madeleine Lemaire. According to critics, Madeleine Lemarie was the artist who, after God, created the most roses. She would have had a formidable competitor in Thérèse who, in her paintings like in her poems, liked to multiply them.

In the spring of 1893, Thérèse ceased her functions of attendant sacristan to help in the formation of novices and to paint pictures that were sold to the faithful. She painted so many roses that she ended up looking like one on the verge of blossoming. Sister Marie des Anges, who, it cannot be overemphasized, was not as naive as was believed, wrote a perceptive profile of Thérèse at age twenty, a profile dated April or May of that year:

> A novice and the jewel of Carmel, its beloved youngest…big and strong with the look of a child in the sound of her voice and in her expression, veiling a wisdom in her, a perfection, a perspicacity of fifty years. A soul always calm, and in perfect control of herself in everything and with everyone. Seeming like a little saint, seeming to be completely virtuous, her bonnet is full of mischief and she does whatever she wants to whomever she wants. Mystic, comic, everything suits her…she will make you cry with devotion and just as easily make you collapse with laughter during our recreations.

Was Thérèse gathering the fruits of her endless consideration and angelic patience? Was the "jewel of Carmel" finally recognized by its companions? To be at the same time a mystic and a comic is infinitely rare and should have attracted many warm feelings to her. But in Carmel, as in every other community where mediocrity and conformity are standard, whatever was original was the least appreciated, not to say scorned. When Thérèse asked, in September, for the prolongation of her novitiate, it surprised no one. It was just another trick played by our Sister of the Child Jesus and of the Holy Face, who no longer knew what to come up with to make herself stand out!

Indeed, ordinarily one left the novitiate three years after one's profession. Thérèse should have left it in September 1893. According to the constitution, no more than two sisters from the same family could be admitted to the chapter. As Marie and Pauline were already in it, Thérèse accepted the situation and claimed a place that she considered hers and that no one should want to take from her: the last place. She would never enter the chapter and would never have the right to vote. For Carmel, and especially for her two sisters, she would remain "little Thérèse," who, from the height of her five feet, four inches, was not so little, to evoke only her physical dimension.

In fact, the eternal novice was not in the least interested in standing out. She took to heart her responsibilities as attendant to the novice mistress and had not forgotten the difficulties of her own beginnings in Carmel; she was all the more understanding toward the beginners. She'd had to look after Sister Marthe, Sister Marie-Madeleine du Saint Sacrement, and then in the spring of 1894, there was a newcomer, Sister Marie de la Trinité, a Parisienne who did not seem very serious-minded and who had the pace of a "wild rabbit." Thérèse, whose slow gait was the model of Carmelite pace, would have to teach the "wild rabbit" to measure her steps, her gestures, her words.

Sister Marie de la Trinité was in good hands: Sister Thérèse of the Child Jesus' pace was considered excessively slow by Sister Saint Vincent de Paul, who had nicknamed her "the big baby goat." Another nickname given to Thérèse, this time by Sister Saint Stanislas, who thought to stigmatize what she took for lethargy: "Sister So Be It."

In June, Thérèse was given a third function, that of bursar's tierce.* In September, she was named second porter. She filled these roles admirably, all without ceasing her interior work, reflected in the letters that she wrote to Céline in the summer of 1893: "Your Thérèse is not on lofty heights at the moment, but Jesus is teaching her 'to profit from everything, from the good and the bad that she finds in herself.'...He is instructing me to do *everything* by love, to refuse Him nothing, to be happy when He gives me an opportunity to prove to Him that I love Him, but it is being done in peace, in *abandon;* it is Jesus doing everything and I am doing nothing,...I never become discouraged, I abandon myself in the arms of Jesus."

---

* A sister charged with accompanying the bursar when a man entered the convent. The custom has today fallen today into disuse.

Never to become discouraged, that was one of the instructions that Thérèse gave to Céline and that she put into practice herself, every day. And she needed a strong will, to do four jobs at the same time and yet devote all her time to God. It was a miracle, a miracle accomplished every day by Sister Thérèse of the Child Jesus and of the Holy Face in her twentieth year.

38

The Two Shepherdesses

(21 January 1894)

On 2 January 1894, Thérèse came of age. She took advantage of this to straighten up her handwriting, which slanted over too much, evoking the beginner that she had been earlier, bent over under the severities of Mother Marie de Gonzague. From then on, Thérèse and her writing held themselves up very straight. It was with her new penmanship that she wrote her first play, her first "recreation," *The Mission of Joan of Arc*, which had to be ready for the name-day feast of her sister and mother superior, Mother Agnès de Jésus, on 21 January.

It is to Saint Teresa of Ávila that we owe the introduction of these "recreations," these diversions intended to break up the monotony of Carmelite life. They celebrated Christmas, Easter, and the main events of the liturgy with plays that were exclusively religious in subject matter. In the Carmel of Lisieux, they also celebrated, with special splendor, the mother superior's name-day feast. Every year, it had been Mother Marie de Gonzague's day of glory. On the occasion of the final celebration of her administration, Sister Agnès de Jésus had been charged with writing this entertainment. Now that she was the mother superior, Mother Agnès de Jésus no longer had any time to spare and entrusted her drama-writing duties to Thérèse, who, along with her other four jobs, now had a fifth to accomplish, the most difficult of all. If Molière acknowledged with alacrity that it was difficult to make upright people laugh, it was not easy, either, to entertain Carmelites!

Each Carmel was supposed to put to best use the competencies of its sisters. Balzac was aware of this when he made his Duchesse de Langeais, an expert on various instruments, the organist of the convent of the discalced Carmelites in which she had taken refuge. Let us note in passing that Antoinette de Langeais had taken the name Sister Thérèse, which would also be that of Thérèse Martin. (One can daydream, long enough for a restful parenthesis, about a meeting between these two Carmelites, the fictitious one and the real one, the worldly seductress and the mystic seductress.)

If she was not familiar with *La Duchesse de Langeais,* which was forbidden reading in convents, Thérèse had read *Jeanne d'Arc,* by Henri Wallon, which was in the library of Carmel and constituted a good historic study of the Maid of Orleans. Thérèse also recalled that Joan had been one of the heroines of her childhood, and that she had thought for a time of becoming the shepherdess of Alençon.

In January 1894, Joan of Arc was everywhere. She had not yet been sanctified, but Leo XIII had declared her Venerable. She inspired dramatists, musicians, sculptors, and painters. They had stopped counting paintings representing *Joan in the Dungeon* or *Joan Facing Her Judges.* Since the defeat of 1870, Joan was more than ever considered the liberator of France. Those who were locked up in Carmel did not retain any less of their patriotic fiber, or stare any less at the blue line of the Vosges. They lived in the hope of reconquering Alsace and Lorraine.

With her childlike simplicity that knew no barriers and that allowed her to address God or His saints directly, Thérèse, in her recreation, identified with Joan of Arc. Her Joan no longer died for France, she died for Jesus—an important nuance. Thérèse gave her heroine extra splendor.

With the authorization, indeed the complicity, of her mother superior, Thérèse gave herself the leading role, which she tailored to
herself. To be her own author and her own interpreter, what could
be better? When she proclaimed:

> For You alone, O my God, I will leave my father
> All my beloved relatives and my village so beautiful,

Mother Agnès de Jésus and Sister Marie du Sacré-Cœur could only
exchange a look of connivance. This father was theirs, Louis Martin. Like Thérèse, Joan said, "I want the cross…I love sacrifice."
One could go on forever, noting the similarities between the shepherdesses of Domrémy and Alençon.

Thérèse had drawn from deep within herself to give birth to this
Joan of Arc, intended to celebrate the feast of her mother superior
and to edify the other sisters, since the recreation finished with a
vibrant plea to the Venerable Joan to deliver France a second time
from ungodly besiegers. The plea achieved a great success. Congratulated as an author and as an interpreter, the modest Thérèse
suffered torments.

She had barely put the finishing touches on her *Mission of Joan
of Arc,* which had as subtitle *The Shepherdess of Domrémy Listening to Her Voices,* when, tireless, Thérèse wrote a poem to celebrate
Mother Marie de Gonzague's sixty years on 20 February 1894:

> For sixty years, on the earth,
> Divine Jesus, you have contemplated
> A flower that is very dear to you
> With your graces you water it.

The graces that Jesus showered on Mother Marie de Gonzague hardly
splashed back over the community, which quietly endured the dis-
sension that had soon opposed the new mother superior to the former
one. Mother Marie de Gonzague had quickly seen that Mother Agnès
de Jésus was not as malleable as she had hoped.

Divided between these two forces, Thérèse discovered in herself diplomatic abilities. She succeeded in satisfying the one without displeasing the other. Better yet: She was fully blossoming in a very uncomfortable situation. That also was a miracle.

39

The Death of a King

(29 July 1894)

Since coming of age, Thérèse had practiced the fasting that was observed at Carmel. Between the fasts imposed by the order and those decreed by the Church, one fasted often.

During these numerous days of penance, Carmelites ate nothing before 11:00 in the morning. At that time they took a light meal composed of soup, fish, and vegetables. There was a second meal at 6:00 in the evening: seven-and-a-half ounces of bread, along with cheese and fruit. It was not much. It was not enough for a young woman of twenty-one. Thérèse's organism offered less resistance to the tuberculosis that began to attack her slowly and manifested itself in the spring of 1894 with a sore throat and chest pains. Her hoarseness was attributed to too many words: Sister Thérèse of the Child Jesus spoke too much to her novices.

Because of the persistence of the symptoms, Doctor Francis La Néele, who by his marriage to Jeanne Guérin belonged definitively to the clan, was called in consultation and could find no explanation other than the abuse of edifying words.

Tuberculosis was, at the end of the nineteenth century, what AIDS is at the end of the twentieth. Not much was known of this illness, which struck the rich as it did the poor. The rich sent their consumptives to die on the Riviera. The poor contented themselves with drinking milk, reputed to fight the scourge, which seemed to have a clear predilection for beautiful and young victims like Marguerite Gautier, Marie Bashkirtseff, and Thérèse Martin. With little food, little sleep, no heat, and no hygiene, Carmel of Lisieux, like other convents, offered a favorable terrain to tuberculosis, which was seen with the sense of grieving fatality caused by a cataclysm against which nothing can be done.

Whenever she had a sore throat and chest pains, when she spoke with difficulty, even suffering the loss of her voice, Thérèse, to express herself, resorted to pen and inkwell. She wrote, seizing the slightest occasion of a feast or a birthday to write a letter or a poem, as she did for Céline's twenty-fifth birthday, giving her as a bonus some reflections on the guardian angel that accompanies every human. "Céline, do not fear the storms of the earth....Your guardian angel is covering you with his wings."

Céline did not hide the fact that she felt somewhat alone in caring for her father, now that Léonie, unstable Léonie, seemed to have settled in the Convent of the Visitation of Le Mans, where she took the habit and the name Sister Thérèse-Dosithée, on 6 April.

Sister Thérèse of the Child Jesus immediately congratulated Sister Thérèse-Dosithée, to whom she offered, on 22 May, this pious challenge: "Which of the two Thérèses will be the most fervent? She who will be the most humble, the most united to Jesus, the most faithful in carrying out all her actions by love!...Everything is so major in religion...to pick up a pin with love can convert a soul. What a mystery!"

A mystery that Thérèse burned to clarify. In the meantime, she found herself once again faced with the mystery of death. Her father passed away on 29 July 1894, at the Château de la Musse, where he had been staying with Céline and the Guérins.

For Thérèse, there was no doubt: Her king had gone straight to heaven. This was confirmed for her by the account that Céline gave of Louis Martin's last moments:

I had never found myself at the bedside of a dying person. I was praying: "Jesus, Marie, Joseph, help me in my final death throes!" At that moment, my darling father opened his eyes and looked at me with inexpressible affection and gratitude. And then he closed them again forever.…He looked like Saint Joseph on his deathbed.

Louis Martin's face wore "an expression of beatitude." This caused Thérèse to say, "Papa's death does not seem like a death to me, but like true life." She did not know that, a few centuries before Jesus Christ, a Greek poet that Marguerite Yourcenar would translate had said the same thing:

> Who knows? Perhaps death is supreme life
> And what we call life is agony and death.

It was echoed also by Fr. Pichon, who wrote to Céline from Canada: "Should we cry for a death that is definitely a birth in heaven?"

Knowing that their father was in heaven did not stop the five Martin girls from crying. Once the first sobs had subsided, Marie, Pauline, Léonie, and Céline followed the suggestion of the one who had been the deceased king's little queen: "Let us look to heaven, seeing there a father and mother who have given us to God."

Judging that there are never enough precautions to ensure eternal rest, Mother Agnès de Jésus had her Carmelites pray for Louis Martin, dead at one month short of seventy-one years old.

40

The Intrepid in Carmel

(14 September 1894)

Like her illustrious contemporaries Pierre Loti and Anna de Noailles, Thérèse suffered from being unable to stop time. She was overwhelmed by the brevity of existence, by the sense that everything is ephemeral, even the century and even Louis Martin, who had just left it. "My life is but one day that is escaping from me and fleeing," she wrote in a poem entitled "My Song of Today."

Shortly after her father's departure, Thérèse wrote, in August 1894 and for herself alone, "Prayer of the Child of a Saint." The child was herself, and the saint was Louis Martin. In this poem, she enumerated the kindnesses that Louis had done for his five daughters. Each verse was imprinted with nostalgia for the lost treasures of paternal tenderness.

In this very personal text, which she signed with one of her nicknames, "the Orphan of Berezina," Thérèse reviewed the situation, for herself and for her sisters. In the stanza that she devoted to Céline, she evoked her possible arrival in Carmel. Céline had remained in the outside world only to care for her father. Freed of this obligation, she could at last satisfy her religious aspirations.

Fr. Pichon, who had been informed of this, secretly urged Céline to become a nun in Canada. Canada or Normandy? The question tormented Céline; she asked her three sisters, who temporarily abandoned their dignified poise of eminent Carmelites to stamp their feet in indignation. How dared Céline ask such a question? As if she did not already know the answer....It was in Normandy, it was into Carmel of Lisieux that she must enter!

Mother Agnès de Jésus, Sister Marie du Sacré-Cœur, and Sister Thérèse of the Child Jesus had to call upon all of their capacities for Christian charity not to malign Fr. Pichon, guilty of trying to break up the circle, the clan, the cocoon of the Martin sisters, united as the fingers of the hand. True, Léonie was in Caen. But Caen was not Montreal! Confronted with her sisters' indignation, tears, and pleas, Céline capitulated and gave up Canada.

When she announced to the Guérins her intention of entering the Carmel of Lisieux, they looked put out, especially Jeanne and her husband, Doctor Francis La Néele. According to them, Céline did not have a vocation: She had been born to be the mother of a family, following the example of her mother, the unforgettable Zélie.

Faced with the small effect produced by this argument, Jeanne and Francis then accused Céline of being nothing more than an ingrate. Why leave them so quickly! All of Lisieux would immediately think that she had not been happy with them....

More conciliatory than his daughter and son-in-law, Uncle Isidore soon gave his consent. Now Céline had to obtain the agreement—decisive—of Carmel's prior, Fr. Delatroëtte, who was not far from thinking that the Martin girls had been put on earth only for his torment. "I fear that the admission of a fourth sister into Carmel would be against the spirit, and even the letter, of the Rule. We will examine this serious question, which is so important, with the concerned parties," the prior answered Céline solemnly. "The concerned parties" meant the bishop of Bayeux, Monseigneur Hugonin, who also must have wondered what he had done to the Lord to be perpetually disturbed by a young Martin daughter wanting to enter Carmel. Well, let her enter, and let there be no more talk about it. If she was refused, Céline would be capable, like Thérèse, of going to throw herself at the pope's feet. Against all expectations, concerned

with preserving his tranquillity and avoiding a new scandal in the Vatican, Monseigneur Hugonin acquiesced. In turn, Fr. Pichon hid his disappointment and gave his blessing.

In Carmel of Lisieux, one of the nuns, Sister Aimée de Jésus, was fiercely opposed to the admission of a fourth Martin sister. Abruptly, she changed her mind, without anyone understanding this abrupt turnaround. Anyone except Thérèse:

> One day when the difficulties seemed insurmountable, I said to Jesus during my thanksgiving: "You know, my God, how much I want to know if Papa want straight to heaven; I am not asking you to speak to me, but give me a sign. If my sister Aimée de Jésus consents to Céline's admission or does not obstruct it, that will be the answer that Papa went straight to be with you."

No sooner was the request formulated than it was granted. At the end of her thanksgiving, the first person Thérèse met was precisely Sister Aimée de Jésus, who no longer wore her fierce look and who spoke of Céline's imminent arrival with tears of emotion.

Thanks to this sign, Thérèse knew that her father had gone straight to heaven. She was even more strongly convinced of it because she had asked her king to intervene on her side to overcome Fr. Pichon's hesitation and Fr. Delatroëtte's opposition: "At last, from up in heaven, my beloved king, who on earth disliked delay, hastened to straighten out his Céline's affairs, so muddled, and on 14 September she was reunited with us!"

On 14 September 1894, Céline, whom her father had nicknamed "the Intrepid," entered Carmel. Thérèse could no longer contain her joy. "The most private" of her desires was fulfilled. Thérèse and Céline would breathe the same air, sit at the same table, sleep under the same roof, as in the past at Les Buissonnets. Who said that happiness is not of this world? On this 14 September 1894, the Orphan of the Berezina and the Intrepid knew felicity.

41

Thérèse at the Stake

(21 January 1895)

It was Thérèse, assistant novice mistress, who guided Céline's first hesitant steps through the rules and the customs that had to be observed at all times in Carmel. For Céline's part, she defined her functions this way: "I am a little hunting dog, it is I who run after the game all day long." And in the evening, Thérèse, exhausted from having watched over her novices, fell asleep during the orison. She admired Céline's vitality all the more!

The Intrepid was twenty-five years old. She had spent more time in the outside world than her Carmelite sisters and had known, at the Musse, what was called "château life," with its comfort, its ease, its frivolities. She radiated youth and beauty. She had refused several marriage proposals.

Before entering Carmel, Céline had described to Thérèse the boredom of such an existence. "We spend our days giggling so much we could collapse, and it gives me a thirst for solitude." She, too, had thirsted for martyrdom, and she had feared she would depend too much on her sister, to whom she had written: "My Thérèse!...Oh! How I have pondered over you, over the affection the two of us share...it seemed to me that...you were too indispensable to me— but guess the rest!" The servant of God guessed, understood, and reassured: "Fear nothing; here you will find more than anywhere else the cross and martyrdom! We will suffer together....Never, never will Jesus separate us…if I die before you, do not think that I will go away from your soul, never will we have been more united."

In entering Carmel, Céline brought the echoes of the outside world, a little of the modernity that was in the air of the times and that was symbolized by the camera she was allowed to keep. Carmel was in a flutter: They were going to take pictures!

Thanks to Céline, today we can look at the face of Sister Thérèse of the Child Jesus. These are the only photographs that we have of Thérèse, who considered the posing sessions lost time. She was more interested in the notebook that Céline brought, which contained numerous passages of the Old Testament that she had copied into it. When Thérèse read these texts that she had previously not known, and for a reason, since they had been forbidden in Carmel, it was an illumination for her. She happened upon a verse of the Book of Proverbs: "If someone is very small, may he come to Me." The very small one was her, Thérèse, who had never ceased proclaiming her smallness.

To reinforce her certainty about absolute smallness, she found another passage, this one by the prophet Isaiah: "As a mother caresses her child, so will I console you. I will carry you on My breast and I will balance you on My knees." Intoxicated by these two messages, Thérèse exclaimed, "Oh! My God, you have exceeded my expectations, and I want to sing your mercies."

For the servant of God, there was no longer any doubt, these two passages of the Old Testament showed her the path to follow, that of childhood and of abandon. She no longer wanted to be anything but a child who abandoned herself in the arms of her Father. Thus, when Doctor Francis La Néele was again called in consultation to cure her persistent hoarseness, it was as a child that she listened to him and took the prescribed medicine. And after all, was not the best remedy Céline's presence?

Sometimes the four Martin sisters got together and rediscovered their intimacy of the past, at Les Buissonnets. Thus, at the end of

1894, Sister Agnès de Jésus, Sister Marie du Sacré-Cœur, Sister Thérèse of the Child Jesus, and Céline, who had taken the name Sister Geneviève de la Sainte Face, were gathered in the only heated room in the convent, besides, of course, the infirmary. It was recreation. Carmelites were free to speak. Thérèse recounted a few childhood memories. Then Sister Marie said to Mother Agnès: "How is it possible that you allow her to write little verses for everyone's pleasure, but she has written nothing of her childhood memories for us?" Mother Agnès hesitated, then ordered Thérèse to write the account for her name-day feast, that of Saint Agnes, on 21 January. Nothing would be ready by the appointed date. Thérèse wrote as she could, when she could. Thus she would take a year, from January 1895 to January 1896, to write this text, which would be the first part of *L'Histoire d'une âme*.

At this end of 1894, Thérèse had to prepare the Christmas presentation, of which she was in charge. Anticipating this, in October she had already composed a recreation entitled *The Angels at the Crèche,* which portrayed her inexhaustible wonder before the Child Jesus.

She played one of the principal roles, that of the Child Jesus' angel, surrounded by angels of the Holy Face, of the Resurrection, of the Eucharist, and of the Last Judgment. All celebrated the beauty of their Master and the greatness of His mercy, which triumphed unequivocally over the exterminating angel who was going to punish ingrates and the lukewarm. The final extermination did not take place. God in His mercy, the infinity of which filled Thérèse with joy, forgave. Here are Jesus' final words, which made the angel of the Last Judgment concede defeat:

> And so in the Holy Land
> My Chosen Ones will be glorious
> In communicating my life to them
> I will make them like so many gods!

Divine love could do everything, even change a man into a god. It is not certain that Carmelites of Lisieux, on this Christmas night of 1894, grasped the audacity, and the novelty, of the message that Thérèse was sending through these verses, and through this final choir of angels who wanted to become children.

The servant of God turned the most certain beliefs of her time upside down, destroyed the Last Judgment, and abolished the punishment of the wicked, without anyone in Carmel complaining. Carmelites had heard angels fly that were not exactly the ones Thérèse had put on the stage. Blessed incomprehension, which can be thought of as the miracle of this Christmas night. For if the nuns, so full of fear of the Lord, had understood this message of mad love and liberation, the scandal would have been even greater than the one she had caused in the Vatican.

On 2 January 1895, Thérèse celebrated her twenty-second birthday by sending her best wishes to Léonie, in Le Mans:

> My beloved little sister[,]
> It is with great joy that I come to offer you my good wishes at the beginning of this new year. The one that has just passed has been very fruitful for heaven, our darling father has seen what "the eye of man cannot contemplate." He has heard the harmony of the angels…and his heart understands, his soul enjoys the rewards that God has prepared for those who love Him!…Do you not find, as I do, that the departure of our darling father has brought us closer to heaven? More than half of the family is now enjoying the sight of God, and the five exiles on earth will not be long in flying off toward their home. This thought of the brevity of life gives me strength, it helps me to tolerate the strains of the road.

And what strains! Thérèse worked like a convict. Incapable of refusing a favor, she added to her own tasks those of others. The servant of the Lord was also that of Carmelites. Despite this incessant labor, she found the time to write, for the feast of Mother Agnès de Jésus, not her childhood memories as she had agreed, but her third theatrical work, *Joan of Arc Accomplishing Her Mission,* which can be considered a sequel to her *Mission of Joan of Arc.*

It was, of course, Thérèse who incarnated Joan. She wore a skirt of dark blue wool trimmed with fleurs-de-lis, and over it armor of silver foil. Céline played the role of Saint Catherine, and Marie incarnated France, appearing at the end, her arms laden with chains. The three Martin sisters achieved a great success; it was "general enthusiasm," all the greater because Thérèse, like her heroine, had almost burned to death. It was Sister Marie des Anges who told of the incident: "She almost was actually burned alive, following an imprudence that lighted the beginning of a fire, but on an order from Our Mother not to move from her place, while we did our best to put out the fire around her, she remained calm and immobile in the middle of the danger, making the sacrifice of her life to God, as she said afterward."

A fine example of obedience to her mother superior and an example as well of confidence in God. If she had perished at that stake, Thérèse would have earned a few lines in the local press and would have been listed in Carmel's records as the author of some poems and of three recreations. The other Thérèse was yet to be born.

In the evening of 21 January, as a "great silence" reigned in Carmel, the servant of God believed herself to be, for an instant, "at the summit of glory." Then she felt immediately "an ineffable light on the vanity of everything here below." At age twenty-two, Sister Thérèse of the Child Jesus and of the Holy Face already possessed the wisdom of Ecclesiastes and could repeat after it, "Vanity of vanities, all is vanity." It was true that she had just stared death in the face and would not soon forget the flames that could have engulfed her like Joan at her stake.

42

To Live a Life of Love

(22 January—14 June 1895)

Beginning on 22 January 1895, to die in order to live in Jesus, thus to live in love, became Thérèse's constant preoccupation, which she expressed on 26 February in a poem called, justly, "To Live in Love."

In the life of every writer, there is a privileged day, during which he wrenches from time his portion of eternity by composing exactly that for which he was put on the earth. This day, for Thérèse, was 26 February of her twenty-second year. She wrote fifteen stanzas upon which there is no point in commenting. What words to add when the essential is said as in this sixth stanza?

> To live in love is to banish all fear
> All memory of the mistakes of the past.
> Of my sins I see no trace
> In one instant love has burned everything...
> Divine flame, O Furnace so very gentle!
> In your hearth I base my sojourn
> It is in your fires that I joyously sing:
> I live in love!

Thérèse had understood that her life had to be a life of love. She wished that every life would also be a life of love. And for that, she was ready to offer herself in sacrifice. On 9 June, during mass, she made a spontaneous offering to merciful love. Anxious to include

Céline in her holy enterprise, she wrote an *Offering of Myself as a Victim of Sacrifice to the Merciful Love of the Good Lord*.

In the very first paragraph, she announced clearly her intention to follow the will of the Lord by becoming a saint: "I want to accomplish perfectly Your will and arrive at the level of glory that You have prepared for me in Your kingdom; in a word, I wish to be a saint, but I feel my helplessness and I ask You, O my God! to be my saintliness Yourself."

On 11 June, the two sisters met in front of the Smiling Virgin, who when Les Buissonnets was abandoned had found refuge in Carmel, and they said the offertory prayer together. To conduct this ceremony properly, they had asked the permission of Mother Agnès de Jésus, who had been satisfied with Thérèse's hurried explanations, trusting her discretion.

After the ceremony, Mother Agnès de Jésus made no attempt to hide her surprise at this text, which she read attentively whereas she had listened with some distraction, she confessed, to the request to make the offering. She was sure to underline the audacious novelties it contained, such as, for example, daring to present oneself before the Lord, in the evening of life, with empty hands but a heart full of love.

Mother Agnès de Jésus and Sister Thérèse of the Child Jesus agreed to submit this prayer to a theologian, Father Armand Lemonnier, who in turn gave it to his superior to read. The latter requested just one change: to replace "infinite desires" with "immense desires" in the sentence "I feel in my heart infinite desires." Infinity has always frightened theologians.

Thérèse, who was not afraid of infinity, obeyed and made the correction. What did this correction matter? She knew that infinity was in her hands, or at least within her reach. She had the proof of this a few days after her act, on Friday, 14 June 1895. She was about to begin, in the chapel, her Stations of the Cross when the love that she felt for Jesus spread like a fire in her veins and in her heart. Thérèse would speak of this experience to no one except Mother Agnès de Jésus, who reported the actual words of her assertion. "My heart felt as if it had been wounded by an arrow of fire. I was burning and I felt that I would not have been able to bear one second more this ardor without dying. Then I understood what the saints say of this state, which they have experienced so many times. As for me, I have felt it just one time, for just one instant, then I fell back into my habitual dryness," explained Thérèse.

In the end, there was nothing pleasant about this experience. The assertion that Mother Agnès de Jésus repeated is not in keeping with what Thérèse said about it in her *Histoire d'une âme:* "My beloved mother, you who have permitted me to offer myself this way to the good Lord, you know of the rivers or rather the oceans of graces that have inundated my soul." Mother Agnès de Jésus evoked fire, and Thérèse, water. Between the inferno of love and the river of love, which must we choose? And what exactly happened? There have been challenges to the reality of this ecstacy—and it's really a question of ecstacy here. Still, Thérèse was repulsed by ecstacies, as by visions. And with good reason. The violence of this first ecstacy did not at all induce her to experience others.

Between 9 and 14 June 1895, between the offering that illuminated and the lightning flash that pierced, something happened. What? It is a secret shared by God and Thérèse, and it would be futile to want to penetrate it.

After that, Thérèse was no longer what she had been. She was aware of the seriousness of the commitment that had set her ablaze, or inundated her, in her entirety. She hid her ecstacy, by modesty and by wisdom. She still remembered the indiscreet questions that had overwhelmed her when, as a child, she had seen the Virgin smile. So that no one would suspect anything in Carmel, so that no one could have suspicions that she was a living offering, she made herself completely disappear in littleness, in insignificance, and in what some of her companions called her "incapacity."

43

Thérèse the Poet

(1895)

The year 1895 for Thérèse was the year of poetry. Like any inspired woman in love, she constantly put her love for Jesus into verse. The titles of the poems that she wrote that year speak for themselves: "Song of the Gratitude of the Fiancée of Jesus," "Who Has Jesus Has Everything," "Jesus My Beloved, Remember!" and "To Live in Love," which was her masterpiece.

In "Céline's Hymn," Thérèse demonstrated that through Jesus, she possessed the world, even the most distant islands. In *My Desires Close to Jesus Hidden in His Prison of Love,* she was the key of the tabernacle, the lamp of the sanctuary, the stone of the altar, a living monstrance. She was also a prisoner of love. What was she not? She was everything, since she was Love, in the image of the Creator who created us by love, without measuring the consequences of his act. In reading certain of these poems of 1895, one seems to hear Berlioz's melody that begins, "The ardent flame of love consumes my youth...." It was unfortunate that Berlioz was not sung in the Carmel of Lisieux; Thérèse would have recognized in him a brother in passion.

From poem to poem, Thérèse was creating for herself a world of love and of light that did not have much to do with the world that surrounded her, which raced along. In Paris, Satan led the dance. Thérèse had only a slight echo of these infernal dances in Carmel.

She was attentive mainly to news of her family, particularly of her sister Léonie, who had done it again.

On 20 July, after a third attempt at religious life, Léonie again left the Convent of the Visitation. She was no longer Sister Thérèse-Dosithée. She was no longer anything but "poor Léonie," who took refuge with her uncle Isidore. Her cousin Marie Guérin took her to visit Carmel. There she sat before her four sisters, who could not believe their eyes. "Our emotion was very great in seeing her, we could not get her to say one word, she was crying so much, finally she ended up looking at us and all went well," reported Thérèse.

After having been the cross of her mother, Léonie was now the cross of her sisters, and of her uncle Isidore, who decreed: "She has a weak nature, incapable of helping herself."

As if to compensate for the disappointment caused by Léonie, who seemed to be abandoning her religious vocation, Marie Guérin entered the Carmel of Lisieux on 15 August. The Martin clan was enriched with a new recruit. Four sisters and a first cousin was a lot for the same convent...M. Guérin's generosity, like that of M. Martin in the past, was enough to appease the murmurs.

For Marie, whom she had sustained with her letters and advice during her progression to Carmel, Thérèse composed her *Canticle of a Soul Having Found Its Place of Rest,* which could also be sung to the famous melody of *Mignon,* "Do you know the country where the orange tree blooms?" *Mignon*'s "It is there that I would like to live," in Thérèse's song, turns into "It is there that I want to follow you."

Custom required that the postulant sing "something" to the community on the evening of her admission. The Carmelites were thrilled with Marie Guérin's soprano, which emphasized each word, each intention, of the author, whose modesty had once more to suffer, faced with such success. Thérèse echoed it in a letter to her cousin Jeanne: "Her beautiful voice makes us happy and is the delight of our recreations."

If Jeanne had not tried to hide her opposition to Céline's entering the convent, she had no more hidden her sadness at seeing Marie disappear behind Carmel's grille. These two departures, almost simultaneous, her cousin's and her sister's, perturbed the wife of Doctor La Néele. She felt a helplessness that Thérèse did her best to dissipate: "Yes, already sweet peace and the happiness of your little Marie have escaped the cloister's bars to pour into your soul."

On 8 October, Carmel's prior, Canon Delatroëtte, died. If she did not write a poem to mark this event, Thérèse surely must have prayed for the one who had scorned her so. Up in heaven, how surprised Fr. Delatroëtte must have been to see in what esteem God held his servant. But Thérèse did not have time to linger on vain meditations, or conjectures, about the departure of her prior. On 21 October, Mother Agnès de Jésus entrusted her with her first spiritual brother, Maurice Bellière. He was twenty-one, almost the exact contemporary of Thérèse, who was twenty-two and delighted with the arrival of this new relative. She felt a joy swell up in her that she qualified as "childlike." To help a future missionary with her prayers and sacrifices, when she herself dreamed of going off on a mission, fulfilled one of her dearest wishes.

Maurice Bellière, who was a seminarian at Bayeux, had put in his request to have a spiritual sister who would pray for him on the exact day of the Feast of Saint Teresa of Ávila, 15 October. For this reason, Thérèse saw it as a gift from her founding mother. She promptly wrote a prayer for Maurice Bellière, who was to go off and acquire souls for Jesus. Meanwhile, he entered the barracks in November to carry out his military service. The servant of God sensed the dangers, the temptations, to which her protégé could be—and was—exposed during this time. Consequently, she began to pray.

On 30 November, Thérèse encouraged one of her novices, her "wild rabbit," Sister Marie de la Trinité, to make her offering of love. She finished the year as she had begun it, writing poems, along with a liturgical celebration, *Little Beggar of Christmas*.

On 25 December 1895, the community was gathered for the evening's recreation, in front of the crèche. An angel incarnated by Marie Guérin asked the Carmelites to come and adore the Child Jesus, who had found only indifference in the world. The mother superior made an Act of Adoration. Then she withdrew, randomly, one of twenty-six notes that had been placed in a basket. On each one were a few verses written by Thérèse, constituting for each of the nuns something like a personal message from the Child Jesus.

Jesus asked his wives successively to be a throne of gold, a bit of milk, a crown of birds, a star, roses, a laughing valley, harvesters of apostles, a bunch of grapes. It was this bunch of grapes that chance, which is not always the *"grand maladroit"* denounced by Natalie Barney, gave to Thérèse, who would forget its symbolism:

> My sister, how sweet is your destiny
> It is you, this chosen bunch of grapes
> Jesus will press you very strongly
> In his beloved little hand.

Each Carmelite had to sing the message that she had drawn. It was with a very husky voice that Thérèse sang her bunch of grapes.

The year ended as it had begun, in truly celestial poetry. "A year of peace, of love, of light," as Thérèse herself acknowledged, was ending. A happy year in a life of love.

44

Thérèse's Double Failure

(20–21 January 1896)

To forget somewhat the terrible rigors of the winter 1895–96 that once again transformed the Carmel of Lisieux into a "hell of cold," Thérèse, shortly after her twenty-third birthday, finished the account of her childhood, and on 20 January she gave it to Mother Agnès de Jésus. She in turn put the text, written in a schoolgirl's notebook, away in a drawer, without reading it. It was unbelievable, inexplicable, but so it was.

It was true that the mother superior was seeing the end of her reign and that the Carmel was on the verge of elections that were to take place in March. Mother Marie de Gonzague, who wanted to be reelected, was very restless. It was likely that Mother Agnès de Jésus simply had no time to devote to her little sister's prose.

Luckily, Thérèse knew nothing of the pride of authorship and did not seem to suffer from this silence. On the morning of 21 January, she gave Mother Agnès de Jésus a new poem for her name-day feast, "Saint Agnes's Responsories," from which here is the last stanza:

> And so I fear nothing, neither sword nor flame
> No, nothing can trouble my ineffable peace
> And the fire of the love that consumes my soul
> Will never go out!

In the evening of that day, Thérèse would have great need of recalling the "ineffable peace" that she evoked in that stanza!

Charged by Mother Agnès with composing a recreation in honor of this same feast, the servant of God had chosen as theme and title *The Flight into Egypt*. Despite appearances, this text was right in the present. Anticlerical decrees of the Third Republic were in the process of dispersing congregations. It was feared that the convents would suffer the same fate. To escape the persecutions, would the Carmelites have to flee, like the Holy Family, into Egypt or elsewhere?

In this recreation, Thérèse gave free rein to her fantasy. She imagined that during its flight, the Holy Family stopped in a cave of brigands. The leader's wife had a leprous child who was healed after having been bathed in the water that had been used to bathe the Child Jesus. This little brigand would become the Good Thief. The robbers' return to the cave took on the appearance of an operetta. To the tune of *Estudiantina*, the brigands sang:

> Let us use our youth
> To build a treasure for ourselves
> So that in our old age
> We may be swimming in gold.

These seemed like the words of Meilhac and Halévy for an operetta by Offenbach. Mother Agnès de Jésus was not pleased, and she made no attempt to hide her displeasure. She brusquely interrupted the presentation. "Your recreations are too long and they tire the community," she snapped by way of thanks to the author, who lowered her head. Two failures in two days. The failure of the account of her childhood, which Mother Agnès had not even deigned to leaf through. The failure of this recreation, after the triumph of the two plays about Joan of Arc. Even if, as bears repeating, Thérèse had no pride of authorship, she did not hide the fact that she was wounded by so much harshness coming from Pauline, as Céline relates: "I surprised her behind the scenes, furtively drying a few tears, then, having sat down again, she remained quiet and gentle under the humiliation."

Her play, which did not merit such rejection, was the perfect illustration of what she believed in the most, the infiniteness of divine mercy, "great enough to erase the greatest crimes."

It has never been clear what could have offended Mother Agnès de Jésus in this *Flight into Egypt* and motivated her intervention. Thérèse, who feared neither flame nor sword, as she expressed in the last stanza of "Saint Agnes's Responsories," learned to fear the moods of the nun who had once been her Pauline.

In the evening of this 21 January, she could only put into practice the verse that she had not known was premonitory: "No, nothing can trouble my ineffable peace." It was unfortunate that Mother Agnès de Jésus and Mother Marie de Gonzague did not share this peace and were already at war!

During the final days of Mother Agnès de Jésus' term as mother superior, two nuns, Sister Geneviève de la Sainte Face (Céline) and Sister Marie de la Trinité (the "wild rabbit") were to make their professions. And Marie Guérin was to receive the habit, thus becoming Sister Marie de l'Eucharistie.

Mother Marie de Gonzague wanted these three ceremonies to take place only after her election, which she considered as assured. Even worse, she did not hide her intention, as soon as she recouped her power, of sending Sister Geneviève to the Carmel of Saigon. There followed between the two mother superiors discussions that degenerated at times into altercations and that divided the community.

The anti-Martins declared, "Our Mother Marie de Gonzague has every right to test our Sister Geneviève."

"But it involves a sort of test that must not be imposed," retorted Thérèse, who rebelled against such a plan. It was her one and only revolt against authority, and it would bear fruit, since her Céline, her double, her soul sister, her Siamese twin, would not be sent to the Carmel of Saigon.

On 24 February, Céline made her profession. On 17 March, she took the veil. On 27 March, Marie Guérin received the habit. These were the final victories of Mother Agnès de Jésus. On 21 March, after seven interminable rounds of balloting, Mother Marie de Gonzague was reelected, narrowly—she was appalled by this—by the sixteen nuns who had the right to vote.

The new mother superior should have named Mother Agnès the novice mistress, as was the custom. Mother Marie de Gonzague named her simply an adviser and contented herself with confirming Sister Thérèse of the Child Jesus in her role of auxiliary novice mistress. Thérèse would also be the sacristan, painter, and the nun responsibile for the linens. As was her habit, she accepted these tasks without balking.

As for Mother Agnès de Jésus, she did not hide her pleasure at no longer being the mother superior, summarizing thus what her priorship had been like: "Mother Marie de Gonzague could not bear for me to take on too much authority. She would have wanted me always under her domination. How I suffered and cried during those three years! But I realize that this yoke was necessary for me. It matured me and detached my soul from honors." It was unfortunate that Mother Agnès de Jésus had not extended her indulgence to the author of *The Flight into Egypt*, who had already forgotten all, forgiven all.

Thérèse no longer allowed herself to be affected by such trifles, which provoked in her only a few sobs, quickly suppressed. This was far, very far, from the inexhaustible torrents of tears of the past. From that double failure of 20 and 21 January, she was able to learn the lesson—she turned the exterior defeat into an interior victory. She who always compared herself to a "little flower" was in the process of becoming a fruit approaching its maturity. Yes, Thérèse had made a lot of progress since her entry into Carmel, eight years ago already. How time passes.

45

The Entry into Night

(Easter 1896)

Thérèse observed the fast of Lent 1896 in all its rigor. She maintained that she had become invigorated by it, a vigor that lasted until Holy Week. Today the benefits of fasting are recognized, and it is possible that the servant of the Lord felt better afterward. But it seems clear that she was exhausting her forces. In short, she was wasting away.

In the night of Holy Thursday to Good Friday, from 2 to 3 April 1896, Thérèse hemorrhaged for the first time: "I felt a kind of flood that was rising, rising and bubbling, up to my lips. I did not know what it was, but I thought maybe I was going to die and my soul would be inundated with joy....It seemed like blood that I had vomited....It was like a gentle and distant murmur heralding the arrival of my Husband."

Alone in her cell, in the most complete darkness, Thérèse had to await the morning to certify that it had indeed been blood that she had spit up. During this night as holy as Christmas night, Thérèse's blood joined the blood that Jesus was preparing to shed on the cross. In this coincidence, in this hemorrhage occurring on the day of the anniversary of Christ's death, she saw the sign of her imminent death.

It was with renewed fervor that she attended the Good Friday liturgy and participated in the ritual of forgiving. As she did every year, the mother superior gave a short speech on charity, and the

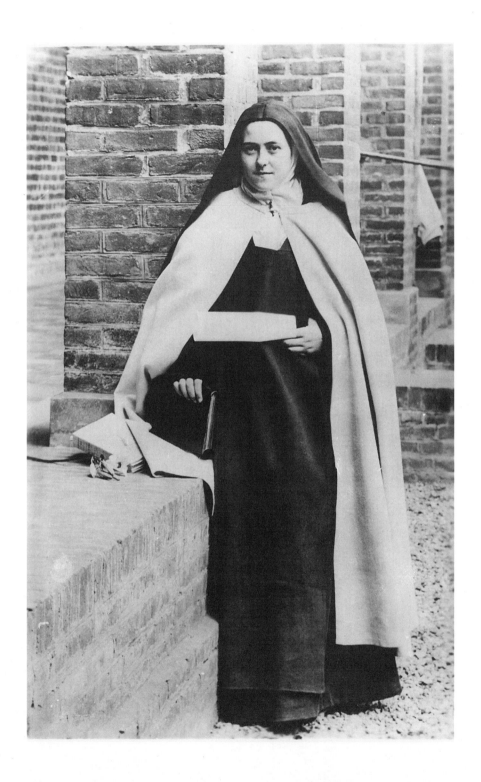

Carmelites embraced one another in asking mutual forgiveness for their faults. While embracing Mother Marie de Gonzague and imploring her forgiveness, Thérèse dared to confide in her about her hemorrhage, which she presented as a "hope" and a "happiness." She maintained that she was not suffering and begged "Our beloved Mother" not to say anything to anyone, not to be alarmed, and to give her "nothing in particular." Faced with this will to martyrdom, the mother superior yielded.

Never had the austerities of Carmel and of Good Friday seemed so "delicious" to Thérèse, who bravely climbed a ladder to wash the windows. "Struck by her pale and haggard appearance," Sister Marie de la Trinité offered to take the place of the servant of God. The servant refused, continued her chore, and finished her day by administering the discipline to herself.

The next night Thérèse had a second hemorrhage, which she greeted with as much joy as she had the first one. This joy did not last. On Easter morning, to the physical test was added the moral test, more appalling still, the one that opened the doors to the shadows of doubt. "He [Jesus] permitted that my soul should be invaded with the thickest shadows, and that the thought of heaven, so sweet to me, should no longer be anything but a subject of conflict and torment. This test would not last a few days, a few weeks, it would abate only at the time indicated by the good Lord."

Then began, for the twenty-three-year-old Carmelite, the test of faith that would last until her death. Thérèse had just entered into the worst of nights, the night of doubt, that of nothingness, the night without a single star.

46

The Dream of a Soul

(10 May 1896)

We have seen that Thérèse's treatment for her body was fasting and discipline. After Easter 1896, she seemed like no more than a soul. *Soul* was the latest expression, and it was all the rage in England, where young ethereal women, cultivated and elegant, formed groups that were baptized, in all simplicity, "the souls." With the help of Anglomania, the "souls" spread into France. One could not pay a greater compliment to a woman than to say of her, "She is a soul," meaning that she was detached from material contingencies and concerned only with art or mysticism.

This fashion constituted a reaction against the lack of soul of the times, which Jean Lorrain stigmatized in his novel *Monsieur de Phocas*: "Modern eyes? There is no more soul in them. Even the purest have only immediate preoccupations: lowly coveting...Lawyers' and cooks' souls....We march along staring at our shoes: our gazes are the color of mud."

To be a soul or not to be, that was the question. In France as in England, the "souls," in their way of being and of dressing, refused the invading materialism and galloping industrialization. The "souls" were decried, even molested, and were often caricatured in newspapers that, thankfully, did not enter behind the walls of Carmel.

Thérèse, though she kept her feet on the ground, was nevertheless a soul, which only increased her companions' incomprehension, their

exasperation. Some of them even wondered if she was really as ill as she was said to be, if it were not just posing, the way she coughed all the time. Others, more compassionate, prayed for healing for Thérèse, who increasingly neglected her body to concentrate on her soul. To wash windows when one is spitting up blood is madness. But the servant of God had madness to spare, to escape from the shadows that had invaded her soul. Washing relentlessly, she hoped to forget her interior torments. Nothing was less certain. The hands can be occupied without the soul finding profit in it, or respite....

Sister Marie de la Trinité, the novice of whom Thérèse had taken such care—it had not been easy to turn a "wild rabbit" into a Carmelite—made her profession of faith on 30 April 1896. For the occasion, visibly inspired, Thérèse wrote two poems dedicated "to our dear little Sister Marie de la Trinité et de la Sainte Face," "Souvenir of 30 April 1896" and "Commentary on the Divine." In the first, in two of the verses she revisited the theme of the offering:

> To give one's life for those whom one loves
> There is no greater love.

In the second, based on a text by Saint John of the Cross translated by the Carmelites of Paris, Thérèse expressed her life, and her death, of love:

> Leaning with nothing to lean on
> Without light and in darkness
> I go burning with love.
> Of Love, I have had experience,
> Of the good, of the bad that it finds in me
> It knows how to benefit (what power)
> It changes my soul into itself.

The lawyers' and cooks' souls denounced by Lorrain could not comprehend the splendors of such a metamorphosis. In offering this text, Thérèse did give a few explanations to the addressee, to whom she cited a thought by Saint John of the Cross: "Love knows how to benefit from everything: from the good, from the bad that it finds in us." This thought was one of those that the servant of God preferred, and that she repeated often. Sister Marie de la Trinité followed, in the end, Sister Thérèse of the Child Jesus' example, benefiting from such a thought. Thus, both believed in the power of love, capable of engendering every metamorphosis.

On 10 May 1896, Thérèse saw in a dream Mother Anne de Jésus, who had been Anne de Lobera in the outside world before becoming Saint Teresa of Ávila's counselor and the one for whom Saint John of the Cross wrote his Spiritual Canticle. The eminent nun had introduced Teresa's reforms to France in 1604.

In this dream, Thérèse saw three Carmelites dressed in their cloaks and great veils, which seemed to come from heaven. She wanted to see the face of one of them. Barely formulated, her wish was granted. It was Mother Anne de Jésus, who lifted up her veil and covered Thérèse with it, showering her with demonstrations of affection. Thus the servant of God received in a dream the consolations, the tenderness, that she so needed and was deprived of in Carmel. Faced with this benevolence, she dared to ask: "Oh, My Mother, I beg of you, tell me if the good Lord will leave me a long time on the earth? Will he come to get me soon?"

With the same tenderness, the mother murmured, "Yes, soon...I promise you."

Insatiable, Thérèse asked another question: "My Mother, tell me also if the good Lord asks something more of me than my poor little actions and my wishes. Is He happy with me?"

"The good Lord asks nothing other thing [sic] from you, He is happy, very happy," answered the mother. Thérèse awoke with the feeling that she was loved in heaven, even if she was hardly loved on earth. There was a heaven, which she had still doubted before her dream, since the Blessed lived there and deigned to take the trouble to pass through the dreams of humans, consoling them.

Thérèse was all the more touched by the Venerable Anne de Jésus' celestial visit because she had never invoked her and had felt only indifference toward her. Thérèse's heart melted with love for she who had loved her despite this indifference. Or perhaps because of it? Saints are unpredictable.

We could go on forever, making concluding remarks on this dream of 10 May 1896, which illuminated the shadows of a soul little accustomed to finding its nourishment in dreams. Jean Lorrain and his spirited cohort of Franco-English souls stated formally: Dreams are the bread of souls. And the dreams of a soul like Thérèse's were clearly destined to make future generations dream.

47

Lucifer's Fiancée

(21 June 1896)

Mother Marie de Gonzague gave Thérèse at least one joy. On 30 May 1896, she entrusted her with a second spiritual brother, Father Adolphe Roulland of the Foreign Missions. He was to leave for China, this China that so worried the countesses with whom Marcel Proust was at the time hobnobbing, and that inspired poets like Tristan Klingsor:

> Asia, Asia, Asia,
> Magical Old Country of Nursery Tales

It was a poem that Maurice Ravel would later put to music. How Thérèse would have liked to sing that melody, and with what passion she would have sung out, "I would like to go off with the schooner." She dreamed of discovering new countries to find new suffering there, as others travel in search of voluptuous pleasures they believe to be new. She had not completely given up the hope that she had once nourished of being one of the nuns of the Carmel of Hanoi, and of finding martyrdom in Indochina. Thanks to this second spiritual brother, Thérèse could imagine that she was leaving for overseas, putting her footsteps in his. Imaginary trips are sometimes the most beautiful.

On 12 June, for the Feast of the Sacred Heart and for her sister Marie du Sacré-Cœur, Thérèse wrote "What I Will Soon See for the

First Time," which can be seen as a prolongation of her dream of 10 May, a reminder of the promise whispered by the Venerable Anne de Jésus, the hope of soon seeing the Lord. In it, the presentiment of her imminent death is expressed unequivocally. She was still "on the foreign shore." She hoped "to contemplate the wonders of heaven" before too long. And, for the first time, she would see her Beloved's smile, "the divine splendor" of his "Adorable Face."

Since Mother Marie de Gonzague had not worried too much about Thérèse's "pale and haggard appearance" after the two hemoptyses, Sister Marie du Sacré-Cœur did not seem very alarmed about the haste that Thérèse showed in wanting to die. Perhaps she saw in this just one of those exaggerations favored by poets? And who would have thought that Thérèse had only one more year to live when she carried out without fail, between coughing fits, the chores and penances of daily life in Carmel?

June 21 was the summer solstice, and above all it was the name-day feast of Marie de Gonzague, who had wanted this ceremony to unfold with the greatest solemnity to clearly demonstrate that she was once again the queen of Carmel. Disregarding the fiasco of *The Flight into Egypt,* which she had loved as much as Mother Agnès de Jésus had hated it, the mother superior had ordered Thérèse to write the recreation for her feast.

Mother Marie de Gonzague was now sixty-two years old. She had lived under the illusion that she would be mother superior for life. Mother Agnès de Jésus' seizure of power had been just an unfortunate intermission that should have ended with the triumphant return of Mother Marie de Gonzague.

Alas, the elections of 21 March had not brought the expected triumph: It took seven rounds, we will recall, to arrive at the result. She who had believed herself "loved by her dear flock" had been forced to yield to the facts. Whom could she trust? The mother superior did not attempt to hide her bitterness, and her health was impaired because of it.

Thérèse tried to persuade Mother Marie de Gonzague that she had not been betrayed. Her power of persuasion was expressed in a story, *Legend of a Very Little Lamb,* a masterpiece of Carmelite diplomacy that the mother superior must have appreciated.

On this 21 June 1896, the Feast of Saint Louis de Gonzague arrived just at the right moment to dissipate the malaise that reigned in the nuns' spirits. Thérèse wrote her recreation with particular care, calling it *The Triumph of Humility,* which was intended as a comic presentation. The community needed to laugh a bit after those trying rounds of the election. Already the Carmelites could not keep from smiling at the title of a play written in honor of Mother Marie de Gonzague, whose primary virtue was not humility....

To the smiles succeeded laughter, which broke out as soon as the curtain rose. Three sisters were on the stage—the author herself, flanked by Sister Marie-Madeleine and Sister Marie du Saint-Esprit. Each played her own character in the convent. It was up to Thérèse to open fire by asking, not without some mischief, of Sister Marie du Saint-Esprit: "What do you think of the feast of our mother? Have you ever seen anything in the world as delightful as this union of hearts, this gentle gaiety?" Then Sister Marie du Saint-Esprit praised the "special charm" of Carmel name-day feasts, stressing "the family spirit" that prevailed. It seemed as if, on this 21 June, they were as united in Carmel as they had been within the House of Atreus....

Listening to this *Triumph of Humility* was like overhearing a conversation between three nuns. Their remarks sounded completely natural. Sister Marie-Madeleine was not afraid to recall that she had been a shepherd before becoming a Carmelite. She was surprised at having been chosen by Jesus to be his wife. Thérèse reminded them that in the eyes of God, "the most humble condition is the greatest." Had He not just proven this with Diana Vaughan, whom the author did not hesitate to present as "the new Joan of Arc"? When we know what Joan of Arc represented for Thérèse, it was certainly the highest compliment that she could pay to this enigmatic Diana, who was widely spoken of at the time.

The daughter of an American and a Frenchwoman, Miss Diana Vaughan counted among her ancestors one who had made a pact with Satan. In 1884, at age twenty, she had been initiated into *palladisme,* a Masonic Luciferien spiritualism. This "beloved daughter" of Lucifer was engaged, in 1889, to the demon Asmodeus. Since 1893 she had lived in the most infernal city of all, Paris, where she had become friends with Doctor Bataille and Gabriel Jogand-Pagés, a Marseillais whose nom de plume was Léo Taxil. Bataille and Taxil were notorious freemason renegades.

There was every reason to hope for Diana Vaughan's prompt conversion. Catholic France ardently hoped that Lucifer's fiancée would become Jesus' fiancée. The newspaper *La Croix* launched a campaign and, on 8 May 1895, invited its readers to pray for this to Joan of Arc. The result was not long in coming. On 6 June, Joan liberated Diana, whose conversion was confirmed on 13 June. Catholic France released a unanimous sigh of satisfaction.

Diana Vaughan proved to be a choice recruit, since she threw herself into the anti-Masonic fight and published *Mémoires d'une ex-palladiste.* In the spring of 1896, in a major article, the newspaper *L'Univers* established Diana's fame; no one had ever met her, but everyone was talking about her. It was Isidore Guérin who gave Miss Vaughan's memoir to Carmel; Thérèse immediately understood its importance, since it told of the eternal struggle between the God of Light and the Prince of Darkness. Hence the allusion to Diana Vaughan, which gave to her "Triumph of Humility" a tinge of current events.

With her trio of sisters and their lengthy discussions, with her apparitions of Saint Michael, Lucifer, Asmodeus, and Beelzebub, and the final choir of triumphant angels singing a closing verse inviting the audience to remain "always little," since "humility makes the wrath of Hell," this *Triumph* achieved a true success, confirmed by Marie du Sacré-Cœur, who found in it "more pleasure than anything that can be concocted in the world to entertain oneself."

The failure of *The Flight into Egypt* was erased. Even Mother Agnès de Jésus was conquered; she asked Thérèse to write a poem to encourage Diana Vaughan in her mission. The inspiration did not come; Thérèse was unable to write even one verse! She contented herself with addressing a letter to Diana, in which she enclosed a photo of herself as Joan of Arc being consoled by Saint Catherine.

Miss Vaughan thanked the Carmelite effusively. Thérèse was elated and read *La Neuvaine eucharistique* [*The Eucharistic Novena*], written by Diana, which Leo XIII himself acknowledged having read "with great pleasure." The pope and the Carmelite were united in Diana Vaughan, the "new Joan of Arc who will deliver France from the freemasons."

The freemasons were presented at the time as dreadful demons. This is to overlook that some persons who were above all suspicion, such as the explorer Alexandra David-Néel, belonged to a lodge. Like Thérèse, whose contemporary she was since she was born in 1868, Alexandra was in search of the light that she finally found on a path leading not to the Carmel of Lisieux, but to the monasteries of Lhassa.

48

Pure Love

(6 August 1896)

A few days after the presentation of the *Triumph of Humility*, on 28 June, Thérèse wrote a poem for Father Roulland's ordination, "To Throw Flowers." As in "What I Will Soon See for the First Time," she calmly announced that she would "soon" go to heaven to throw flowers with the angels. It was, after all, as good a way as any to occupy one's eternity! But the servant of God did not need to go up to heaven to indulge in this activity. Every evening during this month of June, with the help of five other novices, she gathered rose petals in the garden, throwing them on the granite crucifix that adorned the inner courtyard. Thus she acted like Veronica, replacing the veil with flowers to dry the tears of the Beloved.

It was a charming, and symbolic, ceremony, which the poem composed for Father Roulland reflected perfectly. We can also see in it a foreshadowing of Thérèse's posthumous mission, a premonitory heralding of her future "shower of roses" that would be passed on to posterity.

The Racinian sonority of two verses stands out: "The slightest sighs, the greatest distresses," and "Lord, with your beauty my soul is in love."

After having been Esther at the feet of the pope, Thérèse was now the Iphigenia of Carmel.

On 3 July 1896, Father Roulland, who was then twenty-six years old, said his first mass in the Carmel of Lisieux. Afterward he talked for a long time with his spiritual sister, to whom he confided: "I am leaving happy." On 2 August, he was off to China. Before his departure, he received the first of the seven letters that Thérèse would send to him:

> My Brother,
>
> You will permit me, will you not, to no longer call you by another name, since Jesus has deigned to unite us by the ties of the apostolate?
>
> It is so pleasant for me to think that for all eternity our Lord has formed this union that will save souls for him, and that he has created me to be your sister....If I go to heaven soon, I will ask Jesus for permission to come and visit you in Szechwan and we will continue our apostolate together....I would even like for my brother to always have the consolations and me the trials; perhaps this is selfish? But no, since my only weapon is love and suffering, and your sword is that of the word and works of the Apostle.

Beginning in the summer of 1896, the thought of her imminent death no longer left Thérèse and can be seen in her poems as well as in her letters, in which she constantly referred to her profound convictions, abandon in love and confidence in suffering, as if she wanted to persuade her interlocutor or to leave a trace for the future. Even if she continued to pass through a tunnel of shadows, she kept her weapons in hand permanently, like a tireless amazon.

Thérèse had received permission from Mother Marie de Gonzague to keep the photograph of the missionary and to have a map of Szechwan in her cell so that she could follow the journey. She could thus, in thought, transport herself into China whenever she wanted to. Was it the effect of these imaginary wanderings or the result of several weeks of a fortifying diet? Whatever the case, she no longer coughed, and she announced the good news to Léonie: "Well! My dear little sister, I am no longer coughing at all. Are you happy? It

will not stop the good Lord from taking me when he wants to; since I am making every effort to be a very small child, I have no preparations to make. Jesus will have to pay Himself all the expenses of the trip and the price of admission to heaven."

It is clear that the obsession with her imminent death and her acceptance of this no longer left her. In a declaration of love to Our Lady of Victories, she went as far as to propose:

> To save one soul
> I would like to die a thousand times.

Beginning in the summer of 1896, during her twenty-third year, it was not only death that Thérèse asked for but also martyrdom. And if she did not obtain it for herself, she would be the sister of a missionary martyr on whom the Chinese would inflict tortures that made even the most valorous servants of God shudder.

. But before these Chinese tortures, Thérèse underwent a more endurable compulsion: She was treated by Doctor Alexandre de Cornière, a friend of the Guérins' and Carmel's regular doctor. He did not understand much about his patient's state; she seemed to accept everything as a grace from heaven. Moreover, how could he have understood anything about it? The treatments that were administered to tuberculosis patients were only in their infancy. And, besides tuberculosis, Thérèse, who called herself a "prisoner of Carmel," suffered as well from the aches that affect people who, always shut up between four walls, complain of various pains in the stomach, heart, or lungs.

Once again, she stood out from the ordinary and did not complain. She even thought that she was too well cared for. Why these consultations and these medicines, which were expensive for the community, when the best doctor was God?

On 6 August 1896, Thérèse composed an Act of Consecration to the Holy Face, which her two most faithful followers, Sister Geneviève and Sister Marie de la Trinité, also signed. The consecration began with this blazing affirmation: "The smallest movement of pure Love is more useful to the Church than all other works combined."

Thérèse also thought that this pure love could be enough to disperse the shadows in which she continued to struggle, without anyone suspecting it, maintaining all the while her immutable smile that infuriated some of her companions. Decidedly, in the Carmel of Lisieux, Sister Thérèse of the Child Jesus and of the Holy Face would always be on the margin!

49

Mad Love

(8–17 September 1896)

From the evening of 7 September to the morning of 17 September 1896, Thérèse went on her private retreat, which she felt would be her last, as she wrote to her older sister, Sister Marie du Sacré-Cœur: "Oh my darling sister! You ask me to give you a souvenir of my retreat, a retreat that will be the last....Oh my darling sister, you would like to hear the secrets that Jesus confides to your little girl."

What secrets? In her extreme solitude, Thérèse had drawn from holy Scripture two verses that illuminated her shadows: "If someone is very small, may he come to me," and "Mercy is granted to the little ones." As others are intoxicated by the idea that they have of their own greatness, the servant of God got drunk on her own smallness, which she constantly accentuated more and more, until she considered herself a grain of sand, or of dust. Who can worry about a grain of dust? Yet the smallest of souls could arrive at the summit of love. How? By abandon and gratitude. Such were, essentially, the secrets that Thérèse disclosed in her letter to Sister Marie du Sacré-Cœur, of whom she was, we will recall, the goddaughter. A goddaughter teaching her godmother, this was yet another of Thérèse's eccentricities, and valiantly she carried on with her demonstration.

She was little, but is a spark not enough to light a fire? Thérèse wanted to enlighten souls "as the prophets" did. In a burst of mad

221

love, she dared to affirm that to be the wife of Jesus was not enough for her. She felt also in herself "the vocation of a Warrior, of a Priest, of an Apostle, of a Doctor, of a Martyr." She had remained, it can never be stressed enough, the child who had said, "I choose everything." She had the ambition to rise up out of her nothingness, and even to transform this nothingness into fire. On the infernos of exaltation, she joined Saint Teresa of Ávila and Saint John of the Cross. She was aware of having crossed the border that separated pure love from mad love. Her audacity had an excuse: "My excuse is that I am a child, children do not think about the impact of their words." It was an angelic coquetry on the part of Carmelite, who used her innocence the way Carmen used her fan.

In reality, she was perfectly aware of the importance of the words that she spoke, since she wondered about the reality of the desires that pierced her. She did not want to be the victim of an illusion. With implacable lucidity, she went as far as wondering if she was not enjoying more sweetness in her actual martyrdom and in her actual madness than she would soon enjoy in heaven. Faced with infinite heaven, she asked for her powerlessness and her smallness, whereas it was from her smallness that she drew her power. It was a little doctrine, a little way, which after Thérèse's death would attract so many little people who were tired of being scorned and rejected by those who believed themselves to be big.

In the silence and isolation of her cell, Thérèse ended her letter to Sister Marie du Sacré-Cœur, signing it "the very little Thérèse of the Child Jesus and of the Holy Face." The "very little one" did not realize that she had just written a text that instantly ranked her among the great mystics. Lost in the narcissistic contemplation of her nothingness, she could not imagine such a consecration. Nor could her sister Marie, who remembered of this declaration of mad love only the desire for martyrdom, which she did not much share. Here, indeed, was one of Thérèse's ideas, to want to be flagellated, crucified, thrown into boiling oil! The soft Sister Marie du Sacré-

Cœur shuddered at the idea and, in her answer to this letter, did not hide how much she dreaded what her godchild valued so highly. She noted that Thérèse was "possessed by the good Lord, but possessed to the point...absolutely, as the wicked are by Evil."

Even so, Sister Marie du Sacré-Cœur would have liked to be thus possessed. She would have liked to know how one achieved it, "but just two words, for what I have is enough for my happiness and my sorrow." "Two words": It was clear that Marie was protecting herself from her sister's interminable effusions. How could Thérèse express all that she felt in two words? On 17 September, she responded at length to her sister's request: "How can you ask me if it is possible for you to love the good Lord as I love you?...O my darling sister, I beg of you, understand your little girl, understand that to love Jesus, to be his victim of love, the weaker we are, without desires or virtues, the more suitable we are for the magic of this consuming and transforming love."

Marie was quite willing to love, on condition that she not have to run risks, or face the madness that such passion can engender. Thérèse loved with no conditions. She was ready for all metamorphoses and all consumptions to attain this love. In the end, the "very little one" was able to take what she called a "giant's course" toward the saintliness that she so desired.

50

Jesus' Prisoner

(1 November 1896)

On 17 September 1896, Thérèse finished her retreat, fertile as could be, since she had succeeded in explaining her little doctrine and her mad love in her letter to Sister Marie du Sacré-Cœur. On 18 September she took up once again the rigors of daily life. She fasted again and increased her penances, without worrying about her health.

To this personal retreat succeeded the community's retreat, preached from 8 to 15 October by Fr. Godefroid Madelaine. A friend of Canon Delatroëtte's, Fr. Madelaine was more understanding than the deceased prior. Thérèse sensed this and confided to him her temptations against faith. The priest saw only one remedy for these doubts: to carry the text of the Creed always against her heart. It was as good a remedy as any, and, in her shadowy helplessness, Thérèse asked only to try it. As she knew nothing of half measures, she chose to write the Creed in her blood. One can imagine the scene, which could be from a novel by Barbey d'Aurevilly, whose death in 1889 was completely unnoticed in the convent of Lisieux. Barbey would have liked the sublime childishness of the beautiful young Carmelite who cemented with her blood the foundations of a faith she believed to be shaky.

At the end of her life, George Sand observed that she had "remained a child in many ways." Sensing her imminent death, Thérèse could make this observation her own, brandishing as proof this bloody Creed. Children sometimes have a strange taste for this sort of entertainment, which they practice, hidden from their parents, in the secrecy of attics or woods.

Saint Gregory affirmed that "active life is servitude, contemplative life freedom." The "prisoner of Carmel," in the midst of so much constraint, had succeeded in building herself an interior freedom, proven in this way of using her blood to write a prayer.

Thérèse was relatively free in her correspondence as well, since, with Mother Marie de Gonzague's authorization, she could write whatever she wanted to Abbot Bellière, freed from a tedious military service during which he had experienced temptations and trials from which he had emerged victorious. The Carmelite echoed this in her letter of 21 October, hoping that he would be "not only a good missionary, but a saint all ablaze with the love of God and of souls; I beg you to attain this love for me as well so that I may help you in your apostolic work. As you know, a Carmelite who was not an apostle would be growing away from the goal of her vocation and would cease to be the daughter of the seraphic Saint Teresa, who wished to give a thousand lives to save a single soul."

To give a thousand lives, to suffer a thousand deaths, to save one soul, such was the mission with which Thérèse now felt herself vested. Indeed, on 15 October, for the Feast of Saint Teresa of Ávila, she had pulled from the basket of notes from which each Carmelite drew a lesson or a subject for meditation, a piece of paper bearing this affirmation by the saint: "I would give a thousand lives to save one soul." Thérèse avidly seized on this formula, in which she saw a course of conduct that she hastened to communicate to Abbot Bellière in her letter of the twenty-first.

Ten days later, the first mail from China arrived. Father Roulland asked for reinforcements for the Carmel of Saigon, where he was making a stopover. Thérèse, who was aiming for absolute deprivation, wondered if in Saigon, she would not reach more quickly the destruction she wished for. Decidedly, it seems as if the servant of God knew every temptation, including that of "elsewhere," where it is believed that all desires are fulfilled. To justify her desire for martyrdom, and for exoticism, she reminded Mother Marie de Gonzague that she, too, in her youth, had wanted to go off into exile in Saigon—"it is thus that often mothers' desires find an echo in their children's souls."

Wisely, the mother superior used the poor health of her novice as a pretext not to pursue this desire. Thérèse insisted, alleging that she was too spoiled in Carmel—the mind boggles—and that in Saigon she would finally experience "the exile of the heart," which, however, was her lot in Lisieux. In short, the prisoner wanted to change prisons, to experience something different from her Normandy.

In any case, concluded Thérèse in ending her plea, to which Mother Marie de Gonzague listened with commendable patience, she no longer belonged to herself. She belonged to Jesus, who would do with her whatever it pleased Him to do. Jesus and Mother Marie de Gonzague refused to let the "jewel of Carmel" leave for Saigon. To allay her thirst for Asia, Thérèse contented herself with reading *La Vie du P. Nempon* [*The Life of Father Nempon*], an apostolic missionary in western Tonkin, by G. Monteuuis, a gift from Father Roulland that arrived on 31 October in the same mail from China.

In her letter of 1 November to Father Roulland, Thérèse revealed a precious confidence about her possible predestination: "Our Lord, wanting for Him alone my first glance, deigned to ask for my heart from the time I was in the cradle, if I may put it that way."

In this same letter, she evoked, in a limpid style, the grace that she had received during Christmas night 1886, almost ten years earlier: "Jesus changed me in such a way that I no longer recognized myself. Without this change, I would have had to remain many more years in the world." Obstinately, she stated once more her happiness at being in prison: "Before being Jesus' prisoner, I had to travel very far to take the prison that I preferred to all the palaces of the earth...I understood that truly one single day spent in the house of the Lord is worth more than a thousand anywhere else."

This letter abounded in confidences, in clarifications, in phrases full of oddness of which here is an example: "Like Joshua you fight in the plain, as for me, I am your little Moses." An unbelievable liberty of tone reigned in this dialogue between Carmelite and the missionary. Across frontiers and oceans, two souls, in complete harmony, answered each other. And it was like hearing the choir of angels.

Saint Gregory was right: The contemplative life is freedom. The prisoner of Carmel left the walls of her cell when she wanted to, as she wanted to, to go off, in thought, to Saigon, where she united in prayer with her spiritual brother. It was a magnificent example of celestial feeling. The heart knows nothing of prison. Or rather it knows only one prison, that of its love.

51

Thérèse's Windows

(November 1896)

On 4 November 1896, Sister Marie-Antoinette, who had tuberculosis, died. She was thirty-three years old. This premature death comforted Thérèse in her conviction of the imminence of her own death. The possibility did not frighten the servant of God, who joked about it with her Aunt Guérin: "I am as merry as the cicada, like it I sing all the time." Thérèse as a cicada, Thérèse as a ball, Thérèse as a flower, Thérèse as a bird—one could go on forever listing all the forms that she had amused herself with taking during her existence. She was Thérèse-Proteus. She was the first to make fun of her metamorphoses; they entertained themselves however they could in Carmel. In any case, and even Carmelites who did not like her admitted it, Thérèse was gaiety itself. She had the gift of amusing others, she had proven it with *The Triumph of Humility*. Laughter and smiles were for this prisoner so many secret weapons under which she hid her sadness and despair.

Thérèse was also the first to laugh at her nascent renown, which had gone beyond the confines of the Carmel of Lisieux. In other convents, they were beginning to talk about this Sister Thérèse of the Child Jesus who was so good at writing poems and recreations. She was thought of as a tree of stanzas that it sufficed to shake for octosyllables and alexandrines to immediately fall from it. She wrote on request, nothing stopped her, not even an acrostic on the first

228

name of her cousin Francis La Néele, whom she called the "learned doctor" and "defender of the Church." Thérèse knew how to handle the compliment and did not fear the extravagance of the depiction, about which she was perhaps the only one to smile.

If she subjected herself to these worldly and family obligations, expressed in acrostics and occasional compliments, she was more comfortable with other subjects. Her love of the humble was expressed in a poem that had as title and subject *Carmel Sacristans*. This could have been the height of the conventional, but it was not. Thérèse's genius magnified everything it touched. The duties of the sacristy, which the servant of the Lord knew well since she had been and still was, on occasion, the attendant sacristan, reached supreme proportions: She compared to queens those who had the honor of preparing the bread and the wine of the sacrifice. Thérèse, who did not shrink from any audacity, finished her poem with an evocation of heaven turned into a ciborium. We do not know what the reaction was of the sacristans to this cosmic dimension that the poet gave their daily work.

To "air out" her two prisons, the prison of Carmel and her interior prison, Thérèse would not rest, in this month of November 1896, until she found no more windows. Windows were the holy images that she had contemplated since her earliest childhood and that she now interpreted in the light of her mystical experience, seeing in the slightest detail meanings that escaped the gazes of those who were too hurried, or indifferent. She identified with the Good Shepherd giving His life for His flock against a background of green palm trees or with the bunch of grapes that Jesus pressed between His fingers. These images were invitations to a journey, a journey of the soul to God or a journey of the spirit to magic countries hidden behind a soft pink horizon.

Windows were also books. Thérèse had always accorded a capital importance to reading. It was thanks to a biography that she had become smitten with Joan of Arc. And it was thanks to another

biography that she would discover one of her invisible companions toward the end of her life, Father Théophane Vénard, priest of the Foreign Missions of Paris.

It was Father Roulland who urged Thérèse to read Father Vénard's biography and correspondence; he had been decapitated in the citadel of Hanoi in 1861.

From the window of her cell, the prisoner no longer saw the roofs and the walls of Carmel, but the beaches, the palm trees, the Sea of China, and the rivers tainted with the blood of the martyrs. She escaped, flew away, and when she came back to earth, it was to observe, in December 1896, the aggravation of her tuberculosis, with what that implied of vesicants and painful treatments.

52

The Christmas Spinning Top

(24–25 December 1896)

At the end of 1896, Mother Marie de Gonzague had Thérèse use an ember heater to combat somewhat the mortal cold that reigned in Carmel. She advised Sister Geneviève to rub Thérèse vigorously with a horsehair glove, following the doctor's orders. Rubdowns to combat tuberculosis had hardly any results. Also, to compensate for this lack of effect, the mother superior decided that Thérèse would get an extra hour of sleep. Sister Geneviève would awake the servant of God at 6:40 instead of 5:45.

Neither the heater, nor the rubdowns, nor the extra hour of sleep improved a state of health that was inexorably deteriorating. It was a deterioration reflected in the poem that she wrote at the request of Sister Saint Jean de la Croix, that had as title "How I Want to Love":

> Divine Savior, at the end of my life
> Come and get me without the shadow of a delay.

It was as if the sisters of Carmel had passed the word to assail the patient with requests for poems. In turn, Sister Marie de Saint Joseph demanded hers, "Child You Know My Name." Thérèse kept going after that, by composing "The Aviary of the Child Jesus" for Christmas.

This aviary was, of course, the Carmel of Lisieux. For fifteen stanzas, Thérèse carried on her comparison between the aviary and Carmel, the soul and the dove, prayer and the lark. It was all chirping and warbling, taking on a more serious tone in the penultimate stanza:

> One day far from the sad earth
> When they hear your call
> All the birds of the aviary
> Will fly away toward heaven.

The love that Thérèse felt for birds was summed up in this poem, which her companions sang merrily to the tune of "*Au rossignol*" ["To the Nightingale"]. As she sang with them, the author must have seen the birds that had filled the trees of Les Buissonnets fly by, birds that now passed through her dreams of taking flight.

In the heated room, a Christmas tree had been put up. By chance, Sister Marie de la Trinité got a spinning top. This caused a commotion among the Carmelites, who had never seen a spinning top and exclaimed: "How ugly it is! Whatever can it be for?" Sister Marie de la Trinité, who knew, answered: "But it is very entertaining! It could work for a whole day without stopping, with a few good whips!" And then she demonstrated, which filled her companions with wonder.

Thérèse, who had observed the scene without saying a word, wrote a note to Sister Marie de la Trinité during the night of 24 to 25 December. It began with "My darling little wife" and was signed "Your little brother Jesus."

Giving in once again to her passion for metamorphoses, Thérèse imagined that Jesus had turned Sister Marie de la Trinité into a spinning top: "But to make the top turn, you have to whip it....Well then! Let your sisters do you this favor, and be grateful to those who will be the most assiduous in not letting you slow down in your progression. After I have had a lot of fun with you, I will carry you away to heaven above and we will be able to play without suffering."

It goes without saying that Thérèse thought also of herself as a top, Jesus' top, which turned according to the whim of its master, or of the daily rebuffs inflicted by her sisters in Carmel. Jesus' top, the Christmas top, Thérèse whirled as much as she could, in order to better prepare herself to enter into the whirl of the dance of death.

53

Saints and Angels

(8 February 1897)

Thérèse began the year 1897 as she had ended 1896, in writing letters and poems. For her twenty-fourth birthday, she received a new homespun habit that she wore with innate elegance, inventing "Carmelite chic" without knowing it.

Dressed this way, she gave Mother Agnès de Jésus a poem for her name-day feast. Since she was longer the mother superior, Pauline had been feeling neglected and even as if she were "looked at askance." Thérèse wanted to prove with this gesture that there was nothing of the sort. "All my soul is here," she said, holding out the text entitled "My Joy."

> My joy is to love suffering
> I smile while shedding tears
> I accept with gratitude
> The thorns mingled with the flowers.

Between the "I choose everything" of her childhood and this "I accept everything" that she said at age twenty-four, an entire lifetime had passed. In this absolute acceptance, she found her happiness. She suffered without complaining so that Jesus would be consoled. Her suffering turned into joy, since she struggled "ceaselessly to give birth to Chosen Ones."

Suffering and joy, it was her entire soul that Thérèse offered to

Mother Agnès de Jésus, from whom, in a note, she did not hide her hope that she would "soon go up to heaven" in order to return a hundredfold all that she had received from the one she had chosen as a second mother at Les Buissonnets. On this note, Thérèse wrote: "It makes me so unhappy to receive always, without ever giving." One likes to hope that Mother Agnès de Jésus protested.

Thérèse, sparing herself no trouble, gave of her smile, her prayers, her poems. She wanted to be like a guardian angel for each one of her companions. In this same month of January, she gave a few stanzas to Sister Marie-Philomène, entitled simply "To My Guardian Angel."

It seemed as if Thérèse was, at times, already in the other world and that she heard cherubs flying. The end of a century is always a favorable time for the flights of seraphim. In 1897, angels were everywhere, in paintings, sculptures, even in daily life. One spoke with one's angel, one drank one's café au lait in his company. Without such exaggerations, Thérèse felt the presence of this angel who guided her hand and directed her steps. The humbler and smaller she became—and she was more so every day—the more radiant he became. Who, during his childhood, has not heard the threat "You are going to make your guardian angel cry again"? Thérèse's angel certainly suffered the least, and cried the least.

It is significant that the servant of God spontaneously addressed her angel with the informal "you," *tu.* We do not know if he did the same. In any case, he must have been delighted with the eighth recreation, in which the angels had their say: *Saint Stanislas Kostka,* which Thérèse produced at the request of Mother Marie de Gonzague to celebrate the golden jubilee of Sister Saint Stanislas des Sacrés-Cœurs. Sister Saint Stanislas had made her profession in Carmel of Lisieux in 1847. Fifty years of profession was rare, and worth celebrating.

Born in 1824 in Lisieux, she had entered Carmel in her native city in 1845. She had been the bursar, the nurse, the sacristan. In the latter capacity, she had had Thérèse as her attendant. Between the septuagenarian Carmelite and the novice there reigned a seamless harmony, a cloudless affection. It was one of the rare affections that Thérèse enjoyed in the convent. This is to say that she surpassed herself in her efforts to do a good job on this recreation, whose hero belonged to the little group of the young elect, who fascinated her because they had died prematurely, like Joan of Arc and Saint Agnes.

Born in Poland in 1550, dead in Rome in 1568, the rich and noble Stanislas Kotska was canonized in 1726. Thérèse was extremely impressed and inspired by the brevity of the fate of Stanislas, in whom she saw a brother in suffering. Like her, he had been helped by the Virgin. Deprived of the sacrament, he had received Communion from the hands of an angel accompanied by Saint Barbara. After that, he found himself in Rome before the superior general of Jesuits, Francis Borgia. Admitted into that order, he was a novice for only nine months. Thérèse was to be a Carmelite for only nine years. Stanislas hoped to do good after his death, which was also Thérèse's hope.

"What I liked in composing this play is that I expressed my certainty that after death we can still work on earth for the salvation of souls. [Sister] Saint Stanislas, dead so young, was of admirable use in expressing my thoughts and my hopes on this subject," confided Thérèse to Sister Marie de la Trinité. Later, Céline would report that during the last months of her life, her sister was "as if haunted by the desire to come back to earth." This haunting was very clear in the eighth recreation, where saints and angels took over the stage. But for Thérèse, it represented the other life to which she aspired so much. What was just a story for the other Carmelites was for Thérèse an imminent reality. How she would have liked to have no more doubts about it, believing entirely in what she wrote.

54

A Good Little Zero

(March–May 1897)

Despite the obvious decline of her strength, despite the pains provoked by illness, Thérèse tried to fast to mark the beginning of Lent on 3 March 1897. She increased her novenas in order to be allowed to do good after her death, the imminence of which she was truly the only one to sense!

To Abbot Bellière, who, after having read "To Live in Love," asked for more poems, she answered: "These poor poems will show you not what I am, but what I would like to and should be." The humility of the servant of God had no limits! In this same letter, there appeared again, piercingly, the presentiment of her approaching departure, which, however, should not interrupt the mission that she had given herself: "To love Jesus and make Him be loved."

Thérèse wrote also, on 19 March 1897, to Abbot Roulland, who, as soon as he arrived in China, had fallen gravely ill and who attributed his recovery to the constant prayers of his spiritual sister: "You almost already went, my brother, to visit the enchanted country where one can make oneself understood without writing and even without talking...already your suffering has saved many souls."

These were serious words, which Thérèse tempered by telling Father Roulland about how a lobster given to the community had escaped from the pot it had been plunged into, and the cook had called it "bedeviled." Called to help, Mother Marie de Gonzague knew how to deal with the recalcitrant crustacean. Each Carmelite had thus been able to taste a mouthful, regaling themselves especially with the story of the bedeviled lobster that Thérèse evoked with incomparable gusto.

Throughout the anecdote, she was mocking her own death, which she tried to put to flight with a burst of laughter.

In this letter, both Thérèses, the mystic and the comic, which Sister Marie des Anges had discerned, were present, and each showed off the other to advantage.

On 25 March, Marie Guérin made her profession of faith and became Sister Marie de l'Eucharistie. This act inspired Thérèse to write one of her most bellicose poems, "My Arms." In it she presented the Carmelite habit as armor, Poverty as a lance, Chastity as a sword, and Obedience as a shield. She instilled in these three vows a furious conquest movement, able to go as far as the ultimate sacrifice, as expressed in the four last verses:

> Smiling, I brave the hail of bullets
> And in your arms, O my divine Husband
> Singing, I will die, on the battlefield,
> Weapons in hand!

Death was from then on Thérèse the Conqueror's constant companion. In her poems as in her letters, the Reaper was there, like the inevitable death's-head placed among the silks, flowers, fruits, and jewels of those paintings that were called "vanities."

The conqueror lived in constant thoughts of her passage to the beyond that was to be her ultimate victory. The cough and the poor digestion were so many signs that the tuberculosis was perfecting its work of destruction. Thérèse had the spirit to joke about it with Father Roulland: "It is really not convenient to be made of a body and a soul!"

No, it was really not convenient, and Thérèse had another proof of this at the end of Lent: She was exhausted. In the beginning of

April 1897, she had fever and loss of appetite, and the resulting weakness overwhelmed her. Still she did not admit defeat, but little by little, and on the order of Mother Marie de Gonzague, she had to abandon her participation in the choral service, her responsibility for the linen, her teaching of the novices. She even had to give up the recreations of the community, where her laughter no longer resonated. Suffering in her body, Thérèse would now suffer as well in her heart.

The attachment that she had shown for Miss Diana Vaughan, Asmodeus's ex-fiancée, who owed her conversion to the intervention of Joan of Arc and the newspaper *La Croix*, had been broken. Since the fracas that had surrounded Miss Vaughan's conversion in 1896, doubt had slipped into people's minds. Rome had opened an investigation directed by Monseigneur Lazzareschi, which Miss Vaughan had attacked with such violence that it had made Thérèse indignant, and then worried: "It is not possible that that would come from the good Lord." And then Diana caused talk about herself again. She announced a press conference on Easter Monday, 19 April 1897, in Paris. At last she was going to show herself.

Speculations were rife. What did Miss Vaughan look like? There were already a few Americans in Paris whose extreme beauty, extreme youth, and flirtatious eccentricities were widely talked about in the scandal sheets, such as *Gil Blas*. Did Miss Diana Vaughan belong to that sparkling troop of magnificent extravagant women? Instead of a blond Sappho from Washington or a red-headed queen of the Prairie, what appeared was a plump man who compensated for his baldness with a white beard, and who projected for the audience a picture of Joan of Arc in prison. It was precisely the photograph that Thérèse had sent to Asmodeus's ex-fiancée. Thérèse as Joan of Arc was the guest of honor at the scandal! For the scandal was immense at the avowal of this bald, bearded man whom everyone knew, and recognized, as Léo Taxil, and who proclaimed: "I am Diana Vaughan." Then he confessed that he had invented everything, written everything. Yes, he had invented *palladisme,* yes, he had written the *Mémoires d'une ex-palladiste* and that *Neuvaine eucharistique* that had so pleased the pope and the Carmelites. His confession ended under the boos of four hundred journalists who were present and considered themselves to have been appallingly fooled.

Le Normand of 24 April published a long account that filled the Guérins with consternation, overwhelmed the Carmelites, who had prayed so for the conversion of Diana Vaughan, and pained Thérèse cruelly; she threw the letter that she had received from Léo Taxil onto the dunghill.

The servant of God felt more than betrayed and humiliated. She would nevertheless pray, and until the end of her days, for the man to whom she owed such an injury. How Thérèse's naiveté must have been mocked! However, she was not the only one who had believed in the reality of Miss Vaughan. But then, what did the judgment of the world, or of her sisters, matter? As if she had foreseen this attack, on 6 April, Thérèse had confided to Mother Agnès de Jésus: "When we are misunderstood and judged unfavorably, what good does it do to defend ourselves, explain ourselves? Let us leave it alone, let us say nothing, it is so sweet to say nothing, to let ourselves be judged any way at all!"

On 1 May, overwhelmed with the pain caused by this imposture, Thérèse felt her heart "completely filled with a heavenly peace." It was a peace that she attributed to the Virgin, to whom she had prayed so much and whose month was beginning.

Her peace was troubled by an incessant cough, causing her to say on 7 May: "I am coughing! I am coughing! It is like a railroad locomotive when it arrives at the station. I too am arriving at a station: it is that of heaven and I am announcing it!"

Feeling that the arrival was near, she became even more aware of what she believed to be her uselessness, even going so far, in a letter to Father Roulland, as to compare herself to a zero. "As for me, I could do very little or rather absolutely nothing if I were alone; what consoles me is thinking that at your side I may be of some use. Indeed, the zero by itself has no value, but placed next to the unity it becomes powerful, provided, however, that it puts itself on the right side, behind and not in front!"

Thérèse was not one to seek compliments. If she called herself a zero, it was because she was convinced that she was one. Yes, but a zero placed on the right side. A good little zero! All of Thérèse's mischief was contained in this comparison, which is of value as a lesson. One must never take oneself seriously, even at the gates of death, this would be one of Thérèse's lessons and, perhaps, the secret of her ultimate strength.

55

The Little Way
and the Elevator

(4 June–8 July 1897)

On 30 May 1897, Thérèse revealed to Mother Agnès de Jésus that she had had two hemorrhages in April 1896. The latter immediately became once again the Pauline she had been in the past, concerned with sparing her little queen the slightest distress. After this avowal, the harmony between the two sisters was regained, as in the wonderful days of Les Buissonnets. Thanks to the notes and letters that they exchanged, too emotional to speak, we can reconstitute their duo.

Thérèse: "I greatly fear that I have caused my little mother sadness....Ah! I who would like to be her little joy, I feel strongly that I am her little sadness."

Mother Agnès: "My poor little beloved angel, I have, it is certain, caused you sadness, and yet I assure you that it is a grace from the good Lord for me to know what has happened to you, for if I had learned these details after your death, I truly believe that I would never been consoled over it."

Thérèse: "Do not be sad, my little beloved mother, that your little girl seems to have kept something hidden from you, I say 'seems' for as you well know, if she hid a little corner of the envelope, she has never hidden a single line of the letter from you; and so

244

who knows her better than you do, this little letter that you love so much?"

The hardest part for Mother Agnès de Jésus was accepting the fact that her rival, Mother Marie de Gonzague, had known of the hemorrhages that she herself had not been aware of. Secrets of the seraglio, jealousy within the *gynaeceum,* all that was forgotten before the gravity of Thérèse's condition. Mother Agnès, who at last had read the text that her sister had given her more than a year earlier, understood the importance of it. She would have liked for there to be a sequel, and to obtain it, overcoming her pride, she asked Mother Marie de Gonzague to order Thérèse to write it.

In this meeting between power and power, Mother Agnès de Jésus was not afraid to skillfully flatter Mother Marie de Gonzague: "I have no doubt that what you would obtain would be incomparably better than what I have." The mother superior immediately asked the novice to write this sequel. Thérèse, by virtue of her vow of obedience and despite her exhaustion, obeyed. From the first lines, she was crushed by the effort it would take. Then, overcoming her weakness, she began to write.

On 4 June, Mother Agnès, who was aware of the heaviness of the task that she had imposed upon her sister by way of an intermediary, could not keep from saying: "I feel so sorry to have made you undertake you know what. As you well know, the saints in heaven can still receive glory until the end of the world....Well then! I will be your little herald, I will proclaim your feats of arms."

The servant of God must have responded to this promise of glory with a smile. It was obvious that it was not Pauline who was going to the trouble of writing, of building, word after word, *L'Histoire d'une âme,* which would be considered a monument, a pyramid of modern mystical literature. Thérèse, the pharaoh, had no slaves to work in her place. She was her own slave and treated herself roughly. She was constantly interrupted by increasingly violent coughing fits, importunate requests from her companions, for whom intellectual work was nothing compared with the "real" work of sweeping, ironing, laundry...

Bravely, Thérèse continued her letter, the immense letter that she had begun with Mother Agnès de Jésus, continued with Sister Marie du Sacré-Cœur, and that she was finishing with Mother Marie de Gonzague. For this Sévigné of Carmel, it was just a letter that was a little longer than the others.

The epistolary genre allowing for effusions, she multiplied the "beloved mother"s and "darling mother"s. From the first lines, she evoked her "childlike simplicity" to excuse possible breaches or a few familiarities unworthy of a young nun toward her sexagenarian mother superior.

Thérèse, who had been nine years old when she had first met Mother Marie de Gonzague, could hope for favorable treatment, seeing in this fearsome mother superior only a tender mother. For twenty years, she had searched for the mother whom she had lost when she was four.

Still with the same simplicity, she admitted: "As you know, my mother, I have always wanted to be a saint." Alas, she observed that between her desire and reality, there was the difference that existed between a grain of sand and a mountain.

Elevating the tone of her remarks, passing with ease from child-like simplicity to divine simplicity, she announced her intention not to become discouraged. In her desire to be a saint, she was blazing her own trail and inventing her way. It was the famous "little way," which was capable of giving hope to the most desperate, and which she defined this way:

> Instead of becoming discouraged, I said to myself: the good Lord could not inspire unrealizable desires, I can thus, despite my littleness, aspire to sainthood; to make myself grow bigger is impossible, I must tolerate myself such as I am, with all of my imperfections, but I want to find the means to go to heaven by a very direct little way, very short, a completely new little way.

This is a century of inventions. Now there is no longer any need to climb the steps of a staircase; rich people have an elevator to replace it advantageously. For me, I would also like to find an elevator to take me up to Jesus, for I am too little to climb the harsh staircase of perfection....The elevator that must lift me up to heaven is your arms, O Jesus! For this I have no need of growing bigger, on the contrary, I must remain little; may I become littler and littler.

This was Thérèse's message, accessible to all in its extreme barrenness, with simple comparisons such as that of the elevator, that fabulous method of traveling upward she had discovered in the Italian palaces. In writing these words, Thérèse must have thought of those gilded elevators, seeing herself back there in a memory flash, and then coming back to her cell, which was not gilded but whitewashed. After this quick foray into the past, how not to believe that life was a dream? Yesterday the splendor of Italian hotels, or the comfort of Les Buissonnets. Today, the strict necessity of a Carmelite's cell.

After having for a moment daydreamed about the word *elevator,* Thérèse again took flight, in the demonstration of her "little way" that was leading her to the supreme flight. "Beloved Mother, I feel that now nothing is stopping me from flying away, for I have no great desires except for that of dying of love." A life of love could only end with a death of love.

Other strokes of inspiration were born under Thérèse's pen, such as "My Beloved Mother, I am a little paintbrush that Jesus has chosen to paint His image in the souls with which you have entrusted me," and there were other moving confidences, such as this one: "The recitation of the rosary costs me more effort than wearing an instrument of penance." She admitted not being able to keep her mind on the mysteries of the rosary. But prayer, according to Thérèse, was a rush of the heart, a uniting with Jesus, which had nothing to do with the mechanical recitation of a rosary. What she repeated tirelessly was confidence and love in God. It was on these two last words that, on 8 July, she finished her letter to Mother Marie de Gonzague:

> Yes, I feel it, even if I had on my conscience all the sins that can be committed, I would go with a heart broken with repentance to throw myself into the arms of Jesus, for I know how much He cherishes the prodigal child who comes back to Him. It is not because the good Lord, in His kind mercy, has saved my soul from mortal sin that I rise up to Him by confidence and love.

The manuscript was uncompleted. Thérèse did not have the strength to continue. Her three blood sisters, Mother Agnès de Jésus, Sister Marie du Sacré-Cœur, and Sister Geneviève, would do it in her place, by writing down her last words in her last conversations. Beginning on 6 April, Mother Agnès, suddenly becoming aware of the gravity of the situation and not wanting to let anything be lost of what Thérèse said, had got into the habit of writing down her statements in a yellow notebook. Beginning in July, Marie and Céline would follow Pauline's example and write down, for their parts, everything that the little queen confided to them.

56

"Yes, I Want to Spend My Heaven Doing Good on Earth"

(17 July 1897)

From 4 June to 8 July, Thérèse had not only written what can be considered her testament, but also letters to her usual correspondents, explaining to Sister Marie de la Trinité that she was no longer counting on the illness "to go to paradise," but on love. She evoked the same love in writing to Abbot Bellière: "How, when we throw our faults with complete filial confidence into the devouring inferno of Love, how would they not be forever burned?"

After having finished her testament and correspondence, she turned her attention to an interminable photo session with Céline, who proved to be a very demanding photographer.

This chore accomplished, Thérèse felt out of strength. Her side hurt, she was choking, and, starting on 6 July, the hemorrhages started again, daily.

On 8 July she abandoned her cell for the infirmary. Then she realized that she had spent her life waiting, she the impatient one: waiting to enter Carmel, waiting to receive the habit and to make her profession of faith. Now she had to wait for death, which was a long time coming, when she would have liked to be already at the Last Judgment, to discover what was to happen next. Thérèse's curiosity concerning the beyond was infinite.

To allay the waiting, she had Mother Agnès de Jésus recite a poem by Abadie, *"Les Feuilles mortes"* ["The Dead Leaves"], which was in style similar to the homonymous work Prévert would later write. Abadie presented a young tuberculosis patient who knew she was doomed and who was to die in autumn:

> My days are doomed, I am going to leave the earth
> I am going to say good-bye to you
> with no hope of return;
> ...
> When you see the dead leaves falling, falling,
> If you have loved me, you will pray to God for me.

Seeing herself carried off to heaven in a flight of dead leaves, Thérèse imagined that she would behave with God like a demanding wife: "The good Lord will have to do everything I want in heaven, because I never did what I wanted on the earth." She who incarnated absolute submission hoped to have her restitution when she would be welcomed up in heaven, as a legitimate Mme Jesus who was aware of her rights. Yet she recognized that she had always been a spoiled child of the good Lord, as she said in a letter to Abbot Bellière of 13 July 1897: "The good Lord has always treated me like a spoiled child...He has always made me wish for what he wanted to give me."

On 14 July, she declared to Abbot Roulland that she would be "much more useful in heaven than on earth" for him. She also announced to him, "with happiness," her imminent entrance into the city of God. She gave the same assurances to her uncle and aunt Guérin, promising that she would spread graces over the entire family when she was up in heaven. The prospect of being able to soon do limitless good made the moribund Thérèse as gay as a lark.

This gaiety succeeded in deceiving certain of her companions who were unrelenting: It was yet another one of the Martin clan's pretexts to put one of their own in the spotlight!

On 16 July, the Feast of Notre-Dame-du-Carmel and also that of author Thérèse, Sister Marie de l'Eucharistie sang two of her works, "You Who Know My Extreme Smallness" and the fourteenth stanza of "To Live in Love." And it was the next day, 17 July 1897, that Thérèse spoke the words that have been repeated so many times since then: "Yes, I want to spend my heaven doing good on earth. It is not impossible, since in the bosom itself of the beatific vision, the angels watch over us....I do not want to rest as long as there are souls to save."

What was possible for the angels must also be for Sister Thérèse of the Child Jesus and of the Holy Face!

57

The Five Sisters

(18 July 1897)

Léonie, who was living at the Guérins' and came regularly to the convent's parlor to learn news of the patient, wrote to Céline, on 18 July 1897: "How she must be perfuming you with her virtues! If you could write all of that down, how consoling it would be for me to have it all, for I do not have, as you do, little sisters so beloved, the happiness of being near my cherished sister."

After this appeal, the three sisters, who, each one on her own, had begun to write down what Thérèse said, renewed their ardor and transcribed more than ever. They felt the urgency of not letting anything be lost of this speaking treasure, too long ignored. And each had her portion that she believed to be unique.

To Mother Agnès de Jésus, Thérèse confided her concern with giving her "little way" to souls, not knowing how to go about it. "I am a little grain, we do not yet know what will come out of it." She explained that it was not death that would come to get her, but the good Lord. She did not think that death was a horrible specter brandishing a scythe. She firmly believed in what she had learned in catechism: "Death is the separation of the soul and the body." She promised Pauline that she would call her to heaven as soon as possible, after she was there, extending as well this favor to her other sisters. She would not keep her promise: Her four sisters would all reach a more than respectable age, approaching or passing their eightieth year.

To be the sister of a saint who had died prematurely assured one of a fine longevity and the promise of a fine place in heaven...perhaps Thérèse anticipated these future favors, since she liked to repeat: "We were all born crowned." Five sisters, five nuns, five wives of Jesus, since after Thérèse's death, Léonie would definitively enter the convent of the Visitation in Caen.

In the summer of 1897, the five sisters found themselves united as in the time of Les Buissonnets. There was no more mother superior, or sisters, or "poor Léonie." There were only Pauline, Marie, Céline, Thérèse, and Léonie. It was a grace that they appreciated, despite the gravity of the situation. To Pauline, Thérèse affirmed that "everything is grace." And to Marie, she announced her famous "shower of roses."

When Marie said to her, "What grief we will have when you leave us," she answered, "Oh! No, you will see how it will be like a shower of roses."

Marie asked then, "If you had to start your life again, what would you do?" She answered, with her usual simplicity, "I would do as I have done." But it was for Céline that she reserved the best of her affection, knowing that it was she who would suffer the most from her death: "Ah!...It is my little sister Geneviève who will feel my departure the most." She even called her right side "Thérèse's side" and her left side "Céline's side."

The two rediscovered the language of their childhood, a jargon that they where alone in speaking and in understanding, causing Sister Saint Stanislas, the head nurse, to say, "How nice they are, those two little girls with their unintelligible jargon!" They were two lifelong accomplices, two birds nesting forever in the arch of divine Love.

Thérèse did not deny herself the feeling of a surplus of affection for Céline, who realized this and said to her: "People will not know that we have loved each other so much." And Thérèse corrected her immediately: "There is no point in hoping that people believe it, the main thing is that it is so." Then, with unbelievable assurance, she added: "Yes, but! Since we will both be on the good Lord's knees!" Céline explained that one of her sister's favorite expressions had been this "Yes, but!" The companions who had nicknamed Thérèse "Sister So Be It" could also have nicknamed her "Sister Yes, But!"

The five sisters had the feeling that they were all together for the last time. But did they not also know that they would see one another again up in heaven, with the family? "Yes, but!" as Thérèse would say.

58

The Pity of God

(31 August 1897)

Absorbed in waiting for death, and in the hope of doing good afterward, Thérèse put her final days to the service of others, in the total self-effacement that she had practiced for nine years. It was a fine example of faithfulness to an ideal that the proximity of death did not change.

She advised Sister Marthe de Jésus, who had bouts of depression: "It is a great test to see everything in black, but it does not completely depend on you; do what you can, detach your heart from the concerns of the earth and especially from people, then be certain that Jesus will do the rest, He will not be able to allow you to fall into the dreaded quagmire....Be consoled, beloved little sister, in heaven you will no longer see *everything in black* but *everything in white*....Above all, let us be *little,* so little that everyone may trample us underfoot, without us even seeming to feel it and suffer from it."

Until the end, Thérèse would teach her little way, as certain Buddhists teach the Doctrine of the Little Vehicle. To remain little, to suffer, and to rejoice in this suffering that leads to God, this is what Thérèse preached with obstinacy.

On 17 July, she wrote her last letter to Léonie, who, "poor Léonie" though she was, could also, according to Thérèse, become a saint. "If you want to be a saint, it will be easy for you, since deep in your heart the world is nothing to you."

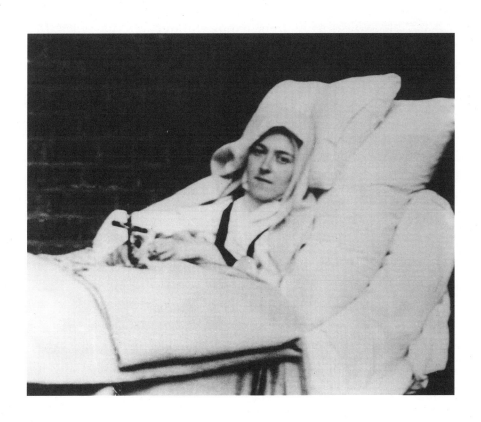

For Abbot Bellière, who was desolate at the thought of soon losing his spiritual sister and who was feeling some difficulty in turning this pain into joy, Thérèse explained: "Ah! If for a few instants
you could read my soul, how surprised you would be! The thought
of celestial happiness not only causes me no joy, but I even wonder
at times how it will be possible for me to be happy without suffering."

A terrible avowal: How to be happy without suffering when, for
Thérèse, happiness and suffering went hand in hand? To the appre-
hension about eternal happiness were added doubt, aridity, and the
shadows that tortured the Carmelite. She continued to keep others
off the track, making them believe that she was not suffering, and
she did this to such an extent that one of her companions exclaimed:
"But why do people speak of my sister Thérèse of the Child Jesus as
if of a saint? She has practiced virtue, it is true, but it was not a
virtue acquired by humiliations and especially not by suffering."

Thérèse, to whom these remarks were reported, commented on
them in this way: "And I who have suffered so from my earliest
childhood. Ah! How it does me good to see the opinion of people at
the moment of my death!"

Nothing was spared to the prisoner of Jesus—not the malevolent
comments of some of the Carmelites, not the attacks of flies that she
did her best to shoo away, without killing them. She affirmed that
she had only flies left as enemies, and since God had commanded us
to pardon our enemies, she refused to kill them. To harm not even a
fly, now the little queen had arrived at the limits of compassion for
everything that is born, lives, and dies.

On 28 July began the suffering of the death throes. On the thirti-
eth, hemorrhages and choking succeeded each other. As it was believed that Thérèse would not survive the night, in the early evening
she received extreme unction from the hands of the prior of Carmel,
Canon Alexandre Maupas. The community awaited the death of
Thérèse…who did not die! The daughter of Zélie and Louis Martin,

embarrassed about disappointing such an expectation, joked about the funeral preparations of which she was the object.

The Orphan of Berezina adorned her bravery with a smile intended to be confident. She even managed to hum, to the stupefaction of the community, a refrain from the distant past of her childhood:

> At last we have you,
> Little gray mouse,
> At last we have you
> And we will keep you!

And like Job, she repeated: "In the morning, I hope not to reach the evening, and in the evening I hope never again to see the morning."

A disappointed hope. Doctor Alexandre de Cornière had been mistaken: He had given his patient two weeks to live, and Thérèse was still here, humming and citing Job. Faced with such a tenacious moribundity, the doctor considered himself beaten and left on vacation. Thérèse hailed his departure by saying to her sisters:

> If you want to give a souvenir of me to M. de Cornière, make an image for him with these words: "What you have done to the least of my people, so you have done unto me."

Fearing that she would quickly be forgotten, Thérèse wanted to leave tangible souvenirs to those who had known her. On 10 August she declared to her first spiritual brother, Abbot Bellière, that she was bequeathing him as a legacy a reliquary, a crucifix, and the last image that she had painted.

On 15 August there was a sudden aggravation of the illness. On the seventeenth, Doctor Francis La Néele, who was replacing Doctor de Cornière, was called in consultation. He could only state the irremediable: The right lung was lost, and a third of the left lung was stricken. Confronted with this diagnosis, Thérèse contented herself with citing Saint Ignatius of Antioch: "I too must be ground up by suffering, to become the wheat of God."

To resign oneself to die at the age of twenty-four was not common. As certain among her companions saw in this resignation an obvious proof of sainthood, she replied eagerly: "No, I am not a saint, I have never done the actions of saints. I am a very little soul that the good Lord has filled with graces, that is what I am." Nevertheless, she was surprised to suffer so, "like a little child." And like a child, she wanted chicken, chops, rice with sorrel and tuna. But she could hardly express what she wanted; she had less and less strength with which to speak.

On 19 August, she offered her last Communion for Hyacinthe Loyson, the priest who had denied papal infallibility and who had married and had a son. After this Communion, she contemplated the crucifix for a long time and sighed. "As for Him, He is dead; I prefer to see Him represented dead, because I think He is no longer suffering."

This speaks volumes about the intolerable pain that she was enduring: "It is enough to make you lose your mind," she murmured. She asked that the medicines not be left within her reach, for, if she had not had faith, she would not have hesitated for an instant to give herself an overdose. She now understood the temptation of suicide. The intestinal pains were terrible, the stomach "hard as a rock," the natural functions were no longer accomplished except in atrocious suffering, and when they sat her up, she felt as if she were on "pointed irons."

The Carmelites came to look at Thérèse, some as an object of curiosity, others as a living Stations of the Cross. The servant of God was dying in public. This lack of privacy brought more suffering. In the infirmary, she was deprived of the blessed isolation of her cell. She was presented to all gazes and for all comments.

To stop the chattering of her sisters, she said, "There is nothing to say." And since they insisted, saying, "All is said, isn't it?" Thérèse answered with a nod, not even opening her mouth again to say "Yes." At last she obtained a little silence. "They are harassing me with questions, it makes me think of Joan of Arc in front of her tribunal," she complained once. She knew that she would have to suffer until the end, and fall prey to hideous thoughts, which she confided to Pauline: "If you only knew what hideous thoughts obsess me!...It is the reasoning of the worst materialism that imposes itself on my mind."

Thérèse had had to fight all her life. Now that her life was ending, she had to continue fighting. She had predicted that she would die with weapons in hand. Her prediction was proving true. She had to struggle not to think like the materialists and deny the existence of God. She exclaimed: "Why must I have such thoughts as this when I love the good Lord so much?" Her love was stronger than the doubt that gnawed at her and provoked, perhaps, her inextinguisible thirst. She was thirsty, she was thirsty, she was thirsty. Neither water nor milk nor lime tea could allay it. "My thirst is never quenched. If I drink, the thirst increases. It is as if I were pouring fire inside." She was thirsty, she was hungry, and she could swallow almost nothing. She said she was ready to devour everything, while she dined sometimes on two grapes and two swallows of wine. She had a rotten taste in her mouth that she was able to dissipate only with a little Botot water.

On 31 August, she no longer had the strength to make the sign of the cross. Her extreme weakness was confirmed that same day by Doctor La Néele, who said to her: "It will be soon, my little sister, I am sure of it." She contented herself with answering: "My God, have pity on me!...I have nothing more than that to say."

59

Joining the Stars

(30 September 1897)

Like Job on his dunghill, in the beginning of September 1897 Thérèse attained wisdom, which caused her to say: "It is because we think of the past and of the future that we despair." Next she recommended prudence concerning corporal mortifications, and being wary of excesses that could bring problems—indeed, suspect pleasures. "One must be very moderate on this point, for mingled with it is often more nature than anything else."

How had this Carmelite of twenty-four years and nine months acquired such knowledge of nature and its possible aberrations? Without having left her convent, Thérèse had seen and understood everything.

Resigned to the incessant questions of Mother Agnès de Jésus, who asked what, exactly, Thérèse meant by "to remain a little child before the good Lord," she answered slowly, catching or trying to catch her breath after each word that she spoke: "It is to recognize your nothingness, expect everything from the good Lord, as a little child expects everything from his father, it is to worry about nothing." With these words, Thérèse had just spoken her credo of littleness, the grand aria of the "little way."

On 3 September, as she was being told about the honors accorded to the czar of all Russia, who was visiting France, she said she was not impressed by this splendor and pomp. "Talk to me about the good Lord, of the example of the saints, of all that is truth," she asked. She was living closer and closer to the saints, especially Saint Teresa of Ávila. To Mother Agnès de Jésus, who dared to ask her, "Do you really prefer to die rather than to live?" she responded with the simplicity that never abandoned her:

> O my little mother, I do not like one thing better than another, I could not say, like our Mother Saint Teresa: "I am dying of not dying." What the good Lord likes best and chooses for me, that is what pleases me more.

What to do other than submit to the will of God, faced with the death that seemed to run away as soon as it was called? On 5 September, Doctor La Néele said to his patient: "You are like a ship that goes neither forward nor backward."

On 8 September, for the anniversary of her profession of faith, she received the visit of a robin that hopped on her bed, then a gift from Léonie, a music box the melodies of which she listened to with pleasure, and a spray of wildflowers. She did not know how to say thank you for so many gifts, and she cried with gratitude.

Bird, music, flowers—Thérèse could imagine she was already in paradise, such as she thought of it, with the angels playing the harp and God, who, like a father, at last held her in His arms.

On 10 September, Doctor Alexandre de Cornière, back from vacation, declared that he was "filled with consternation" about Thérèse's state; she listened to him with the philosophic attitude that results from frequent contact with doctors. "They say something and then they go back on their word," she observed, disenchanted.

Since she had gone into the infirmary, on 8 July, it had been exactly two months and two days that she had been dying. Always thinking of others, she asked that those who were at the gates of death be treated especially well, repeating: "Oh, how we must pray for the dying! If you only knew!" She knew. She lived her dying night and day. She was able at times to distract herself from it with trifles, the sight of the Virginia creeper that she saw from her window and that turned red in the autumn, of the leaves falling from the chestnut trees.

In the afternoon of 20 September, Thérèse's tunic was changed, and she was so thin that Mother Marie de Gonzague was called. She exclaimed: "Why is this little girl so thin?"

"A skeleton," answered Thérèse, who, pretending to be a little girl, said "'keleton" to amuse Mother Marie de Gonzague. The latter had no desire to laugh and made no attempt to hide her surprise at the amplitude of the disaster. A skeleton in Carmel, this was what had become of Sister Thérèse of the Child Jesus!

Curiously, her face had retained its roundnesses and seemed to know nothing of the ravages of her body. Which caused Doctor de Cornière, who did not understand this at all, to say: "She is an angel! She has the face of an angel, her face is not at all changed despite her great suffering. I have never seen anything like this. With her state of general emaciation, it is supernatural."

The angel now wanted to run in the meadows of heaven, which she had dreamed of so much, no longer speaking anything but the language of angels. With precisely the patience of an angel, seeing Mother Agnès imperturbably taking notes on the suffering that she was enduring, she contented herself with whispering: "Oh, my mother, it is very easy to write nice things about my suffering, but writing is nothing, nothing. You have to be there to know."

On the morning of Wednesday, 29 September, she could no longer breathe, she gave the death rattle, it seemed to be the end. The community gathered around the dying Thérèse and prayed for one hour. Then Mother Marie de Gonzague dismissed the sisters. Distressed about this new delay, Thérèse asked the mother superior: "My mother, are these the death throes? How will I go about dying? I will never know how to die." The servant of God, who since entering Carmel had been preparing to die, yet found herself unprepared before the imminence of death. Would she know how to go through the passage that led from this life to the other?

After Doctor de Cornière's visit, she questioned Mother Marie de Gonzague to find out "if it is to be today." Then she caught herself and said, "If I died right away, what happiness." In fact, she was afraid of suffocating to death: She was breathing with more and more difficulty. She was able to make a final confession to Abbot Pierre Faucon, Carmel's occasional confessor, her usual confessor, Abbot Youf, being ill. Father Faucon would attest to the "simplicity, clarity, and sobriety" of his penitent. "There was in her spiritual conduct nothing that denoted the least affectation. She…forgot herself and thought only of God."

In the evening of the twenty-ninth, she asked to be alone. Until then she had not accepted being watched over. She did not see why she should be this night. Finally, she consented that her godmother, Marie, Sister Marie du Sacré-Cœur, remain. Then she was concerned only with not disturbing she who was to watch over her and who fell asleep.

On Thursday, 30 September 1897, she was exhausted, breathless. She gave up trying to say what she felt. She was able, with difficulty, to sit on her bed. "See how strong I am today. No, I am not going to die. I am going to last months yet, maybe years," she said.

And she wondered: "If these are the death throes, what is death?" She suffocated so much that she called the Virgin to her aid: "Never would I have believed it was possible to suffer so much! Never! Never!" She added: "Everything I have written about my desire for suffering, oh! It is still really true! And I do not regret having given myself to Love. Oh! No." It was an affirmation that brought definitive illumination, chasing away her abominable interior shadows. After that, Thérèse could consider that all had been accomplished, that she had nothing to regret, and especially not that she had lived a life of love.

Toward five o'clock in the evening, the final death throes started. Death rattling, sweating, involuntary crying out. At a few minutes past seven o'clock, she asked once more of Mother Marie de Gonzague, "My mother, are these not death throes now? Am I not going to die?"

"Yes, my poor little one, they are death throes, but perhaps the good Lord wants to prolong them for a few hours," answered the mother superior.

God only prolonged these death throes for about twenty minutes. At about 7:20, before the assembled community, Thérèse died while looking at her crucifix and murmuring, "My God, I love you."

"She had hardly expired," tells Céline, "when I felt my heart breaking with grief, and I rushed out of the infirmary. In my naiveté, I thought I was going to see her in the sky, but the firmament was covered with clouds, it was raining. So, leaning on one of the cloister's columns, I said while sobbing, 'If only there were stars in the sky!' I had hardly spoken these words when the sky became serene again, the stars shone in the firmament, there were no more clouds."

On 30 September 1897, Thérèse achieved her ultimate victory: she joined the stars. It was her turn to twinkle in the sky, where she now adored, for eternity, her God of love.

—Paris, 18 November 1995

60

Afterword

When she died, Thérèse began another life, in the stars or else-where. A different book would be needed to tell of that exist-ence. Upon her arrival in heaven, did she go up to God, as she had said she would, curtseying and saying, "Happiness for all those I love"? And then repeating her curtsey and her request before each saint?

Obviously, we would like to know if she found paradise to her liking, such as she had imagined it in her simplicity as the eternal child, with celestial meadows and choirs of angels. Had not Jesus explained that there are many houses in his Father's kingdom? Per-haps Thérèse lives in an ideal Carmel, or in a Buissonnets built on some cloud....What is certain is that the servant of God settled down in countless hearts.

It is notable that Thérèse kept her promise of doing good after her death; she has accomplished myriad miracles. Her prophecies have come true. For example, she foretold that after her death, Léonie would return to the Visitation of Caen, never to leave again. She died there in 1941. "She will take my name and that of Saint Francis of Sales," Thérèse had specified. Indeed, on 30 June 1899, she who had been "this poor Léonie" received the habit and the name Sister Françoise Thérèse.

The little queen had also promised Mother Agnès de Jésus to help her with the publication of *Histoire d'une âme,* of which two thou-sand copies appeared exactly on the first anniversary of her death,

30 September 1898. Since then the text has not stopped being reprinted, and it has been translated into more than forty languages and distributed all over the world in millions of copies, unleashing "a storm of glory" on Lisieux.

Beginning in 1899, pilgrims came to gather around Thérèse's tomb, obtaining favors and cures. Since then, this has not ceased. During the war of 1914-18, above the melee, Thérèse divided equitably her protection to soldiers who called on her, whether they were French or German, prefiguring, in her way, the European Union.

In 1903 a Scottish priest, enthused after reading *Histoire d'une âme,* came to Carmel's parlor to elicit a possible canonization of Sister Thérèse of the Child Jesus and of the Holy Face. He came up against the incredulity of Mother Marie de Gonzague, who exclaimed, laughing, "In that case, how many Carmelites would we have to canonize?" Nor did the idea of having a saint in the family enchant the Guérins, who were very concerned with what people would say. With their visions and their levitations, saints have always had a bad reputation.

Besides, it was impossible that someone as ordinary as Thérèse Martin could be a saint, as one of her companions, Anne du Sacré-Cœur, attested. "There was nothing to say about her; she was very nice and very unobtrusive, she was not noticed, I would never have suspected her sainthood." The same echo came from Léonie: "She was very nice, Thérèse, but still, to canonize her!"

Despite the reticence of Mother Marie de Gonzague, Léonie, and the Guérins, Thérèse's canonization would be incredibly rapid. In 1907, Pope Pius X wished for her glorification, naming her, in anticipation of the future, "the greatest saint of modern times."

In 1921, Pope Benedict XV signed the *Decree on the Heroism of the Virtues of the Venerable Servant of God.*

In 1923, Pius XI beatified Sister Thérèse of the Child Jesus, who was canonized by this same pope in 1925. Mother Marie de Gonzague was no longer here to protest: She died in 1904.

In 1927, Pius XI proclaimed Saint Thérèse de Lisieux the principal patron, equal to Saint Francis Xavier, of all missionaries.

In 1944, Pius XII named Thérèse the secondary patron of France,
equal to Joan of Arc. Two of her sisters, Pauline and Céline, were
still alive to attend at this posthumous triumph. (Marie died in 1940,
Mother Agnès de Jésus would die in 1951, and Sister Geneviève in
1959.)

Thérèse had had her head in heaven and kept her feet on the
earth. An inconvenient position it had indeed been, and she suffered
greatly from it. It was because she suffered so much that she was
attentive to the suffering of others. She who refused eternal rest and
who conceived of eternity as a full-time job must be fulfilled today!
The patron saint of missions and patron saint of France has plenty
to keep herself busy with! This is not even mentioning the particular
requests that, every minute, fly toward the one who, following Saint
Catherine of Siena and Saint Teresa of Ávila, may be named Doctor
of the Church in 1997, for the centenary of her death. Then, ringing
across the Vatican, would be heard the laughter of Thérèse, who
preferred wildflowers to the flowers of rhetoric, and divine love to
earthly honors.

Bibliography

As I wrote this biography, three works never left my desk: Thérèse de Lisieux's *Complete Works* (Cerf-DDB); Zélie Martin's *Family Correspondence* (1863-1877, Carmel of Lisieux); and *Story of a Life, Thérèse Martin*, by Guy Gaucher (Editions du Cerf).

Also within reach remained the two volumes of the *Proceedings of Beatification and Canonization of Saint Thérèse of the Child Jesus and of the Holy Face* (Teresanium-Roma); *The Genius of Thérèse de Lisieux*, by Jean Guitton (Editions de l'Emmanuel); *Story of a Family*, by Stéphane-Joseph Piat (Carmel de Lisieux); *Marie Guérin*, by Stéphane-Joseph Piat (Carmel de Lisieux); *Thérèse, Abbey Student*, by Anne-Marie Roué (Médiaspaul); *Léonie Martin, A Difficult Life*, by Marie Baudouin-Croix (Cerf); *Mother Agnès de Jésus*, by Jean Vinatier (Cerf); *Saint Thérèse de Lisieux*, by Lucie Delarue-Mardrus (Fasquelle); *Little Saint Thérèse*, by Maxence van der Meersch (Albin Michel); *The True Childhood of Thérèse de Lisieux*, by Jean-François Six (Le Seuil); *Thérèse in the Carmel of Lisieux*, by Jean-François Six (Le Seuil); *Light of the Night*, by Jean-François Six (Le Seuil); *The Life of Saint Teresa of Ávila*, by Marcelle Auclair (Le Seuil); and *The Brilliant Flame of Love*, by Saint John of the Cross (Arlea).

Index

Abadie, Jacques 251
Alençon, Émilienne d' 19
Annoville, Marguerite d' 91, 99
Arminjon, Abbot 76–77, 79
Aurevilly, Barbey d' 224

Balzac, Honoré de 6
Banneville, Yvonne de 99
Barney, Natalie 197
Bashkirtseff, Marie 175
Bataille, Dr. 214
Bellefond, marquess of 91
Bellière, Abbot 195, 225,
  239, 249, 251, 258–259
Berenger, viscountess of 91, 99, 103
Berlioz, Hector 192
Blino, Father 140
Borgia, Francis 238
Bouchardon, Edme 2
Bouillon, Adrien 93
Boul, Paul Albert 8

Cauchon, Pierre 36
Cavafy, Constantine 81
Chivré, countess of 91, 99, 103
Claudel, Paul 73
Colette, Sidonie Gabrielle 64
Cornière, Alexandre de 219, 259,
  263–264
Coulombe, Mme 18
David-Néel, Alexandra 22, 215
Delarue, Jules 93
Delatroëtte, Jean-Baptiste 86–88, 104,
  110, 116, 125, 130, 139,
  141–142, 157, 164, 178, 180,
  195, 224
Desroziers, Christophe 18

Diderot, Denis 97
Domin, Abbot 60, 66
Ducellier, Msgr. 41
Dupont, M. 137

Faucon, Pierre 265
Fossard, Louis 93
Froment, Pierre 98

Gautier, Marguerite 175
Germain, Msgr. 91–92
Grainville, Edmée de 91, 99, 103
Guérin, Céline (wife of Isidore, uncle of
  Thérèsa) 33, 68, 110, 119, 158
Guérin, Guillaume Marin 24
Guérin, Isidore (grandparent of
  Thérèse) 2
Guérin, Isidore (uncle of Thérèsa) 3, 5,
  15, 24, 30, 33–34, 41, 55, 60,
  68, 85–86, 104, 110, 124, 126,
  145, 194, 214
Guérin, Jeanne (wife of Francis
  La Néele) 34, 37, 110, 145, 174,
  178, 194
Guérin, M. (grandparent of Thérèse) 2
Guérin, Marie (Sister Marie de
  l'Eucharistie) 98, 110, 141, 145,
  194, 197, 200, 202, 240, 252
Guérin, Marie-Louise (Sister Marie-
  Dosithée) 3, 16, 26–29
Guérin, Mme 35
Guérin, Zélie (wife of Louis
  Martin) 1–5, 6–9, 11–14, 16–19,
  21, 23–30, 32–36, 40, 42, 56,
  58, 70, 108, 178, 258
Guibert, Msgr. 15
Guitton, Jean 77

Halévy, Ludovic 199
Hugo, Victor 39
Hugonin, Jean-Baptiste 145
Hugonin, Msgr. 39, 87–88, 91–92,
    97, 104–105,129–130, 142, 145,
    153, 178, 180

Ingres, Jean Auguste Dominique 4
Isaiah 137

Janin, Jules 2
Jay, Danièle 11
Jogand-Pagés, Gabriel 214

Klingsor, Tristan 211
Kotska, Stanislas 238

La Gigne, Valtesse de 19
La Néele, Francis 145, 174, 178,
    182, 195, 230, 259, 261, 263
La Roque, Jeanne de 91, 99
Lamartine, Alphonse de 39
Larminat, Antoinette de 91, 99, 103
Lazzareschi, Msgr. 241
Legoux, Msgr. 101
Lemaire, Madeleine 166
Lemonnier, Father Armand 190
Leriche, Mme 30
Lorgeril, viscount of 91
Lorrain, Jean 206, 210
Loti, Pierre 67, 177
Loyson, Hyacinthe 148, 260
Luther, Martin 150

Mac-Mahon, Marie-Edme-Patrice-
    Maurice de 1–2
Madelaine, Father Godefroid 224
Marais, Louise 12, 26–27, 32–33, 37
Martin, Captain (grandparent of
    Thérèse) 1
Martin, Céline (Sister Geneviève de la
    Sainte Face) 5–7, 11–12, 15, 17,
    19, 21–23, 25–26, 28, 30, 32,
    34, 37–38, 43, 45–46, 52, 54,
    56, 64–67, 70–71, 73–74, 76–78,
    83, 87, 90, 93–96, 100–101, 103,
    105, 107–108, 110, 119, 122–125,
    131–132, 135–136, 138, 141,
    144, 146–148, 150–151,
    159–160, 166, 168–169, 175–177,
    180–182, 184, 186, 195, 199–200,
    219, 233, 238, 248–249, 253–255,
    266, 270

Martin, Hélène 5, 57
Martin, Joseph Jean-Baptiste 5
Martin, Joseph Louis 4–5
Martin, Léonie (Sister Thérèse-Dosithée)
    5, 7, 15, 22, 25–27, 29–30, 32–33,
    35, 37–38, 52, 54, 56, 62, 64–65,
    70–71, 73, 102, 110, 122, 124,
    131–132, 136, 160, 175–176,
    178, 185, 194, 217, 253–254,
    256, 263, 268–269
Martin, Louis 1–4, 7–8, 12–14, 18,
    21, 24–25, 30–33, 35–39, 41, 54,
    55–56, 58, 60, 64–65, 67, 70,
    73–74, 76, 78, 82, 84, 88, 90–93,
    95, 100–103, 108, 110, 119,
    1–125, 129, 131, 136–138, 144,
    160, 172, 175–177, 258
Martin, Marie (Sister Marie du Sacré-
    Cœur) 4–5, 7–8, 15, 21–22,
    25–26, 29–30, 32–33, 35, 37, 40,
    43, 52, 54–57, 59, 61, 64–65,
    70–71, 77, 90, 108, 114–116,
    118–120, 123, 127–128, 132, 137,
    143, 160, 166–167, 172, 176, 178,
    184, 186, 211–212, 215, 221–224,
    246, 248, 254, 265, 270
Martin, Mélanie Thérèse 5, 7
Martin, Pauline (Sister and Mother
    Agnès de Jésus) 4–5, 7, 15–16,
    21–22, 25–26, 29–30, 32–33, 35,
    37, 39–40, 43, 50, 52–55, 57,
    59–60, 68, 77, 86, 90, 93, 98,
    104–107, 114–116, 118–119,
    122–124, 127–129, 132, 134,
    137–139, 141, 147, 160–161,
    164–167, 170, 172, 176, 178,
    184–185, 190–191, 195, 198–200,
    202, 212, 215, 236–238, 242,
    244–245, 248, 251, 253–254,
    261–263, 268, 270
Maudelonde, Henry 158
Maudelonde, Marguerite-Marie
    147–148
Maupas, Alexandre 258
Meilhac, Henry 199
Meriman, Émily 148
Mesnard-Dorian, Mme 14
Molière (Jean-Baptiste Poquelin) 171
Monteuuis, G. 226
Mother Anne de Jésus 209
Mother Geneviève de Sainte Thérèse
    87, 98, 112, 116, 123, 128, 140,
    147

Mother Marie de Gonzague
52, 54, 57, 61, 87, 98, 105, 112, 114–115, 117, 119, 121, 128–129, 134–135, 137, 144, 161, 164, 170, 172, 198, 200, 202, 205, 211–213, 217, 225-226, 233, 237, 239, 241, 245–246, 248, 264–266, 269
Mother Saint Léon 50

Noailles, Anna de 28, 177
Notta, Dr. 25, 54–55, 57

Offenbach, Jacques 199
Otero, Caroline 19

Papinau, Valentine 68, 108
Paquet, Achille 93
Pasquer, Victoire 37, 43
Pichon, Father 58–59, 65, 70, 120–122, 140, 176–178, 180
Pope Benedict XV 269
Pope Leo XIII 91, 96–98, 100, 171, 215
Pope Pius X 269
Pope Pius XI 269–270
Pope Pius XII 270
Potel, Théodore 93
Pougy, Liane de (Anne-Marie Chassaigne) 19, 45
Pranzini, Henri 80–85, 94, 148
Prévert, Jacques 251
Prou, Father Alexis 153, 156
Proust, Marcel 211
Racine, Jean 99
Ravel, Maurice 211
Regnault, Marie 81
Révérony, Maurice 88–89, 92–94, 100, 102–104
Roulland, Father Adolphe 211, 216–217, 225, 239–240, 242, 251

Sade, Alphonse François 15
Saint Agnes 15, 95
Saint Anthony 94
Saint Augustine 78
Saint Barbara 238
Saint Catherine 215
Saint Catherine of Siena 270
Saint Cecilia 95
Saint Francis of Assisi 86
Saint Francis of Sales 268
Saint Francis Xavier 270

Saint Gregory 225, 227
Saint Ignatius of Antioch 259
Saint Joan of Arc 36, 48, 171–172, 186, 199, 214–215, 230, 238, 241, 261, 270
Saint John of the Cross 63, 139, 143, 147–148, 150, 153, 159, 161–162, 208–209, 222
Saint Martin 92
Saint Michael 214
Saint Monica 78
Saint Paul 61
Saint Peter 98
Saint Sebastian 15, 95
Saint Teresa of Ávila 5, 41, 53, 63, 78, 115, 140, 148, 170, 195, 209, 222, 225, 263, 270
Sand, George 15, 224
Ségur, Comtesse de (Sophie Rostopchine) 5, 13, 27, 48, 141
Siméon, Brother 144
Sister Aimée de Jésus 116, 180
Sister Anne de Jésus (Anne de Lobera) 212
Sister Anne du Sacré-Cœur 269
Sister Agnès de Jésus (See Martin, Pauline)
Sister Fébronie de la Sainte Enfance 121–122, 128, 156
Sister Geneviève de la Sainte Face (See Martin, Céline)
Sister Geneviève de Sainte Thérèse (See Mother Geneviève de Sainte Thérèse) 140
Sister Henriette 48–49
Sister Madeleine du Saint Sacrement 156
Sister Marie de Jésus 110, 116
Sister Marie de la Trinité 168, 195, 200, 205, 208–209, 219, 234, 238, 249
Sister Marie de l'Eucharistie (See Guérin, Marie)
Sister Marie de Saint Joseph 116, 233
Sister Marie des Anges 117–118, 121, 135, 141, 144, 167, 186, 240
Sister Marie des Anges (Jeanne de Chaumontel) 115
Sister Marie du Sacré-Coeur (See Martin, Marie)
Sister Marie du Saint-Esprit 214
Sister Marie Gertrude (Bigot) 18
Sister Marie-Antoinette 228

Sister Marie-Dosithée (See Guérin, Marie-Louise)
Sister Marie-Madeleine du Saint Sacrement 168, 214
Sister Marie-Philomène 118, 237
Sister Marthe 138
Sister Marthe de Jésus 118, 161, 168, 256
Sister Saint Jean Baptiste 116
Sister Saint Jean de la Croix 233
Sister Saint Stanislas des Sacrés-Cœurs 147, 168, 237–238, 254
Sister Saint Vincent de Paul 116, 128, 168
Sister Teresita de Jesus 53
Sister Thérèse de Saint Augustin 54, 116, 163
Sister Thérèse-Dosithée (See Martin, Léonie)
Stylites, Simeon 37

Taillé, Rose 8–9, 11–13, 65
Taxil, Léo 214, 241–242
Turgot, Victor 93

Vaughan, Diana 214–215, 241–242
Vénard, Father Théophane 232

Wallon, Henri 171
Wiseman, Nicholas 14–15, 48

Youf, Abbot 147, 265
Yourcenar, Marguerite 176

Zola, Emile 98